The Upper Room
Disciplines
2004

The Upper Room
Disciplines
2004

UPPER
ROOM BOOKS®
NASHVILLE

THE UPPER ROOM DISCIPLINES 2004
© 2003 by Upper Room Books®. All rights reserved.

The Upper Room Web site: http://www.upperroom.org

Cover photo: Corbis
Cover design: Ed Maksimowicz
First Printing: 2003

ISBN: 0-8358-0989-7
Printed in the United States of America

Contents

Foreword

Lost in New York City, a person hails a taxi: "How do I get to Carnegie Hall?" "Practice, practice, practice," replies the cabbie. So runs the old adage.

You have embarked on another year of using *The Upper Room Disciplines*—and *practices, training, methods,* or *exercises* are all good synonyms. Each term conveys a slightly different image of the spiritual journey. Every athlete, musician, artist, or writer knows the value of simple practice: You do your stretches, learn your scales, place yourself before a bare canvas or a blank computer screen. I like to play the piano, but when first learning a piece by Andrew Lloyd Webber or George Gershwin, I am merely pushing the keys, playing the notes. Somewhere along the way, I am ready to give up. I walk away. But if I return, often at that very point the music becomes part of me. I am no longer playing notes but making music.

The New Testament uses several Greek words to convey healthy meanings of "discipline." *Paideia* comes from the Greek *pais,* meaning "child," from which we get the word "pedagogy." First, then, approach scripture with a childlike habit of mind, curious to learn, even from life's adversity. "Endure trials for the sake of discipline [*paideia*]" (Heb. 12:7). Each time we want to re-enter the kingdom of right relationships, we need to come as a child, playfully and prayerfully.

A second key word for spiritual "discipline" is *gymnastikos,* meaning "training," from which we get "gymnasium." Like an athlete, we are required in training to become spiritually "naked" (*gymnos*), letting go of extra baggage. Living out our baptism, we die with Christ, stripped "naked"—then rising to put on the clothing of compassion and love (Col. 3:9-14). Divesting our attachments, we embrace our vulnerabilities and become spiritually resilient. "Train (*gymnazē*) yourself in godliness, for while physical training (*gymnasia*) is of some value, godliness is valuable in every way" (1 Tim. 4:7-8).

Third, following this image of the gymnasium we can also

view disciplines as spiritual "exercises." I learned from a back injury that a pinched nerve causes muscles to atrophy. Without exercise our spiritual muscles atrophy; thus prayer is the vital nerve that nurtures the muscles of faith. John Calvin spoke of prayer as "the chief exercise of faith." Ignatius of Loyola gave us a treasured book *The Spiritual Exercises* to pattern our lives around the life of Christ. Just as physical therapy exercises help a person regain strength bit by bit, so daily practices strengthen one's heart.

John Wesley referred to spiritual practices or disciplines as "methods," so his followers were dubbed "Methodists." Methods have no value in themselves, except, like conduits in a desert, to carry the life-giving gospel of love to points of need. Spiritual disciplines do not coerce grace but merely train the eyes of one's heart to be awake when the sun rises, to notice the bush when it blazes.

But what specific disciplines do we practice? Richard Foster in *Celebration of Discipline* lists thirteen. But if the spiritual life could be reduced to merely two, they would be the discipline of solitude and the discipline of community. We can see these two in the life of Jesus as he retreats into the solitude of the mountains to pray, then returns the next day to call the community of disciples to surround him (Luke 6:12-16).

Without the discipline of community, solitude degenerates into self-absorption and isolation; without the discipline of solitude, community degenerates into codependency and enmeshment. The trumpeter who does not practice has trouble playing in the band, yet the band also helps the trumpeter to practice.

By praying and meditating on scriptures from the Revised Common Lectionary using the *Disciplines* in your own solitude, you are simultaneously practicing with disciples of Christ around the globe as the word of love becomes flesh in community.

—KENT IRA GROFF
Director, Oasis Ministries for Spiritual Development
Camp Hill, Pennsylvania
Author of *The Soul of Tomorrow's Church*

The Promise

January 1–4, 2004 • Helen R. Neinast[‡]

THURSDAY, JANUARY 1 • Read Ecclesiastes 3:1-15

Cynicism. Absurdity. Predestination. Despair. All of these have been used to describe the mind-set of the writer of this passage from Ecclesiastes. Yet none of them addresses the heart of the matter. The Teacher in Ecclesiastes does not despair in the cycle of human life; he rejoices in it. The cycle is good, dependable, secure. It provides order, meaning, and purpose, even when life's turns threaten to undo us. The Teacher assures us that God is with us throughout the whole cycle of life.

The first cycle in the list, "a time to be born, and a time to die," is obviously out of human hands. The rest of the list, however, lies squarely within human grasp, requiring that we make choices and make them wisely.

Some pairs on the list are straightforward—a time to weep and a time to laugh, a time to mourn and a time to dance. Others have meanings that could be missed if we simply look on the surface. "A time to keep, and a time to throw away," for instance, is not a warning against junk and clutter. "Throwing away" refers to generosity—giving away good things to those around us. "A time to tear" refers to the Jewish custom of rending garments in grief. "A time to sew" gives the grieving family permission to sew the rips back up when the time of mourning is over.

Whatever else the Teacher's list shows us, one thing is clear: "I know that whatever God does endures forever…God has done this, so that all should stand in awe."

PRAYER: O God, you give us life. You give us time. Make us wise in our choices. Give us joy to praise you through all the days and times of our lives. Amen.

[‡]Former United Methodist campus minister, Emory University, Atlanta, Georgia; ordained elder in the New Mexico Conference of The United Methodist Church.

Psalm 8 is the first song of praise in the Book of the Psalms. It is also the first biblical text to reach the moon. Seventy-three nations were invited to contribute writings to accompany Apollo II when it landed on the moon on July 20, 1969. The Vatican chose this psalm.

It's easy to see why. The words are a startling affirmation of the glory of humanity's vocation as God's creation. Wondering at the heavens, marveling at God's majesty, the writer is in awe of God's work in making us "little less than God" and crowning us with "honor and glory" (RSV). The true wonder, of course, is that God chose to be mindful of us in this way. God chose to make us partners.

And such a risky choice that was! The history of humankind is marred by war and death, chaos and disrespect for our world. Yet sometimes we humans rise to the level of God's choice of us as partners in creation; we do the right things for the right reasons. Sometimes we listen for God's call and follow it in love.

The genius of God's majesty is the hope and trust God has placed in us. That is the spirit—the divine spirit—within us that God would have us tend. Praise of God is a good place to start the work of getting a sense of our place in the world as partners with God.

PRAYER: I am grateful, Creator God, that you care for me. I wonder at your mindfulness of me, your human creature. Make me wise in the service of your creation. Amen.

This passage from Revelation contains some of the most beautiful, dramatic, and joyous images in the entire Bible. John's vision here centers squarely in the community of faith and in the faith community's relationship with God. Our relationship with God, John says, and our relationships with one another are the very means God uses to bring to a new earth the new heaven. God's presence had before been hidden. Now God dwells with God's people in intimate closeness. Three times in verse 3 John repeats that God is "with them." The particular word John uses carries a special sense of God's belonging with the people and the people's belonging with God. The sense of promise, of rightness, is unmistakable. This is how life with God is meant to be.

Verse 4, traditionally read at funerals and memorial services, is a word of comfort to the bereaved. To imagine a world where death, crying, and mourning will be no more is a moving expression of God's power. But these words are much more than just words of comfort. They are words of challenge, because they represent a vision of a world that has not yet come, that is not yet redeemed. They remind us that God calls us to change our lives, to change the life of the world so that the old ways—death, poverty, privilege—will be transformed into the new ways John's vision proclaims.

PRAYER: **God, help me today to pray and work and live in ways that bring comfort and change to the world. May your will be done on earth as it is done in heaven. Amen.**

The rich and glorious images of light call out from the darkness that covers the earth and its peoples. Isaiah describes with joy God's light and the salvation it brings. "The LORD will arise upon you" the scripture says, "and nations shall come to your light."

The promise is clear and great. Light will replace deep darkness; vision will replace blindness. Radiant hearts will rejoice—hearts that had been weighed down by darkness and exile.

This passage is about coming home, coming home to God, coming home to salvation, coming home to joy. Isaiah wrote these words to the people of Israel during a very dark time—the time of their exile in Babylon. These words from God carried the promise and hope to Israel in its time of desperate need.

At Jesus' birth God's promised light came into the world, fulfilling Isaiah's redemptive message for all peoples. The light of Christ now lives in us and among us, enabling the church to bear witness to the light wherever darkness and suffering are found.

Where in your life do you need to hear God's words of light and promise? What dark places in the world need the witness of God's light? How are you called to be a bearer of light and promise to others?

PRAYER: Lift my eyes, O God, to your light. Let me arise from my prayers to carry your light into the world. Amen.

Fire and Water

January 5–11, 2004 • *Maxine Clarke Beach*[‡]

MONDAY, JANUARY 5 • Read Isaiah 43:1-7

We prepare for the remembrance of Jesus' baptism as this week's texts lead us wonderfully into a minicourse in Christian life. We will celebrate our redemption that takes away all fear, remember our baptism that signifies an intimate relationship with God, and recall the touch of the Holy Spirit that assures us of our wholeness. We begin with today's text from Isaiah.

This text reminds us that in the rehearsal of the story of Israel we often find these essential symbols of water and fire. These two basic necessities cannot live together and yet are held together as a sign that God gives to God's people. Redemption has come to these Israelites because God has called them by name. They no longer need fear water or fire. Water and fire shall be their companions.

Water is essential for drinking, washing, cleaning homes and clothing, and also to protect us from fire. However, water evokes fear for the ancient Israelites. Sea monsters live in the water, making the sea a troubling place. The necessary rains are often undependable and future life is put at risk for lack of water.

Fire is also a basic need; to cook meat and other foods, to stay warm, to light the dark night. God appears as fire in the bush to Moses and leads the people as a pillar of flame. Fire is often the reality of God's wrath.

Water and fire: essential elements for purification and life and a fearful reminder of God's presence.

SUGGESTION FOR MEDITATION: **Remember God when you thirst and take the necessary drink. Feel that blessing of water as you shower. Go for a walk in the rain without an umbrella. Remember God whenever you light a candle or simply feel the warmth of a fire.**

[‡]Vice president and dean of the Theological School at Drew University, Madison, New Jersey.

TUESDAY, JANUARY 6 • **Read Isaiah 43:1-7**

EPIPHANY OF THE LORD

Isaiah encourages those in exile in Babylon to return to Israel to reestablish the nation. There is much to fear. The Temple is in shambles, and the religious cohesiveness that had formed early Israel is gone. The Babylonian exile has lasted for seventy years. Now Isaiah challenges the people to leave the land they have known and return to the land of their ancestors, a land they know only by story and the memory of others. Babylon is familiar. Who will they be if they leave it? Yet God calls them by name! "I have called you by name, you are mine."

God does not deal in generalities. The call to return to the Promised Land is sent not to all the nations of the world but to Israel. The ancient understanding of the power of a name had led the Israelites to shrink from addressing God by name. But now God calls them—by name—to a frightening task. We all yearn for God to know our name and to call us by that name, yet we stand in awe of the frightening possibilities that might flow from such intimacy.

Here the text is clear. Much will be asked because we are known by God through the intimacy of a name, but we need not fear; God will accompany the journey. The long scary journey to become Israel will be companioned by God. God desires to be with us in our own journey as well: "When you pass through the waters, I will be with you; and through the rivers, they will not overflow you. When you walk through the fire, you will not be scorched, nor will the flame burn you."

At each baptism in our church community we are asked to remember our own baptism, to recall that moment when our naming by God started us on our spiritual journey. We cannot know in such moments what might lie ahead, only that the God who names us will accompany us.

SUGGESTION FOR MEDITATION: **By what name does God know you? How have you felt God's presence in your faith journey?**

Again we find in an ancient text the power of water to pull forth great emotion. God is enthroned in the crashing of thunder and rising flood waters. This psalm like others rehearses the powerful appearance of Yahweh in a thunderstorm. If God is this strong, may God give strength to people! May God's people be blessed with peace!

As a child I loved a good thunderstorm. I grew up in big sky country in western Nebraska, where you can watch the storm roll across the plain. The lightening bolts are visible miles and minutes before you feel rain or need to worry about where the bolts will hit ground. The big sky storms are part of me.

But while living for a time in Nashville, I found thunderstorms to be quite frightening. I watched with fear as our large trees swayed and lightning cracked. I could not make friends with these storms. They were not my comfortable storms.

I could not see these storms, hidden in the mountains and amongst the trees. They snuck up on me. Storms had changed, and I now feared what once had given me a strange comfort and sense of security. I developed a new awareness of the power of creation—yes, a kind of theophany.

What does it mean when the appearance of God no longer seems familiar, when it actually brings fear? Sometimes our understanding of God becomes too comfortable. Perhaps the appearance of God should at times bring trembling. We worship an awesome God who will be as God will be. I rejoice that God will not be confined to my limited experience and keeps coming to me in fresh and awesome ways with new kinds of thunder.

SUGGESTION FOR MEDITATION: **How does God appear to you? Where do you see the divine? The Bible tells us that God is like a crashing thunderstorm but also like a mother hen or a rock. What metaphors best reflect your experience of God?**

THURSDAY, JANUARY 8 • **Read Acts 8:14-17**

Peter and John go to pray with the new Christians at Samaria that they might receive the Holy Spirit. "For as yet the Spirit had not come upon any of them."

The people of Samaria reside in the margins of our faith story. Worship in Samaria had developed as an alternative to worship in Jerusalem. Jews believed the Samaritans to be impure because of intermarriage and a different understanding of the purity codes. Jesus, however, used the example of a Samaritan to tell one of his most famous parables (Luke 10:29-37). The Samaritan is the one who does what is right and just. He does not let the purity laws of the time or the demands of the present moment interfere with the need to help a stranger in distress. To the early hearers, the parable would carry a double sting: Recognized religious leaders offered the hurt man no help, and the hero turns out to be one on the margins of proper society.

Jesus also shocked the established system by walking through Samaria and having a conversation with a woman at a well (John 4:7-25). There he offers redemption in the form of "living water." Sent back to her community by Jesus, the Samaritan woman became a missionary who bore great fruit. Yet the charge of impurity and unacceptability continued to haunt the Samaritan community.

Hearing that this marginal community of faith has accepted the word of God and is anxious for a new start, Peter and John go to the Samaritans to pray that they might receive the Holy Spirit. Now a new birth in a relationship with God will erase the past.

SUGGESTION FOR MEDITATION: **What difference would the presence of the Holy Spirit have made in the Samaritan community? What difference does it mean to our churches that the Spirit comes upon us? Where are the margins of our society? Who is waiting for the Holy Spirit? What role might you play in bringing the Spirit to them?**

Having been sent to the people of Samaria, Peter and John lay hands on them, and the Samaritans receive the Holy Spirit. The laying on of hands evokes the presence of the Spirit.

We too reach out and lay hands on one another so that we might share the Spirit. We are also sent by God to lay hands on those who have not yet received the Holy Spirit. Like Peter and John we can become the vehicles for others to experience a new awareness of God's presence.

What places await the touch that will release such power? Where are we to go? And what is the quality of our touch?

Many have been touched inappropriately and yearn for a touch that brings the Holy Spirit. Memories of abuse and broken dreams of possibilities have left many of us hurting, yearning for a touch of wholeness that affirms the sacred place within us. So many are broken, and so many ache for a touch that heals.

We live in a broken world. As those who have been blessed by the touch of the Holy Spirit, we carry responsibility to touch others so that they might believe. This is evangelism: the power of our lives lived in union with the Holy Spirit that sends us to another—not to judge or to condemn but simply to touch and be there. It is the work of the Christian.

SUGGESTION FOR MEDITATION: As you begin this new year, are you aware of the power of the Spirit in your life? Or are you one of the broken, touched by others in such a way that you are hurt? Resolve to be with men and women who reflect the power of the Holy Spirit. Receive their touch and experience the possibilities of a new beginning. If you are full the Spirit of God and know that blessing, resolve to find the hurting ones. Reach out with the healing touch of friendship and new visions.

SATURDAY, JANUARY 10 • Read Luke 3:15-17, 21-22

John the Baptist celebrates water baptism but, he indicates that the fullness of that baptism will come in the fire of the Holy Spirit. Water and fire: an unlikely mix that somehow brings completeness.

In Luke the act of baptism is followed by Jesus' prayer, the opening of heaven—an expected way for God to be revealed. Ezekiel remembered, "As I was among the exiles by the river Chebar, the heavens were opened, and I saw visions of God" (1:1). Isaiah prayed, "O that you would tear open the heavens and come down, so that the mountains would quake at your presence" (64:1).

Jesus' prayer brings forth from the opened heaven great blessing in a bodily form of a dove. This perhaps is an unexpected revelation of God. In Acts 2 the Spirit will come from heaven like the rush of a violent wind: "Divided tongues, as of fire, appeared among them, and a tongue rested on each of them" (2:3). Psalm 29:7 reminds us, "The voice of the LORD flashes forth flames of fire."

The voice from heaven makes an unexpected claim: "You are my Son, the Beloved." Like the ancient Israelites, Jesus is given a name, a name that reflects great intimacy—like that between parent and child. Later Jesus will call God Abba, "papa," reflecting a new relationship with this awesome God.

SUGGESTION FOR MEDITATION: **Find a quiet place. Look up to the heavens and imagine that God wants to break through and pour blessings upon you. Do you understand God as a God of blessing? What would blessing look like in your life? What would God call you?**

BAPTISM OF THE LORD

We remember our baptism and are grateful. As redeemed, named, touched children of God, we acknowledge that we are changed by the power released in the baptism of Jesus. We remember the connection of our ritual of baptism to this amazing moment of God's declaration of Jesus as the beloved one. At the moment of baptism we become Jesus' brothers and sisters. God says to us, "You are my beloved child."

I was baptized in a little church in rural Iowa, together with my only sibling. As I look back I can see the path of sacred journey that was claimed in my name in that little church. More and more has been revealed as I have attempted a walk that is worthy of being named and called by God. I am so grateful for my baptism and the body of Christ that undergirds it. Our baptism is twofold: the water cleanses us; the fire of the Spirit commissions us. Faithful people responding to that commission have formed my life. We are connected in an incredible journey of the Christian faith; we respond in gratitude.

At this time in the Christian year as we remember the baptism of Jesus, we need to recommit ourselves to our calling. Each time we participate in the baptism of another, we need to take seriously the responsibility we assume for that one. Thus we become part of the continuing community of Christians who nurture new faith by witnessing with lives well lived.

SUGGESTION FOR MEDITATION: **What memories of baptism come to your mind? Who loved you into baptism? Who assumed responsibility for your spiritual nurture? How have you fulfilled your responsibility for others? Rejoice and be glad. You are a child of God.**

A Glorious Superabundance of Grace

January 12–18, 2004 • Gerald Kirksey[‡]

MONDAY, JANUARY 12 • Read John 2:1-11

We have all experienced events similar to the dilemma at the wedding in Cana. Maybe at a wedding reception the punch bowl began the evening filled with carefully blended punch and a fruit ring decoration but later in the night it was replenished by pouring ginger ale and orange juice straight from the bottles into the bowl. After all, why serve the best or worry about proportions after palates have been dulled?

Few would blame the headwaiter's incredulity at the bridegroom's saving the best wine until later in the feast. Had the waiter known that the best wine came from the purification jars—water used to wash feet and in the ritualistic hand washing related to meals—he would have been even more shocked.

Jesus' miracle signifies that a time of change is coming to Israel. The Torah's emphasis on ritual will be supplanted by Jesus' emphasis on grace, the unmerited love of God for God's children. Jesus brings a message of hope for the downtrodden and the poor in spirit: the last will be first!

Can the disciples chosen by Jesus during the previous few days understand what awaits them? Do we fully understand the change in emphasis that following Christ brings? What the disciples are just beginning to understand—what we know—is that following Christ brings change to our lives. But following Jesus also gives us the best life has to offer: the reserve wine.

SUGGESTION FOR MEDITATION: "He rules the world with truth and grace, and makes the nations prove the glories of his righteousness, and wonders of his love." (Isaac Watts, *The United Methodist Hymnal* [UMH], 246)

[‡]Layman, member of Belmont United Methodist Church, Nashville, Tennessee.

Isn't changing water into wine at the wedding feast of a family that has run out of wine a social blunder, a rather mundane miracle? How could Jewish people steeped in the stories of their ancestors—Moses who parted the Red Sea and Joshua who commanded the sun and moon to stand still—get excited about such a minor miracle?

How can the miracle of the wedding wine serve as a "sign"of Jesus' glory to his disciples? John, the Gospel writer most concerned with Jesus' divinity, relates the miracle of the wedding wine immediately after beginning his Gospel with the powerful images of Jesus coming as the light of the world. Perhaps he wants us to understand that Jesus, God's only Son, the Word, also became flesh and dwelt among us.

Dwelling among the Jews of Galilee at the time of Christ meant that Jesus worked as a carpenter, worshiped at synagogue, attended the temple in Jerusalem, and went with his disciples and mother to a wedding in Cana. He truly dwelt as a physical person among his peers. Although he has left his body of flesh, he also dwells among us.

Jesus is with us during times of illness and trouble as well as during times of joy—weddings, births, baptisms into the family of God. Following Jesus does not mean that Christians must wear black and avoid parties. After all, the Jesus of John's Gospel defends Mary, sister of Lazarus, when she anoints Jesus' feet with a pound of costly perfume. Jesus, the Word made flesh, even serves the reserve wine at a wedding feast!

The miracle of the wedding feast signals that Jesus is our constant companion. He is always "with" us, not only when we need healing but also during times of joy and celebration.

SUGGESTION FOR MEDITATION: "Come, thou long expected Jesus, born to set thy people free; from our fears and sins release us, let us find our rest in thee." (Charles Wesley, UMH, 196)

On the CD *Garrison Keillor & the Hopeful Gospel Quartet,* Garrison Keillor sings an ode to fresh sweet corn. He describes a scene from his youth when the family returned home from church for Sunday lunch. While his mother got the rest of the meal together, the children went to the corn patch and gathered the fresh sweet corn—sixty-seven ears in Mr. Keillor's account. After the corn was briefly boiled and blessed, the family feasted on the sweet, sweet corn.

Keillor observes that fresh sweet corn is a sign of God's goodness even to the least of God's children. Such grace, unmerited but freely given, can only come from the boundless love of God.

The psalmist in today's scripture reading must have tasted sweet, sweet corn when he wrote of the "abundance of [God's] house" and the "river of [God's] delights." William Barclay writes in his commentary on Jesus' miracle at the wedding in Cana of "a glorious superabundance in the grace of Christ."

As I write this week of meditations, the last leaves of the most glorious fall in years are falling, and the trees are becoming bare. As you reflect on these meditations, another celebration of Jesus' birth will have just passed, a time of great beauty, wonderful music and worship in all of Christendom. The glorious superabundance of God's grace surrounds us at all times of the year and in all seasons of our lives.

The God of steadfast love in the psalm, the God whose son began his ministry at a wedding, and the God of Garrison Keillor's youth is the same God who provides reserve wine and sweet, sweet corn to even the least of God's children.

SUGGESTION FOR MEDITATION: "O God, thou giver of all good.... The life of earth and seed is thine; Suns glow, rains fall by power divine; thou art in all; not e'en the powers by which we toil for bread are ours." (Samuel Longfellow, *The Book of Hymns,* [BOH],) 515)

God's chosen people often didn't act like chosen ones. The children of Israel were a "stiff-necked" lot, always getting in trouble and turning their backs on God.

When the Israelites made a golden calf to worship while Moses received the law on Mount Sinai (see Exod. 32:7-14), God had had enough. It was time to accept the fact that God had chosen the wrong people and to start again! Only after Moses begged for mercy did God relent.

Hundreds of years later at the time of Isaiah, God's chosen people continue to struggle. Judah is part of the Assyrian empire, and much of the Jewish countryside lies desolate. The poetry of Isaiah expresses anger at the occupiers and laments the state of Israel and God's chosen people.

But the book of Isaiah, particularly the later chapters, also contains messages of hope: God will restore Zion and the land now termed desolate will be married to God. God will rejoice over Israel as a bridegroom rejoices over his bride. God's chosen people, a stiff-necked lot, still benefit from God's boundless love.

Hundreds more years into the future, at the time of a wedding at Cana, Israel will again be occupied, this time by the Roman Empire. But Jesus will come to reclaim God's chosen people not with great military victories but with a glorious superabundance of grace.

As followers of Jesus, we join the ranks of God's chosen people, sharing in the goodness of God's delights and married into a fellowship with God through the glorious superabundant grace of Jesus. We receive this grace not through any claim of entitlement but because we are infinitely loved by Jesus, the light of the world.

SUGGESTION FOR MEDITATION: "Happy the souls to Jesus joined, and saved by grace alone; walking in all his ways, they find their heaven on earth begun." (Charles Wesley, BOH, 535)

In a popular early seventies song, Janis Joplin begged the Lord to buy her a Mercedes Benz. I didn't care for Joplin's music or lifestyle, but that song has stuck with me—perhaps because I'm secretly praying for my Mercedes Benz! It's easy for Christians to believe that we are entitled to special treatment because we share in God's glorious superabundance of grace. Like the children of Israel, we are "stiff-necked!"

The psalmist in today's reading knew better: God's love is bestowed on all people. Wesleyan theology places a strong emphasis on prevenient grace, God's protection and guidance of our lives even before we are aware of God's love for us. Grace is given freely to all, not to a particular sect or group of believers. Even animals are saved by God.

But the grace of the Wesleyan tradition is more—a grace that converts us to a new life walked with Christ, a grace that perfects and sanctifies us. The road to perfection is not traveled with prayers for a Mercedes Benz. It is lived out through ministry. Our charge is to share the superabundance of grace that we have received with all of God's creation, even the animals. We must carry the "light" throughout the world!

Jesus didn't begin his public ministry in the marble temples of Jerusalem. He chose instead to minister to the people of Galilee, a poor region of an insignificant, occupied nation. He didn't perform his first miracles in the Temple; rather, he bestowed a glorious superabundance of grace on the weak, the sick, and the downtrodden.

If we claim to be followers of this Christ, we are also called to share the glorious superabundance of the grace of Jesus Christ with all people, whatever their condition or place in life.

HYMN FOR MEDITATION: "The sovereign grace to all extends, immense and unconfined; from age to age it never ends, it reaches all [hu]mankind." (Charles Wesley, BOH, 130)

The Corinthians were much like us: Self-aggrandizement was a way of life. Surely preaching and interpreting are more important than healing or faith. But didn't Jesus heal the sick? So goes the constant bickering among the Corinthians as to the importance of their individual gifts.

Paul is tired of the Corinthians' uninformed faith: No one can claim Jesus as Lord except through the Holy Spirit, a gift of God. Faith, not spiritual perks, reveals the Spirit's presence at work. And each person's spiritual talents are to be used for the common good.

Just like the Corinthians, we modern Christians have all received a glorious superabundance of gifts: Some of us can sing; some are called to preach; some are teachers; and others heal the sick and poor in spirit.

I find offering an extemporaneous public prayer difficult; I need time to compose my thoughts. Give me a computer, some books, a meaty topic, and time to ponder; and I am happy. Thank God for the Christian layperson who prayed a loving, gentle prayer as my grandfather spent his last hours with us. The quiet words remain vivid in my memory twenty-two years later— surely the Holy Spirit was with us as Granddaddy slipped away.

Mother Teresa never ascended to the pulpit at St. Peter's; she never published a best-selling book. But Mother Teresa and the self-sacrificing life she lived stand as a model for all modern-day Christians.

God is good, God's grace is everlasting. All of God's gifts are important to and sufficient for the common good of all people.

HYMN FOR MEDITATION: "What can I give him, poor as I am? If I were a shepherd, I would bring a lamb; If I were a wise man, I would do my part; yet what I can I give him: Give my heart." (Christina G. Rossetti, UMH, 376)

Today Christians the world over will gather around the table of Christ. Some will partake of the Eucharist; others will receive Holy Communion; still others will share the Lord's Supper. Some will receive a wafer the size of a thumbtack head dipped in the holy wine. Others will receive an individual measure of wine in a plastic cup no larger than a thimble. Still others will tear a morsel of bread from a loaf and sip from a common cup.

Isn't it strange that Christians only receive the smallest of portions when partaking of the Holy Meal? Can we be observing the commandment of the same Jesus who changed over one hundred gallons of water into wine at a wedding in Cana, who with five loaves and two fishes fed five thousand men plus women and children and had twelve full baskets left over? Forgive me if I drink deeply from the cup and tear an extra portion from the loaf. Today I'll SUPER SIZE mine!

I need not upset the Communion servers by taking more than my normal share of wine and bread. The size of my physical portion is not important. The grace that I will receive as I partake of the bread and the wine has already been SUPER SIZED! As we hear the words of the Great Thanksgiving, we remember once again that God's love remains steadfast, even when we turn from God. Through the Holy Spirit, we are made one with Christ and with one another, and one in ministry to all the world.

We have no need to SUPER SIZE the elements we receive because, through the holy mystery, Christ in all his love and glory comes again to us. We have already received and will continue to receive a glorious superabundance of God's grace. We have tasted the sweet corn and the reserve wine!

HYMN FOR MEDITATION: "Amazing grace! How sweet the sound that saved a wretch like me! I once was lost, but now am found; was blind, but now I see." (John Newton, UMH 378)

The Grace of the Law

January 19–25, 2004 • Andrea La Sonde Anastos[‡]

MONDAY, JANUARY 19 • Read Psalm 19:1-6

God continually pours out an amazing bounty to bless the universe. Day after day, from the beginning of time, we have been surrounded with abundance. The psalmist reminds us that the beauty and grace of the cosmos are a jubilant proclamation of wonder and joy—even in the profound silence of wordlessness.

As this week begins, we are invited to allow wonder and joy, beauty and grace, and infinite abundance to transform us. Perhaps we will come to know ourselves as persons permeated with the wisdom and knowledge of the Holy One who liberates us from all aspects of temporal life that imprison us: from violence and anger, alienation and despair, resentment and stress, self-righteousness and prejudice, from addiction to substances or work or body image and from idolatrous worship of money or power or prestige.

We are invited to live in the light of the sun (and the Son) as it runs its course and from which nothing is hidden. In the clarity of that radiance, we understand the simple truth that when we focus on praise of God's grandeur, we have no time or energy for pettiness, greed, or arrogance. We are freed to be who God created us to be: reflections of God's own image.

SUGGESTION FOR MEDITATION: Write your own psalm of praise for the world you see outside your window. Look with God's eyes. With attention and love, notice the miracles of God's handiwork around you.

PRAYER: God of grandeur, empty me of all the clutter of my life to allow space for your abundance. Amen.

[‡]Intentional interim minister with the United Church of Christ; spiritual director and retreat leader; writer; member of the Consultation on Common Texts, living in Greenfield, Massachusetts.

When my daughter was about three years old, she loved to hear the story of her birth. For several months, she asked me to tell it every day, sometimes three or four times. This story explained to her who she was, told her that she was loved, and reminded her that she *belonged* to a community of family.

The Hebrew people, returned from exile, settle into their towns. Then they gather to hear the reading of God's word, to hear *their* story of belonging to community and to God. From early in the morning until midday, the scrolls of Moses are read to "those who could understand," and the people respond by offering prayers of thanksgiving and by praising God.

How many faithful churchgoers today would respond with such excitement to three or four hours of scripture reading? I suspect that most people find God's word uninteresting because they hear it as something that has nothing to do with them.

How different would our lives be if we heard God's word and God's law as *our* story, a story about how we are loved and claimed by God? as a proclamation of our emancipation from our slavery to worldly agendas? as a description of the beloved community we have been empowered to create with God here and now? These verses from the book of Nehemiah invite us to return to our story again and again to find ourselves and, in finding ourselves, to be filled with enormous gratitude because we are God's own people.

PRAYER: Holy Creator, you called me into being and claimed me for your own. You call me back from every exile and claim me as your own. May your word name me and your law shape me today, so that I may see your reflection in me and know in whose image I am created. Amen.

In a society like that of the twenty-first century United States, many Christians seem strangely resentful of God's law, as if the law were a prison, denying them access to "the good life." Yet the people of Nehemiah's time weep for joy when the law is read aloud to them and then interpreted so that they can understand it fully.

It is hard to believe that these former exiles were masochists; they must have understood something that many of us miss when we hear God's word. Perhaps they recognized the *abundance* in the law that invited them into continual connection with the divine source of life. Perhaps they recognized the *loving interdependence* of the law that allowed them to live generously in community, honoring and respecting one another. Perhaps they recognized the *freedom* of the law that allowed them to trust one another to act with integrity.

As we move through this week, we are offered the chance to look again at the gift of God's law and to receive it with celebration and thanksgiving.

SUGGESTION FOR MEDITATION: Consider the gift of the sabbath. What would you do with a true sabbath from work, errands, and chores? Plan a sabbath day that is truly a time of rest and renewal and post it beside your calendar or tuck it into your date book. Speak with the other members of your household, and then schedule a sabbath and "celebrate the law."

PRAYER: Holy Lawgiver, open my heart to the hidden treasure of your law. Allow me to feast on its abundance and to celebrate its liberating power. Grant me the grace to write it on my heart and follow in its way with joyful feet. Amen.

In my first pastorate, I was blessed with the companionship of Bessie, a woman in her early 70s when we met. Bessie had faced much pain and loss in her life, but she had a lightness of heart that brought joy to everyone around her. People smiled in her company. Indeed, people sought her out when they were feeling low because her very presence was healing.

One afternoon as we sat drinking tea together, I learned Bessie's secret. I asked her how she could face life with such equanimity. "Why, I suppose it's that I never worry about decisions. I don't waste any time agonizing over what's the right thing to do. It frees up a powerful lot of energy to have fun, and I sleep like a baby at night. And," Bessie's eyes twinkled as she said, "I don't have nearly as many wrinkles as some of my friends."

We laughed, and then I asked her how she managed to make decisions so easily. "Well, pastor, I just follow the Ten Commandments: I love the Lord first and I don't let anything get in the way of that. Then, of course, I don't need to *decide* about whether to tell little lies or cheat on my taxes or whether someone will overhear me speaking badly of them. It makes life mighty simple and gives me time to appreciate what God has showered on us all."

For Bessie, the law was "sweeter than honey, and drippings of the honeycomb." In the twenty years since I met her, I have yet to find a better prescription for joy or restful sleep. (And it continues to work for Bessie, who is still going strong in her 90s.)

SUGGESTION FOR MEDITATION: Think about a decision you made recently that caused you stress or sleeplessness. How might you feel if you had used Bessie's approach? In what ways might the decision have come more easily? more peacefully?

When John the Baptizer came out of the wilderness, he called people to baptism by water, and he told them that the one who was coming would baptize with fire and the Spirit. In this passage, Jesus reminds us what that means. He announces the task for which he and his disciples are commissioned. He announces what it means to have the Spirit of the Lord resting on us.

It is dangerous work to which we are called. Those in positions of power will be no more receptive to the message today than they were when Jesus spoke it himself. God's message overturns the status quo in every age because it is a message of liberation rather than legalism, of release rather than imprisonment, of forgiveness of debt rather than greed and materialism.

However, the realm of God will only come to fruition through the faithful witness of God's people. God has told us that it will not happen without us because the Holy chooses to depend on our free response to God's invitation. How many times will we ignore these words that invite our wholehearted commitment to God's desire for creation? When will we finally respond, as Jesus did, with the words God longs to hear: "Today this scripture has been fulfilled in your hearing."

SUGGESTION FOR MEDITATION: **Consider one way in which you can fulfill this scripture tangibly. Visualize what it would mean for *you* to "bring good news" or "proclaim release." What words would you speak? What deed(s) would you perform? Allow yourself to realize that your decision makes a difference. Celebrate the fact that you have been empowered to be an instrument of grace.**

PRAYER: **Holy God, you risk entrusting your creation to my hands and heart. Grant me the courage to protect and love it at any cost. Amen.**

When we accept our baptism in the Spirit, we allow ourselves to be revelations of the One in whose image we are created. We each become manifestations of some unique aspect of that glorious One who is All-in-All; together, we become visible incarnations of God's own body in this universe.

Together. Not alone. Together.

Paul alerts his sisters and brothers in Corinth that God has a particular call for each of them. Each has a specific, unique task within God's great plan for creation, just as each part of the body has its own special function in the health and growth of the physical person. Therefore, it is only *together*, respecting and celebrating one another's uniqueness, that they begin to reflect divinity in human form.

We too are called to this awareness. We need to let go of our expectation that God's people will all look alike or act alike or speak the same words. We need to give up the laziness that believes we can piggyback on someone else's faith. We need to refrain from accusations of heresy or judgmentalism when a sister or a brother challenges our perspective. We need to listen attentively to the still small voice that invites us to take up our own individual work on behalf of God's realm.

Paul reminds us that God creates us and arranges us in a community to God's own satisfaction to meet God's hope.

PRAYER: O you who are One and Many-in-One, open my heart to the many who are not like me but to whom I am bound in your plan. Open my heart to rejoice in their difference, to recognize their gifts, to respect their uniqueness. Encourage me to trust your call, to trust my own difference from others, to trust the gifts you give me for the good of the whole that your body may be incarnate on earth. Amen.

Clark was a soloist in the church choir; but when he did not sing a solo, he didn't sing with the choir. As the pastor, I asked the choir director about this. She shrugged and said, "He can't sing in a group and blend his voice with others; he throws everyone else off."

A month later, Clark's wife, Cindy, came to talk with me. She confessed that she was considering a divorce. "I don't know what to do! I love him so much, but we don't have a partnership. Clark won't make decisions *with* me about anything: the children, the house, vacations, investments. He is either in charge or he won't participate."

Only weeks later, Clark was diagnosed with cancer. Suddenly, he could not "go it alone." He needed to trust his medical team to help him weigh treatment options; he needed to depend on family and friends to provide the most intimate care; he needed to delegate decisions within his company. For the first time in his adult life, he knew himself as part of a broader community, a community that was working together to help *him* return to full health.

Clark didn't change overnight, but the crisis of cancer eventually transformed him. He no longer said, "I have no need of you." As his body recovered, his heart and soul also healed from a deep alienation; and he awoke to the profound realization that, as a member of a community (a body), he was empowered to do far greater things than he had been able to accomplish alone.

SUGGESTION FOR MEDITATION: In what ways do you tell others you have no need of them? Where do you see places of alienation in your life? In what ways does being connected to others or dependent on others make you fearful? What would it feel like to let go of that fear and to let others know you need them?

A Standing Invitation

January 26–February 1, 2004 • Ray Waddle[‡]

MONDAY, JANUARY 26 • Read Jeremiah 1:4-10

Jeremiah opens with one of the great mysteries of the life of faith: the sense of calling, mission, vocation. Jeremiah's just a young man when God calls him to the task and ordeal of a prophet. Bamboozled by the idea, he insists on his unworthiness, but God knows better. God knows Jeremiah's potential.

The scarcely conceivable notion that the Maker of the Universe is tapping you for an amazing journey, a new identity or public witness, a revolutionary course inducing joy and sacrifice—well, it happens. As a journalist, I encounter people every day who've heard such a call for themselves, a divine beckoning. How did it come? Every sort of way: the bolt-of-lightning experience that makes page-one news or a sudden whisper or a persistent dream or, as often as not, a long, slow turning in personal perspective, years in the making.

Some people say they literally hear a voice. Was it God? Or conscience? Or the soul's own cry? Perhaps the divine calling breaks in on a person's life when the literal and the metaphorical become one and the same, a vision of justice and kindness; the effect is life-changing.

Then there are the believers who aren't called in a dramatic flourish, who see the mission before their eyes and go about it without fanfare. Jeremiah discovered his way, one of the most famous reckonings in human history. Everybody faces the prospect of a calling, whether it makes front-page news or not.

PRAYER: Eternal Spirit, you've given me eyes for seeing and ears for hearing. Keep me alert to the signs and wonders of your will, and lead me where you will. Amen.

[‡]Writer based in Nashville, Tennessee; author of *A Turbulent Peace: The Psalms for Our Time*, published by Upper Room Books; former religion editor of *The Tennessean* newspaper.

We baby boomers are getting on up there, getting older, just plain old getting old. This psalm, the plea of a person crying out in old age, might one day be the baby boomers' unofficial theme song, the psalm to cherish in the twilight.

A boomer theme song? The vast boomer demographic—78 million Americans, the first wave now closing in on their 60s—always had a complicated relation to faith. About a third of the boomers left church and never came back. Another third wandered away but eventually returned. The other third never really left in the first place. Boomers grew up riding a golden age of pop songs and prosperity. Nostalgia, the sweet memory of the way things were, could be the tempting religion of old age.

The writer of Psalm 71, while reflecting on past deliverance and refuge, lays down a challenge to proclaim the living God in the present. The psalmist has not had an easy time of it. He cries out from feeble health and vulnerability, offering poignant details. The psalmist has been faithful to God during a long lifetime, but now enemies mock. He was once perhaps a teacher in the faith, but his strength is spent. Yet now, reaching deep inside once more and fighting back doubt and fear, he finds a reserve of trust in the divine, a vision of joy. A few verses later, the psalmist asks God for strength enough to proclaim God's might to all the generations to come. It's a big-hearted request, a generous way to spend the remaining fragments of one's old age, taking harp and lyre in hand to proclaim God's wondrous deeds.

We boomers have had a good run. In a jittery new century we should remember our privileges with gratitude, search our hearts, and muster the courage to proclaim the faith again—"for you are my rock and my fortress"—for all to hear.

PRAYER: Holy Lord, you are the rock of refuge no matter how uncertain the times we live in. I pray your name with gladness, thankful for the gift of life. Amen.

The psalmist testifies that it was God who took him from his mother's womb, a declaration of great intimacy and faith. It has echoes in Jeremiah's cry that God knew him in the womb.

What a breathtaking image: God was there when our tiny hearts and minds were yet unformed and now waits patiently for us to come around. Some of us get the message early on, seeing our parents praising God and reading scripture, and we follow suit. Others of us arrive at the party way later, after decades of spiritual sleepwalking or confusion or anger or plain bad luck. God's governance isn't altered by our false turns or inertia. The divine patience arcs across the span of one's whole life. A standing invitation beckons us to step into the drama of redemption.

In Psalm 71, the psalmist declares a lifelong trust in the Lord. But now in old age that lifelong relationship feels tested as never before. Poor health, cruel enemies, and corrosive doubts torment him. There's a momentary slip of resolve: Do not cast me off in the time of old age.

But the logic of divine presence is clear enough—the God who was there in the womb, when we're helpless and silent and unaware, is there at the other end of life too. The psalmist summons determination, puts aside fear, gathers a lifetime's verbal tools of faith, and goes out with a bold witness of praise to God. An entire life is traced here, from womb nearly to tomb, from the prenatal heartbeat to the music of a last leave-taking. When the final credits roll on his life, the psalmist makes sure Who gets top billing.

PRAYER: Dear God, you've been constant from the beginning, a presence our whole lives, even in the shadows of old age. Grant me the voice to praise you with ever-renewing force to the last. Amen.

This is one of the great passages of all scripture. Every time I read it, something fresh leaps out at me. Often it's "Love is patient; love is kind," a reminder that my wife and I read this passage at our wedding. It remains a foundation document for matrimony.

Some days other passages clear their throat and take center stage: "If I have all faith, so as to remove mountains, but do not have love, I am nothing." This is startling to hear in a nation of so much official religion and doctrinal competition to see who can market the strongest faith.

At the moment, though, yet another passage chimes forth with alarming authority: "For we know only in part, and we prophesy only in part." Our knowledge is imperfect. In the world of religion, many of us are reluctant or afraid to admit we don't know the mind of God after all. We're afraid such an admission would look like weakness or spiritual laziness or look bad on the annual evaluation.

But there it is in the Holy Bible, permission to state the obvious: We don't know the whole picture, not yet. We peer, all of us, into the mirror dimly, the glass darkly. Our doctrinal knowledge cannot be perfect. To insist that it is perfect opens the door for arrogance, vanity, and violence. Better to trust actions over words, the actions urged by Paul in First Corinthians: Love is the ultimate action, the needed thing, the grown-up thing in a grieving world.

PRAYER: Dear God, you give us love, and you give us each day to fill with love. May I be a worthy instrument of your love. In Jesus' name. Amen.

Do you take the Bible literally? Many people declare the whole Bible is literally true, and they mean it. For others, *literally* is one of those litmus test words—a gotcha term in religious debate when one side tries to outdo the other for first place and top ranking in the Bible-believer playoffs.

Usually literalism focuses on the six-day creation story in Genesis or on Jonah in the belly of the fish or on the miracles of Jesus. Such debates never get around to this famous passage on love written by Paul in his first letter to the Corinthians. But what if everyone indeed took this passage literally; that is, took it to heart, as if the words had the unflinching, nonnegotiable, divine quality of authority, which they do?

What would the world look like then? What would Christianity be like? Imagine: Ideological tensions would cease. Energy would shift from doctrinal haggling and committee work to incessant acts of random kindness. The culture wars would be mothballed. Religious and ethnic bitterness would lose relevance. Each faith would feel safe enough to trust its own best insights and gifts to the world—the triumph of love, right action over righteous talk, results and not speculation. Divine love would be a verb again and not a pious abstraction. Literally.

PRAYER: Heavenly God, I thank you for your word, laid down in the pages of scripture across the many centuries, speaking to us plainly. Help me read it with courage, that it will enter my heart and move me forward to action. Amen.

From the start, Jesus was acquainted with rejection, even at his birth in Bethlehem where there was no room in the inn. And now, near the beginning of his public ministry, rejection stands ready to isolate him. Speaking to the home-turf congregation in Nazareth, he has just announced a world-shattering manifesto, the old words from Isaiah made new: release to the captives, sight for the blind, freedom for the oppressed. But it doesn't take. People are alarmed and getting mad. The acceptable year of the Lord is anything but acceptable. By any earthly measure, his is a disastrous hometown debut.

Jesus' words always had a way of rubbing people the wrong way. Only committed followers got the picture, and even they misunderstood much of what he was saying. So Jesus never stayed anywhere for long. After he preached, he managed to slip through the clutches of doctrinal hostility, finding daylight, moving on. Divinity on earth is no easy fit. Anything Jesus said was likely to be met with befuddlement or irritation except to a disciple's heart.

Nothing much has changed. It's no easy thing for a preacher to stand in the pulpit and read these subversive words from the old Holy Bible and declare the acceptable year of the Lord, even in the year 2004. Release to the captives. Freedom for the oppressed. Hard sayings indeed. They imply rearranging personal values and questioning public priorities. More than two thousand years after Jesus' ministry, divine messages and earthly life mingle uneasily still. Somehow, though, the good news keeps arriving. It's being fulfilled in our hearing today, every day.

SUGGESTION FOR MEDITATION: What will I do today to help make this the acceptable year of the Lord?

SUNDAY, FEBRUARY 1 • Read Luke 4:21-30

One brief scene in a Nazareth synagogue changed the world. Jesus stood and read from the prophet Isaiah, then sat down and declared that God's time had come to be fulfilled. When Jesus spoke, a vision of compassion, healing, action, and redemption was released into the world. It's been circling the globe ever since, looking for a place of welcome.

It must have been an astonishing moment to hear these words from Jesus, this compelling new testimony to life's possibilities. Afterward, a silence surely filled the room, a long moment of silence, as the words sank in. But it only lasted a moment. The protest from his audience was almost immediate.

They knew this man, his family, his ordinary daily circumstances. He was local, surely too local and familiar to be an honorable prophet.

After Jesus escaped Nazareth, he went to Capernaum and preached out of the synagogue there. It became a base of operations, where he performed mighty acts of healing, though even there he was eventually rejected. Years ago I visited the ruins of the Capernaum synagogue near the banks of the Galilee, the likely spot where Jesus himself preached. It was a disorienting experience—such a small place, crowded, tourist-centered. My tour group was tired and on a tight schedule. Bus fumes were everywhere. How could such a headachy scene be ground zero for history-altering news of spiritual import?

The joke was on me, of course. I was letting everyday irritations get in the way of a biblical truth. From this humble place Jesus' message of kindness and decision was released all those years ago like the dove freed from the ark after the great flood, a vision of compassion still looking for a place to light its feet.

PRAYER: **Dear God, it's my privilege to share this earth and walk this world for a time. It's my responsibility to take up the work of your will and redemption. I rejoice in the power of your Son, his words, witness, and resurrection. Amen.**

Call and Response...An Eternal Dilemma

February 2–8, 2004 • Victor Pérez-Silvestry[‡]

MONDAY, FEBRUARY 2 • Read Isaiah 6:1-7

As the sun rises, I watch from my porch enjoying a fresh cup of coffee. As minutes pass, shadows disappear and everything comes alive. Birds fly around chirping, letting everybody know that night is over and a new day awaits. I can feel God's presence in the fresh breeze, the sunlight, the birds flying, in nature's awakening to a new day. God allows us to enjoy divine presence in the midst of our daily lives.

In today's scripture passage, Isaiah experiences God's mighty presence through a vision. Like Moses, Ezekiel, Gideon, and Jeremiah, Isaiah has an encounter with the awesome God. Such encounters are known as vocation or visionary experiences. All these cases report an encounter with God, a commission to do God's will or speak God's word, and a ritual sign or act symbolizing a designated role. In most instances, the one who is called objects to the vocation and then receives reassurance from God.

Many of us have experienced God's presence in wonderful ways at different times in our lives and have tried to discern how to respond to God's call. Each moment in God's presence makes us aware of our limitations, of our sinful nature. Yet if we, as Isaiah, humbly recognize our condition, God will come to our rescue, the divine touch taking away our guilt. We will be forgiven and given a new start.

Some encounters with God are less intense than others, but each one offers the opportunity to praise God's greatness, mercy, and love for us. Every new encounter equips us better to respond to God's will.

PRAYER: God, we experience you every day of our lives. Make us sensitive to your call and obedient to your will. Amen.

[‡]Director for Continuing Education, the Evangelical Seminary, San Juan, Puerto Rico.

Listening to the weather expert predicting the route of Hurricane Lily reminded me that sometimes in life you would rather be the bearer of good news than the predictor of desolation. In just hours, he said, Lily would hit the coast of Louisiana with great force, bringing possible destruction to the people who lived there. Other than share the data he had at hand, the forecaster could do nothing but warn the people of Louisiana of potential disaster.

God is looking for a messenger to share a message with the people of Israel. Without hesitation Isaiah volunteers for the task. God tells him what to say to the people: a word of judgment, a forecast of destruction and desolation. Not an easy task, but someone has to do it. Begging mercy, Isaiah raises a question about the length of this judgment. The response he receives is unexpected, but still he fulfills his task.

Many times in our lives God chooses us to fulfill tasks that we find uncomfortable. Our first reaction is to reject such a call or to question why it has to be done or be done by us. We try to get a more suitable response or find another volunteer or a better time to go about the task. Usually this doesn't work, and we find ourselves reluctantly fulfilling the task God has given us.

Such times are difficult and stressful, but as with Isaiah, God is counting on us. God never asks if we are able for the task; God asks if we are available. If we respond positively, God will enable us for the challenge. No matter how difficult it is, God will support us to its completion.

PRAYER: Loving God, make us obedient to your will and willing to obey, so that your many tasks can get done. Amen.

One of our major challenges as Christians is to guide others in understanding Christian faith, especially in learning to trust God and patiently wait for God's action and intervention in their daily lives. In God's love we are precious. No matter what our situation, turning to God assures deliverance and the discovery of solutions to our many troubles. God's love for us is accessible if we will but call on it.

The psalmist has experienced God's love in his life, as well as God's faithfulness and readiness to respond. The God of a universe so vast and complex has always had time to come to his rescue. The psalmist is thankful and full of praise.

We seek that close relationship with God, recognizing God's power and might in the universe and praising God as the maker and the sustainer of our lives. No matter how much knowledge, power, or money we might have, we will always emotionally and spiritually need to trust someone. And no one can be as close to our inner being as God, who knows our intimate thoughts and longings, because God has made us.

As we continue our journey in life, let us be reminded of God's steadfast love for us. Sharing our doubts, concerns, and questions with God, we can put our future in God's hands. Like the psalmist, we can trust that "the LORD will fulfill his purpose for me" (v. 8). We will not be left alone, because God never abandons the work of God's hands.

PRAYER: Loving God, open our hearts and minds to understand the greatness of your love for us. Make us patient and wise so we can see your hand reaching to us when we are in trouble. Help us to be content knowing that we can always trust you. Amen.

The members of the congregation expected to participate in our church's usual Holy Communion service, but this time the setting differed. Our pastor had moved the Communion table to the center of the sanctuary: same table, same vestments and elements, but closer to us. As we made the now much-shorter walk to the table, we were reminded again that Jesus offered his life to save us from our sins. Through his death and resurrection we are made one in Christ.

The apostle Paul reminds the Christians in Corinth of the importance of the message he has shared with them, the essential message of the gospel: salvation by faith in Jesus Christ. He has preached to them, probably repeatedly, about the way Jesus suffered, died, and was resurrected. Because they need to understand the theological truth of such events, the foundation of their faith, Paul reminds them again and again, pushing the Communion table a little closer with each reminder. He knows they must become faithful Christians in order to stand firm in their time of trial and tribulation, as Paul has already experienced. They need to be clear about their faith.

Christians all over the world must understand Paul's urgent insistence. If his message was important for Christians of his time, it is important for Christians in postmodern times: We need to be clear about our faith; we need to live with the Communion table in our midst. Many creeds, movements, and leaders claim to have the truth. But Paul reminds us that only in Christ can we find salvation. Because Christ died for us, we can be relieved from guilt and be forgiven. In Christ's resurrection we have been promised eternal life.

PRAYER: Loving God, make us sensitive to your love for us. Help us to keep the Communion table at the center of our lives. Open our hearts to receive the truth of salvation in Jesus Christ your son, who came to this world to fulfill your will. Amen.

While attending a weekend retreat for men, I met a young man assigned to be my table leader. He tried earnestly to keep the group's attention focused on the various subjects presented throughout the retreat. He won our confidence, and we willingly followed his directions. He seemed like a committed Christian trying to help others get closer to Christ.

On the second day of the retreat, the young man spoke to the group about the impact of God's grace in his life. In his testimony we learned that he had been a drug addict, imprisoned for stealing and drug trafficking. While in prison he turned his life to Jesus and promised to serve him by helping others grow closer to God.

God's grace gave the young man an opportunity to reshape his life and use it for the good of others. After several years he came back to the free community and joined a Methodist church, where he now serves Christ through ministry to men in spiritual retreats.

In today's scripture, we meet another man who gave testimony of God's grace in his life. After being a persecutor of Christians, he became, in God's grace, an apostle. Paul gave himself to the task of sharing the message of salvation in Christ, reaching out to the Gentiles; he committed himself to carrying the gospel message to them so they could believe and be saved.

Many men and women have experienced God's grace at work in their lives, changing them for the better. If this is your case, make sure you share your story so that others can learn about God's perfect love for all.

PRAYER: Dear God, make us mindful of the many times you have forgiven our faults and have given us new opportunities. Help us share a word of encouragement with others. Amen.

The spiritual formation team of my annual conference invited all the pastors to a biannual retreat that focused on the spiritual nourishment of pastors. The theme of the two-day journey, "Feed My Shepherds," invited pastors to stretch their current ideas about their relationship to Jesus.

The leader for the retreat challenged the pastors to be open to new ways of prayer, scripture devotional reading, personal meditation, and scripture group reflection. He invited us revisit some practices we had probably employed in the past, but he offered new insights on approaches to scripture and prayer.

We pastors left the retreat with renewed spirits, having been fed by the good shepherd Jesus. Making appropriate use of the spiritual disciplines of prayer, scripture reading, the sacraments, and group Bible reflection, we were fed magnificently and ready to find new ways to feed as we had been fed.

The disciples have been fishing all night without any catch and have decided to call it a day. Jesus asks Simon to go out into deeper waters and cast out the nets. An excellent fisherman, Simon reminds Jesus that they have been working all night and have caught nothing. Yet he decides to obey Jesus' advice. He has recognized Jesus' authority and power and willingly follows his directions.

Perhaps we feel like experts in our differing fields of ministry and service. However, to be truly effective in ministry, we must, as did Simon, accept the advice of the real expert.

PRAYER: Dear God, make us sensitive to your voice so that we can receive appropriate directions in order to get better results. Open our minds and hearts to your wisdom so that we can be effective instruments of your grace. Amen.

Throughout my Christian journey, I have felt called to serve God in different capacities. At the age of thirty-three, I experienced God's call to the ordained ministry and quit my banking career to attend seminary while serving a local church. Later, God gave me the opportunity to serve my church in a leadership role in one of its general agencies. Presently I serve God through the ministry of a theological education institution.

Most of the times when I have experienced God's leading, I have felt unfit for the task but have obediently gone in the direction God showed me. As time has passed, God's grace has enabled me to carry out the assigned task, and I have found great joy in serving in my new capacity.

Simon had made his living, like many of his friends, pulling fish from the water so that others would have something to eat. But his encounter with Jesus changed his daily routine. Jesus asked Simon and some of his friends to quit the fishing business and follow him, calling them to be his partners in the business of bringing people closer to God. Even though they might not have known exactly what Jesus meant, Simon and his friends left their boats and nets and followed him.

Throughout the years since Simon put down his net, many people have willingly abandoned secular professions to become partners with Jesus in the business of bringing others closer to God. These decisions are not easy to make; but those who do, learn that God will never forsake them. When we respond obediently to God's call, we receive sustenance for the journey.

PRAYER: Dear God, help us to be obedient to your call no matter how many times you ask us to change directions in our journey to serve you. Amen.

The Blessed Life

February 9–15, 2004 • Sharon M. Freeto[‡]

MONDAY, FEBRUARY 9 • Read 1 Corinthians 15:12-20

If repetition lends strength to a point, Paul certainly tries to make this one very strong. He wants there to be no doubt for any reader that the resurrection of Christ through the work of God is essential to being a Christian. Jesus' resurrection is a requirement! It is neither optional nor a suggestion. It is an absolute necessity!

Six times over the course of nine verses Paul uses the word *raise* in the perfect tense—that is, Jesus was raised by God. It is not simply Jesus' resurrection that gives validity to the faith, but that this resurrection was willed and carried out by God.

The importance of this seemingly subtle distinction is that all those who are "in Christ" enjoy the same benefits: We both die with Christ and are raised with him through the power of God. Through Jesus' sacrifice our sins have been forgiven, and we are directly linked with the life-giving power of the Creator of the universe. As Paul emphasizes and reemphasizes to the Corinthians, because Jesus *was raised* our faith has not been in vain.

Having just read this verse as I passed the cornerstone of my congregation's new church building one day, I was struck by the words carved on it: "Christ is our cornerstone." Paul would have preferred something a little less concise and more powerful, accurate, and hopeful. He would have preferred, "The risen Christ is our cornerstone." He would have been right.

PRAYER: All-powerful God, we thank you for the resurrection of Christ and the promise it embodies for us all. We rejoice that our faith is not in vain. Help us to understand the promise and hope of your power in that event. Amen.

[‡]Pastor, Blanco United Methodist Church, Blanco, Texas; retired Air Force chaplain.

In this early psalm, Jeremiah contrasts the fate of those who look to God with that of those who look to themselves or others. The psalm's theme is as unmistakable as it is powerful.

"The heart is devious above all else; it is perverse—who can understand it?" laments Jeremiah. Certainly Paul's familiarity with this passage became evident when he wrote, "For we know that the law is spiritual; but I am of the flesh, sold into slavery under sin. I do not understand my own actions. For I do not do what I want, but I do the very thing I hate" (Rom. 7:14-15).

How easy it is to wonder with both the Old Testament writer and our brother Paul what it takes to follow God's blessed way. Each of us is intimately familiar with our shortcomings and discouraged at the ease with which we repeat the same mistakes. Both Jeremiah and Paul make it clear that placing our trust in human strength is doomed to failure. Only our trust in the Lord saves us.

I am reminded of a confirmation class that used a dartboard to talk about sin as missing the mark. All the spaces except the bull's eye were labeled "sin," and in that small center was written the word *love*. When the young people were invited to try their aim, they soon began to complain: "But it is so easy to hit sin, and so hard to hit love!"

When God aims our life, we can hit the mark. What we can never hope to accomplish on our own is made possible by God. We are loved by the God who both knows our intentions and wipes out our sins.

PRAYER: Forgiving God, we thank you for the blessings of your unfailing love, even when we let you down. Enable us through your strength to be a channel of love to others. Amen.

Sometimes called "the psalm of contrasts," this uncharacteristic passage from Jeremiah leaves no room for doubt. Those who trust in themselves aren't misguided, missing the mark, or mean-spirited; they are cursed.

The temptation is to interpret this psalm in the traditional understanding that "good things happen to good people" and "bad things happen to bad people." But the new covenant gives us a different perspective.

In the traditional understanding, curses come to those who turn from God. They have called down trouble upon their heads not through their actions but by who they have chosen to be. They have chosen to be their own person, not God's.

Yet we know from the painful and sometimes horrible circumstances that surround us that God brings the sun and the rain on both the just and unjust. (Or as a friend of mine used to say, "God has a lot to account for.") And when we choose to depend completely upon ourselves, God's blessings may indeed continue, though they may go unrecognized and uncelebrated.

In the new-covenant understanding, doing it "my way" instead of God's way is a surefire formula for disaster, not because God takes revenge (God doesn't) but because our decisions sever us from communion with God, leaving us with only a powerless idol—ourselves.

PRAYER: Loving God, remind us that you bless each of us not according to our worthiness but according to your love for us. Teach us to acknowledge and celebrate those blessings so that we belong to you. Amen.

Luke's version of the beloved Beatitudes brings them down to our level. Jesus does not deliver them from the mountaintop (no Sermon on the Mount here) but from level ground, the "Sermon on the Plain." In Luke, Jesus reaches out to all, coming down to our level to establish a relationship and to be our teacher.

Shortly before Luke begins his account of this sermon, he notes that Jesus has chosen his disciples. These blessings outlined in the sermon are Jesus' first teachings, then, for both the inner circle of the twelve and the greater, less intimate crowd, many of whom have come not to learn from Jesus so much as to benefit from his healing powers.

The Beatitudes do not readily lend themselves to spiritual interpretation. They do not replace the Ten Commandments or additional rules of Jewish law but describe lives configured by the will of God and people who choose to follow God's will. Reversing the societal norms of the time, the Beatitudes introduce a new way of looking at the world—through God's eyes. They remind us of what we would today call "lifestyle issues." They are promises but also descriptions that we, like the disciples and the early crowd, are encouraged to recognize and celebrate.

The Beatitudes have a wonderful immediacy and reality about them that impress upon us, whatever our social status, that God has a special concern for the poor, the hungry, the sorrowing, the persecuted. To such as these does God offer blessing.

PRAYER: God, you remind us that your blessings are poured out on those in need, regardless of their social status. As we view the world through your eyes, may we recognize that in showing your love to others, we are ourselves blessed. Amen.

This part of the Sermon on the Plain reminds me of the old "good news/bad news" jokes. First we had the good news of the Beatitudes. Now we have the bad news of the woes. Even as the Beatitudes are not commandments so much as reminders, so are the woes neither curses nor individual predictions. They are rather declarative statements to help us remember the consequences of refusing relationship with God.

Jesus outlines the logical consequences of choices that take us into the kingdom of God or keep us out. To live in relationship with God is a choice rich with blessings simply because of the company we keep. On the other hand, to live outside God's will and reign, to live under the sway of worldly kings, lesser gods, or hollow values fills our lives with woe. We deserve what we get simply because we hang around with the wrong crowd!

Unlike Matthew's version of Jesus' sermon, which guarantees future blessings for the poor, Luke's version uses the present tense. God's kingdom is already on its way, breaking in amidst the poverty and grief and hunger of the world with the wonderful promise of blessings to come! Jesus gives us every reason to choose to enter God's kingdom and enjoy the rich blessings that flow from God's divine fellowship. Woe to those who choose otherwise.

PRAYER: Great God, ruler of all time, Creator of the universe, give us the wisdom to choose always and everywhere to live under your reign so that we may both enjoy and anticipate the blessings of your fellowship. Amen.

Continuing the theme so beautifully begun in the Magnificat, Luke uses the woes to press home his point about the dangers of wealth. In the Magnificat Mary sings, "He has shown strength with his arm; he has scattered the proud in the thoughts of their hearts. He has brought down the powerful from their thrones, and lifted up the lowly; he has filled the hungry with good things, and sent the rich away empty" (Luke 1:51-53).

The woes are not an "I told you so" from a nagging heavenly parent. They are declarations of judgment about the logical results of living outside of the kingdom of God. Being rich does not, by itself, guarantee residence in the land of Lukan woes, but it does ease our entry there. The danger of wealth resides in its power to preoccupy us with the entertaining and attractive false gods that riches buy. In time we may feel so assured of our own authority that we fail to recognize the Creator's invitation to divine fellowship in the kingdom.

The message is simple if not easy. Any contest between worldly blessedness and heavenly blessedness will always favor the poor. God does play favorites, and they are always the least favored of this world. Luke makes clear the message to those of us who are rich (and that's most of us): to avoid the woes we must seek a threefold repentance of gifts, generosity, and grace.

PRAYER: Generous God, bestow upon us the perception to seek heartfelt repentance so that we may focus on your love rather than on the false love of worldly things. Amen.

This psalm operates beautifully as the introduction to one of the most-beloved of biblical books. What it says about the law and the expectations of the righteous may seem a little strange to the minds and hearts of Westerners, however. Most of us think of laws as those things that fence us in with their demands and expectations. The psalmist's perspective is very different. His classic Jewish understanding of law as a gift of the covenant relationship means law is not a burden but a blessing.

Cast adrift in a world that often seemed illogical and haphazard, our Jewish brothers and sisters found their relationship with their Creator to be one that gave order and meaning to their lives. God's laws were not arbitrary demands nor rules to keep human beings away from all the fun things of life. Instead God's laws were road maps of righteousness. Righteousness was not just a way of living that pleased God. It was a way of living that brought with it the promise of "the good life," one bounded by the rules of a loving parent and filled with the joy of relationship with that parent.

For this reason "their delight is in the law of the LORD, and on his law they meditate day and night" (Ps. 1:2). How best to live is a question that has challenged human beings since the dawn of consciousness. While other peoples have struggled with the pleasing or cajoling of myriad gods, the Jews entered into a covenant based on law with the one God, a God who guided them with steadfast love.

We are beneficiaries of this legacy of law and righteousness. Let us rejoice in the laws of God as the blessings they really are!

PRAYER: God of steadfast love, we thank you for the promise of your continued guidance as we faithfully seek how best to live in this world. Fill us with your Holy Spirit so that we may live righteous lives of holy obedience. Amen.

Experiencing the Holy

February 16–22, 2004 • J. Peter van Eys[‡]

MONDAY, FEBRUARY 16 • Read Exodus 34:29-35

Throughout this week our readings will center upon human encounters with the holy. In our Judeo-Christian faith God is the holy one; thus any experience of the holy is a moment of interaction with the divine. Places where God appears are considered holy. Such a place is Mount Sinai where Moses made repeated visits to converse with God, and it is the setting of our encounter for this day.

When Moses returns from the mountain with tablets containing the covenant, the people notice that his face is shining. His experience of the holy has been such that his face continues to reflect the divine encounter even after returning from the mountain. But because the people fear this development, Moses wears a veil. Nevertheless, a new seed has been planted. Humans not only have moments of experiencing the holy by meeting God; humans may be conduits of God's presence for others.

We live in an age that has an approach-avoidance issue with holiness. Though instant communication lessens our capacity to wait upon the Lord and advanced technology dulls our sense of wonder, evidence points to a renewed interest in spiritual formation and Christian practice. The former would seek the holy, and the latter would reflect the holy.

God expects the covenant people to be holy because God is holy. We will discover over the course of the week that Jesus provides not only our ultimate encounter with the holy but also our most complete witness to living a holy life, one that reflects God to the world.

PRAYER: Lord, lead me this day to experience the holy, that I too might reflect your presence and love in this world. Amen.

[‡]Senior Pastor, Calvary United Methodist Church, Nashville, Tennessee.

TUESDAY, FEBRUARY 17 • Read Luke 9:28-43

It is a beautiful, crisp New England fall day, and I am seated outside on the porch of a bed and breakfast in Cape Cod. Looking up from the computer screen I can see the ocean and an endless blue horizon. I do not see a mountain. Reading this Gospel lesson challenges me to reflect upon lofty heights while gazing at the flat Massachusetts coastline.

Yet thinking on sight lines draws me into this story, for there are multiple references to what the characters see. As Peter, John, and James reach the top of the mountain with Jesus, the appearance of Jesus' face and clothing change, and Luke makes it clear that the disciples notice. Immediately thereafter the disciples see two men, Elijah and Moses, talking with Jesus.

The use of sight is further magnified in the description of the cloud covering the mountain. At first, sight gives way to sound, for the disciples cannot see in the cloud. But upon hearing the voice of God identifying God's own son, they see Jesus and Jesus alone.

The location of this event captures our imagination. The disciples' relationship with Jesus is now markedly and remarkably different. They see Jesus in a new way. However, as I look at people walking their dogs, at geese flying in formation, at the lapping waves on the beach, at the everyday commerce of life, I see the more relevant thread of sight woven into this story. And it is this: Not everyone reading the Transfiguration story is atop a mountain or even in view of one. Nevertheless, we all share the experience of life and the glory of God all about us. No matter what your day holds, look around you for the face of Jesus. It is not something we can script, but it is something we can intentionally seek, even in the clouds of life.

PRAYER: Almighty God, enable me to trust in your presence at all times and in all places, and give me eyes to see your face and encounter your glory. Amen.

One approach to understanding the Transfiguration event is to read it as a resurrection appearance of Jesus. To be sure, this requires us to accept that the Gospel writer is not concerned with historical accuracy. Yet such a reading conveys particular power, and it may be more in line with the author's purpose.

The resurrection of Jesus was central to the theology and identity of the early Christian communities. Consequently, each encounter with the risen Lord not only reinforced Jesus' own foretelling of his passion and new life but also provided a glimpse of the future one receives in communion with Christ Jesus. A dazzling world unfolds before us as Christ is manifest in full resurrection glory, and we discover the God who has been with us all along. In the Transfiguration passage, the future is intimately wed to the creation that is without beginning and end. The inclusion of Moses and Elijah make clear the connection between what God has done, will do, and is doing in Christ Jesus.

The Gospel writer, by moving a resurrection appearance into the corpus of Jesus' earthly ministry, affirms the nature, character, and authority of the communities that become the church. Christ has formed these faith communities as surely and uniquely as Jesus called the twelve disciples to follow him. Ultimately, the discernment that comes to us in a resurrection experience involves more than recognizing the face of Jesus; it is an epiphany moment that God has always been with us.

I too can look back on my spiritual journey and identify moments of profound awareness of God. Such occasions overwhelm me in the present and illumine my heart to a past that has been equally in God's care. From my vantage point today, it would be hard to write an autobiography and not interject the glorious work of God in my life even when I was not aware of my Creator and Savior.

PRAYER: O God, open my heart and mind to your presence in ways that enable me to see that you have abided and will always abide with me. Amen.

This psalm is the last in a group of enthronement psalms. In many ways, this collection captures the heart of the Psalter message that God has and always will reign. Understandably, the events of the exile had shaken the moorings of the faith community and sent the people into a spiritual crisis. Thus, the psalmist employs Moses and Aaron and Samuel in an affirmation of God's sovereignty, reminding the reader of past voices that proclaimed the rule of God.

The fact that such reflection is even necessary comes as much more of a surprise than it should. Openly many of us reject any notion that God is absent or removed, while privately we have all experienced those dark nights of the soul. Such a reality makes Psalm 99 a helpful corrective some days and our own praise on other days.

The psalmist not only announces the reign of God but also gives definition to the relationship between God and humanity. Here is the surprise. God's rule involves initiating justice, righteousness, and equity. The intimacy with God that we so desperately seek is established through patterns of care, conferred in acts of mercy, and realized by guardians of human dignity.

To an audience worried that God had become removed and disinterested in their fate came a word affirming God's glorious rule and, even more to the point, God's particular focus on their struggles. Though the crises of our day are different, the same impulse for an assurance of God's rule is present. Like folks of old, we want to know that God is more than interested, that God is actively involved in our lives. We too look for signs of the holy.

PRAYER: Almighty God, help me know the things that make for justice and righteousness in this world, and help me experience your holiness in my relationship with others. Amen.

This is not the first time Moses has come down from the mountain carrying the tablets of the law. In fact, having been established as the chosen leader of the Hebrew people, Moses has had several road trips high upon the mountain. Sometimes he has been summoned by God, and other times he has sought God to make supplication on behalf of the people. An earlier visit had included receiving the tablets of the covenant. However, upon his return Moses discovered that the people had made an idol and in his anger destroyed the tablets.

So this is a story of new beginnings. God is willing to write the covenant laws upon the tablets again. Human fear and lack of trust had prompted the community's unfaithfulness; shock and anger had sparked Moses' destructive rage. Nevertheless, where humans engender self-defeating patterns God consistently seeks to shape and guide. The divine predisposition to author the laws once more is nothing short of enduring and eternal grace.

This story contains another vital quality. As Moses comes down from the mountain he is not even aware that his encounter with the holy has changed his countenance. His brother and others must bring this to his attention. We might pause to consider the role of others in affirming the personal experiences any of us have had with God. Indeed, the implications of this lesson are threefold: it is the human side of the equation that breaks tablets and laws; our occasions of experiencing the holy are always moments of new beginning; and we need the faith community to recognize fully the new life born of encountering God.

PRAYER: Almighty God, though humbled by your consistent gift of new beginnings and amazed at a love that will not let me go, I would seek your holy presence and commit to life in the covenant community that I might receive, know, and share grace. Amen.

Paul builds upon images we heard in the Exodus reading as he writes about the new covenant God offers humanity, referring to Moses, veiled faces, and the glory of God. Simply put, he suggests that until we look to the Lord, we have a veil on our faces; once we see Christ, we see the full image of God in all God's glory.

Paul clearly wrestles with the failure or refusal of some to respond to the gospel of Christ, but he is absolutely convinced that seeing the glory of God in Christ leads to transformation. Through his writings and through the Acts of the Apostles we know that Paul believed this because he experienced it; his life was changed when Christ appeared to him in a blinding light from heaven.

In Paul's construct, all who see in Jesus the glory of God are being transformed into the same image, though in varying degrees. This transformation equips us for a future life in the kingdom and a present life in Christian community. From Paul's personal perspective, God takes the initiative to connect with us.

We would be wise to cultivate eyes that can see the presence of Christ, assured that the glory of the Lord is forever about us. Such a harvest is reached through disciplined commitment to acts of devotion and mercy. No matter what designs God may have for our lives, it is always appropriate to seek God by drawing closer to Christ.

PRAYER: O God, as I would seek a holy encounter with you this day, help me be aware of your glory around me that it might mold me for life in your name. Amen.

TRANSFIGURATION SUNDAY

A child of six with incurable cancer was soon to die, and she knew it. She had battled the disease for over two years with varying results. Yet she understood the situation far better than her doctors, family, or friends. Most of her days were spent in a hospital, so much so that it became the principal community in which she experienced the daily swells of life and relationships.

Though the hospital was over two hundred miles away, I traveled to see her at least every other week. On one of my visits, I was listening to the child talk when she abruptly jumped up and ran over to another girl being wheeled down the corridor. The two of them vanished, and I sat for quite some time before she returned. She explained that the other girl was about to go through a painful procedure, one she assured me that she knew about firsthand, and "no one should have to endure that alone." I felt sure that I looked upon the face of God as she spoke to me.

The psalmist writes out of a community that was hurting because of the exile, a struggle compounded by its spiritual angst. His words affirm the reign of God and proclaim God's holiness in new ways, capturing the connection between humanity and God known through love and forgiveness. Rather than trembling in fear, we exalt and worship God.

Life in the pediatric cancer ward of a hospital is not the first place we would look for holiness, but I have seen the face of God in a child there and have witnessed true incarnational love there. Indeed, an experience of the holy evoked the praise of the psalmist. In the holy we experience a sharing and affirmation of incredible love in the midst of sorrow, confusion, pain, and the absolute assurance that God reigns and desires love among all.

PRAYER: O God our Creator, I thank you for all the holy encounters I have had with you. May my mouth pour forth your praise. Amen.

The Quiet Shelter of God

February 23–29, 2004 • *Peter Storey*[‡]

MONDAY, FEBRUARY 23 • **Read Deuteronomy 26:1-11**

Whether a landowner with olive groves and flocks of fat sheep or a humble tiller of a small patch of soil that yielded little, at the time of harvest everyone went to the place of worship carrying a basket of produce. This was no ordinary visit. Just at the time when these early settlers in Canaan might have felt most independent and secure, with their barns full, they were required to remember that nothing they had was their own, and all they had was from God. Every inch of the soil that had brought forth their crops was land God had given. Every plant and animal was God's creation. All was gift.

After watching the priest place the produce before God's altar, each person was required to make a humbling statement, beginning with the words, "A wandering Aramean was my ancestor; he went down into Egypt and lived there as an alien, few in number...." There, in front of the altar, the humbling story was recalled, together with God's great acts of deliverance, how God brought them to this land "flowing with milk and honey." All was gift.

People who live on the land usually have a much more acute sense of dependence upon, and gratitude for, each day's gifts than those of us who live where the soil is paved over, where we think we make our own climate and our own living. It might be a good thing if all of us who share in the generosity and prosperity of our culture had to make a similar pilgrimage, a similar tithe, and a similar acknowledgment.

PRAYER: Help me, generous God, to acknowledge all of life as gift. Amen.

[‡]Professor of the Practice of Christian Ministry, Duke University Divinity School, Durham, North Carolina; former bishop in The Methodist Church of Southern Africa.

If you enjoy singing Charles Wesley's hymns, you may have noticed how many times this passionate poet uses the word *all*. His wonder at the all-embracing love of God flows through his hymnology. John Wesley too never tired of telling people that all of them, without exception, were loved and longed for by God.

Paul is equally adamant in this scripture: "No one who believes in him will be put to shame." In case we don't get the message, he repeats it in verse 13: "Everyone who calls on the name of the Lord shall be saved."

The message of salvation is for all. It has no limits or boundaries. None is excluded from its promises. In a world that measures people by all sorts of "litmus tests," the result is too often rejection and exclusion. Human beings seem to be born with a powerful addiction to division, obsessed with determining who will qualify for salvation and who will not. Here we are reminded that none is left out.

Yet there is a caveat. How will people know this amazing news unless someone shares it with them? From 1960 to 1997, I preached almost every Sunday and sometimes understandably wondered whether those thousands of sermons made any difference. Now I often sit in worship as the listener, and, because of the difference in my life when I hear the good news proclaimed to me, I know they did.

We may not all be called to be preachers, but Paul wants us to have no doubt that all of us are called not only to believe in our hearts but to share that belief with all who need to know. And that's everybody.

PRAYER: Jesus, help me today to hold in my heart the conviction that you are alive, and give me courage to share with those who need to hear that you are Lord. Amen.

ASH WEDNESDAY

Today, all over the world, followers of Jesus will line up before the dead, silent ashes to have the sign of the cross marked upon their foreheads. Those ashes usually come from the leaves of last Palm Sunday, burned in shame to remind us of the fickleness of our faith and how quickly our adoration turns to alienation and hostility.

God's words spoken through the prophet burn us with equal shame. As so often in scripture, the people who claim to be God's people are held up for judgment. Lent is a time to be called to account for our transgressions, particularly those that may contradict our proclaimed faith.

The people of Israel are frustrated because, in spite of their carefully choreographed religious rites, including fasting—the unpleasant business of going without food for long periods—their efforts seem to leave God quite unmoved. "Why bother," they complain, "if God ignores us?"

Then comes the devastating reply: far from ignoring them, God sees through them. God denounces their religious posturing as a fraud, demanding instead that they begin a "fast" from injustice, snapping the bonds that bind the oppressed, discovering a new depth of hospitality to strangers, clothing the naked, and feeding the hungry. If they desist from perverting justice and making false accusations, then not only will God honor this fast of the heart, but they will be the people God longs to see. Only then, in a world that is broken and ruined, can they rebuild on God's foundations.

Don't play games with God this Lent. The occasional external sacrifice is not what it's about. It is about recalling who we are meant to be when we walk with the cross on our foreheads.

PRAYER: Mark me, Savior Christ, with the ashes of my shame, but also with the sign of your cross, to remind me of the kind of sacrifice to which you call me. Amen.

This psalm offers perhaps the most poignant and heartrending prayer of repentance in all of scripture. It is traditionally thought to have been David's cry of contrition following his adultery with Bathsheba and his murder of her husband Uriah. This confession has become part of the church's liturgy and serves as a template to assist our own poor attempts to come clean with God.

We tend to minimize, rationalize, and excuse our failures, belonging to a culture that doesn't believe in taking blame. We find notions of "original innocence" much more appealing than original sin. If we are to live a holy Lent, we will need this psalmist's honesty.

Here there is a ruthless peeling away of pretense and a self-knowledge too deep for most of us. Here there is a determination to stare into the face of our sin and acknowledge that our wrongdoing does much more than hurt those we sin against. Here we find the dreadful truth about our sin that will be demonstrated on Calvary—that all sin is sin against God. No wonder all the psalmist can offer is a broken and a contrite spirit.

Yet in the depths of his brokenness, the psalmist clings to a hope that is almost absurd—the hope that he might be forgiven. If his self-knowledge is painfully acute, his trust in the pardoning grace of God is astounding. It is as if there are two realities, one being undoubtedly the degradation of his sin. But the other and greater reality is the amazing mercy and grace of God. Upon this mercy he flings himself.

Sometimes we have nothing else to rely upon than this.

PRAYER: Have mercy upon me, O God, according to your loving-kindness. According to the multitude of your tender mercies, blot out all my transgressions. Wash me thoroughly from my transgressions, and cleanse me from my sin. For your mercy's sake. Amen.

This psalm is more than a statement of confidence in God. It contains not only amazing promises but presumes to read God's thoughts and to speak directly out of God's heart.

The psalmist conjures up a picture rooted in the exposed and dry desert lives of the Hebrew people. For them, every day was a struggle to wrest life from the desert and to survive its vicissitudes. No wonder they spoke of their God in the language of shelter; they needed to know that they could lodge under God's shadow and find there a safe retreat from the dangers surrounding them.

Their God did not simply offer a passive sanctuary from harm, however: Their God also promised that angels would keep guard over them, actively intervening in their risk-laden lives. The idea of "guardian angels" is not universally accepted among today's believers, but in the midst of a world where the influence of dark principalities and powers seems much too real to be wished away, it is comforting to know that there may be an angelic reality committed to our defense. The writer of the book of Hebrews speaks of our being surrounded by a "great cloud of witnesses" (12:1, NIV) and implies that they are rooting for us, much as a crowd in the bleachers would do, as we struggle in life's arena.

God is always willing to be our deliverer, the one who will never leave us in times of trouble. God asks for three signs of trust: that our love be set on God, that we know God's name, and that we be willing to call on God for all our needs. That is all.

PRAYER: God, my shelter, let my love be set on you; let me know your name is love; let me rest in that love. Amen.

It's not often that Jesus gets to be a little sarcastic, but there is sharpness in his judgment on those who make a big show of their virtue, whether through widely trumpeted gifts to charity or ostentatious acts of devotion and self-denial. His biting comment is simply, "They have their reward already."

Jesus makes a valid point. There is a reward for that kind of behavior. Showy piety reaps the rewards of enhanced reputation, perhaps even celebrity, and the admiration of others. Few of us would refuse such rewards in a world where self-promotion is regarded as not only acceptable but necessary. This is not a culture of shrinking violets. Sadly, the church can become infected too, marketing the gospel as a commercial commodity and different religious groups vying for our attention.

Yet Jesus is adamant. For those who need the world to admire their virtue, such reward is all there will be. Later he tells us it's all about whether we want to store up treasures on earth or heaven—to invest in the things that can be corrupted by decay or in those things that have eternal value. Not only should we act in ways that do not seek self-promotion, but when we give, we should not even remember it ourselves. The left hand should not even know what the right is doing.

During this Lent, take note of Jesus' advice to those who fast. If you have decided to deny yourself something of importance to you during this season, try not to tell anyone about it. After all, that is not why you're doing it. Let your sacrifice be between you and God, the one who sees in secret.

PRAYER: God of grace, help me not to need the approval of others so much and to seek instead to please you alone. Amen.

FIRST SUNDAY IN LENT

Jesus has just emerged from a climactic experience. In the waters of the Jordan, he had come humbly to seek the baptism of John. In that moment, God had declared him the Son, the Beloved, upon whom God's favor rests. The Holy Spirit had descended upon him (Luke 3: 21-22). After this great affirmation and full of the Holy Spirit, Jesus now will surely set out on his world-transforming mission.

Yet before Jesus can begin his ministry, he must take another painful step. The same Spirit who fills him also now drives him into the desert wilderness to be tempted by the devil. God's affirmation is not enough; a great renunciation must also come.

Jesus knows who he is and what he must do, but Satan has other plans. Acknowledging Jesus' identity and his goals, Satan simply seeks to corrupt the means by which Jesus will reach them. In the desert temptations, Jesus is invited to abandon his trust in God's way of suffering love and to turn instead to "shock and awe." Satan suggests swift economic power through conjuring food out of stones, political domination of all the kingdoms, and religious signs and wonders to win gullible devotees. After all, will not these means bring the desired end of God's reign?

With incredible resolve and using the power of God's word alone, Jesus renounces the shortcuts of naked power, returning to that other, "less traveled," road that will lead not to his domination but to our salvation.

Nothing much has changed since Jesus' great renunciation. The greatest temptations are seldom about our weaknesses; they play to our strengths. Nor are they usually about ends; instead, they seek to corrupt the means to those ends.

PRAYER: Strong Son of God, give me insight to renounce what I mistake for strength and, through the scripture, reveal your strength as I put my trust in you. Amen.

Models of Faithful Living

March 1–7, 2004 • K. Cherie Jones[‡]

MONDAY, MARCH 1 • Read Genesis 15:1-6

"I will always love you." "I will always be your friend." I have heard those words of promise before. I have spoken them as well. I have watched in dismay as those promises are bent, if not broken. Sometimes I was responsible for the failure; sometimes the other person was. We make these promises with every intention of keeping them but discover that they are so hard to uphold.

Our personal experience with bent and broken promises makes it more difficult for us to trust the promises of God. In our heart, we think that God may not be any different from all those whom we love. So we hold back a bit, hedge our bets, hoping to protect ourselves in case God's promise goes sour.

God comes to Abram once more with a grand promise, "Your reward shall be great" (v. 1) But Abram's desires are more specific. He needs an heir if the promise "I will make of you a great nation" (Gen. 12:2) is to come true. He has been waiting, trying to come up with a way to make it happen, perhaps wondering if God has forgotten the promise. He needs reassurance.

And God offers Abram reassurance through words and actions. God reiterates the promise of a child that shares half of Abram's DNA. Then God takes Abram outside beneath the canopy of stars. See them? Your descendants will be as numerous!

Nothing in Abram's circumstances make him think that this can possibly come to pass. He is an old man and menopause is a dim memory for Sarai. Yet with no concrete evidence, Abram chooses to believe God. He puts aside that understandable, natural wall of self-protection long enough to believe God's promise. And thus is he reckoned as being righteous.

PRAYER: God, you make and keep promises to me. Help me learn to trust you and your word. Amen.

[‡]Pastor, Atascadero United Methodist Church, Atascadero, California.

TUESDAY, MARCH 2 • Read Genesis 15:7-12, 17-18

Seeking to reassure Abram, God uses a familiar rite, that of making or "cutting" a covenant. In this rite, animals are hacked in two, and the covenant makers pass between the pieces, swearing that this and more should happen to them if they fail to uphold the covenant. But in this case, God unilaterally vows to uphold the promise of a land and a people for Abram.

It is tempting to bypass this part of the story. It seems barbaric to us to kill animals, hack them in two, and then walk between the pieces. And yet here is a clue to God's character. By choosing to use this rite, God swears to Abram that the animal's fate would be God's own fate if the covenant is broken. Divine commitment to this covenant is so great that God ponders God's own suffering and death.

Suddenly we catch a glimpse of what will become clearer as we continue through the Hebrew Scriptures and into the Christian Scriptures. The images of the vulnerability of God are breathtaking. This God willingly refrains from judgment on the people's sin and suffers weariness as the people turn away again and again.

In this second week of Lent, we prepare to ponder anew the mysteries of Jesus' suffering, death, and resurrection. In the final days of Jesus' earthly life, we see the depth of God's willingness to suffer even death for the sake of the beloved people. We see the son of God suffering death; we see God the Father suffering grief over the death of a beloved son. The glimpse of God's willingness to suffer in today's reading comes to pass on the cross.

SUGGESTION FOR MEDITATION: **How does the image of God as one who suffers fit in with your understanding of God? What difference might this image make for you?**

The psalmist in today's reading offers a remarkable profession of faith in God. Living in the light of God, the psalmist has nothing to fear as the confidence that God is the source and sustainer of life sinks to the core of his soul. That freedom from fear gives him courage both to seek the face of God and to face adversaries.

In March 1998, a close friend and coworker Donna Smith Farr disappeared. We hoped and prayed for her return. Several days later when police found her car with a significant amount of blood in the trunk, we knew she was dead. Six months later her remains were discovered. In the fall of 2001, her ex-husband was sent to prison for her murder.

Immediately after I learned of her disappearance, this thought came to me: *God has loved Donna from the beginning and always will. And in her baptism and in her response to her vocational call, Donna shows her love for God.* These words from the Holy Spirit became an assurance that whatever was happening at the moment, ultimately Donna was safe in God's hands. That assurance sank to the core of my soul and became a place of peace in the chaos that swirled around those of us who love Donna.

We may never know the depth or strength of our faith until we come face-to-face with our enemies who seek to destroy us and those we love. In those times of distress we discover the sheltering faithfulness of the One who loves us. Certainly following Donna's murder, I, like the psalmist, experienced the breadth of God's protection and care. When the soul dwells under God's protection, the storms of life are powerless to shake it.

PRAYER: O God, I want to live as one who trusts you. Hide me in the shelter of your love. Amen.

I attended the second set of Walk to Emmaus weekends in South Africa in April 1991. Apartheid was almost completely dismantled legally, and I sensed great hope among South Africans. Yet the vestiges of apartheid remained, as seen in the violence and struggling economy.

On the women's weekend, I roomed with four women from the township of Katlehong, on the outskirts of Johannesburg. I remember sitting on my bunk late at night, listening to them talk about their lives, their hopes, and their fears. Much of the time they talked about the effects of living with the constant threat of violence. One woman said, "When you go to bed at night, you do not know if you will live to see the sunrise. And at night you do not know if you will wake up in your bed or in a coffin." The other women nodded in agreement. They went on to tell how their faith sustained them each day. They talked about the pain they felt when their children turned away from the faith. I saw the depth of their faith, honed in times of suffering.

In times of violence, these Christian sisters chose to trust God rather than fall into fear. Like the psalmist, they sought the light and life in God. Their lives reflect the faith of those who have plumbed the depths of God's faithfulness and care.

In this time when the threat of terrorism and war has become part of our daily landscape, I remember how they chose time and again to trust God. They serve as models of faithful living for me. Thanks be to God!

PRAYER: O God, you are faithful to us in times of suffering. Continue to be with my Christian brothers and sisters who are suffering persecution. Amen.

In the past few years the United States has been rocked by business scandals, mostly of the accounting variety, as major corporations claimed greater worth than was true. What happened? In part, executives and employees began climbing a mountain of wealth, intending to dwell there. Blinded by greed, they built an enormous house of cards atop that mountain. Eventually the truth began to emerge, and we watched corporations implode.

Those who scale mountains to achieve earthly goals labor in vain. In today's reading, Jesus and three disciples go to the mountain, not in search of wealth but to find God in prayer. There the disciples learn about Jesus' true nature as he speaks with heavenly visitors. In response, Peter proposes to build three booths or dwellings for them, a response both of faith and of misunderstanding. He wants to capture the moment, freeze it in a new housing development so that they can dwell on that mountain of revelation.

Then the divine voice speaks, the heavenly visitors depart, and Jesus alone remains with the disciples. Without heavenly companions, without heavenly glory, Jesus is the dwelling, the reality of God's abiding presence with us. He leads the disciples down the mountain into the mundane world of suffering and mission. But they do not walk alone; "God with us" is with them.

SUGGESTION FOR MEDITATION: **What mountain are you climbing—the mountain of wealth? the mountain of security? the mountain of God? some other mountain? Where do you choose to dwell?**

As the disciples struggle to make sense of what is happening, a cloud envelops them and God interrupts Peter to repeat the words from Jesus' baptism: "This is my Son, the Chosen; listen to him." *Listen to him.* The verb tense is present imperative so it would be better translated as "keep on listening" or "continue listening" to him. Continue listening to what he teaches you. Keep on listening to his statements about his suffering, death and resurrection. Continue listening to him!

Also implicit is the understanding that the disciples will obey what they hear. It is not enough to go up on the mountain to hear the divine voice; we must also follow the guidance God gives us.

Like the disciples, our faith is a dance of contemplative and ethical action. We are summoned up to the mountain to gaze upon God. We are called to contemplation, wonderment, and awe. So we go on retreats, practice the Sabbath, and attend conferences. We place ourselves in a posture of receptivity, eager to glimpse God, longing to hear a divine word spoken to us. And God reaches us in the right way at the right time.

Often our temptation is to stay on the mountain where we can more easily perceive God's word to us. But we are called to descend the mountain and return to our lives. However, we come back changed. As we gaze upon Jesus, we are transformed and conformed to the mind of Christ. As we continue listening to Jesus, we follow him into the suffering world, beginning with our family, neighborhood, and workplace. In our everyday lives, we live out the word we hear on the mountain.

As we "keep on" practicing the dance of contemplation and ethical action, the more smoothly it flows.

PRAYER: O God, help me to become a graceful, grace-filled partner with you in this dance of contemplation and action. Amen.

SECOND SUNDAY IN LENT

"Join in imitating me" writes Paul. God provides Christian people to serve as role models of faith for us. Not that we need to imitate everything about them, for we are only fallible humans after all. As I think about those whom I can imitate, I think about my mother and how she modeled the practice of prayer and the loving acceptance of others.

My mother's prayers for me began when she learned she was pregnant. She asked God for a scripture to pray for me and was given a passage from Isaiah. She taught me to pray, and we were prayer partners for many years. Her daily prayer list was very long. She was a woman of prayer!

I always knew she loved Dad, my sister, and me deeply and fiercely. My mother died several years ago, and at the visitation prior to her funeral I witnessed her love of others. People came in droves to tell her family members how much they loved her. From twenty-year-olds to retirees, from the entire staff of the dry cleaner's shop to members of a medical school faculty, they told us stories of how she helped them through a difficult time or prayed with them through decisions.

The tableau I remember most vividly is that of two men in deep conversation: one, in his forties, cares for Mom and Dad's yard and the other is a retired CEO of a major oil company. That tableau caught the essence of my mother's deep capacity to love others, regardless of age, ethnicity, or social standing.

Even as I think of my mother, I also think of all the others who have been role models of faith for me, some still living, some now in the communion of saints. Today I give thanks for all of them!

SUGGESTION FOR MEDITATION: Think about the persons who are role models of faith in your life. Offer a prayer of thanksgiving for them.

Making God's Ways Our Own

March 8–14, 2004 • *Susan Muto*[‡]

MONDAY, MARCH 8 • **Read Isaiah 55:1-5**

Come. With this one word God invites us to a symbolic messianic banquet where all who hunger and thirst for holiness will have their fill. The righteous gather to celebrate their liberation, not because of their merits but because of God's generosity. This invitation is so incredible it has to be repeated four times: Come to the water; come, receive grain and eat; come without paying and cost; come…listen, that you may have life.

On God's table is life-giving sustenance to stay hunger, to quench thirst. Renewed at this feast is the everlasting covenant, proving that God hears the cry of the poor. Divine intervention reverses the worst disasters. Sinners who repent and make God's ways their own are pleasing in the sight of the Most High.

PRAYER: Renew in us, almighty and gracious God, your covenant promises as we make the symbolic journey from the land of unlikeness due to sin to the land of likeness enabled by grace. There rainfall turns desert dryness into fertile ground. Feed us on this long road home with the bread of life so that we may be obedient witnesses to the supremacy of your word in our oft fallen lives. Renew and refresh us with delightful fare, abundant and beneficial beyond all telling. Amen.

[‡]Roman Catholic author, teacher, and scholar of the literature of spirituality; executive director of the Epiphany Association, a nonprofit ecumenical center dedicated to spiritual formation, and cofounder and Dean of its Epiphany Academy of Formative Spirituality, Pittsburgh, Pennsylvania.

No food, however filling, can satisfy the hungry heart in search of intimacy with God. We may be invited guests, but we feel like beggars at this holy table.

Our need for mercy never ceases. Wickedness crouches in every corner, and we must not grow complacent. God never tires of hearing us ask for forgiveness and compassion. We are sinners in need of redemption, fallible creatures incapable of penetrating the awesome transcendence of the Infinite. Try as we might, we can never comprehend the ways of God with us. What we can do is to wait and pray for the courage to go into the desert to repent and reform our lives. There we watch with wonder as God takes a recalcitrant people and turns them into a nation of believers.

Isaiah offers us the vision of an ideal city while reminding us that everything we see is a gift from God. Our only effort—and even this by grace—is to respond with reverence to God's irresistible power. Then we can forsake unrighteousness, practice virtue, and turn every obstacle on our path into a formation opportunity. Then we can begin to make God's ways and God's thoughts our own.

PRAYER: Merciful Lord, choose us as your covenant people bound together as one body by the blood of your son. Make us a light to all nations who pray in accordance with the lights you give them for the homecoming you promise. Redirect our desert wanderings to your sacred table that we may glorify and praise you despite the worldliness of our ways. Loving Savior, come near to our wayward hearts even as we forsake any idle expectation of ever being able to penetrate the height and depth of your transcendence. Amen.

It is impossible to make God's ways our own if we do not believe the seemingly impossible truth that the felt absence of the Holy may mark the deepest sense of presence. In this poignant love song voiced in aridity the psalmist shows us what an intimate relationship of love between us and God looks like.

It starts with a declaration of faith in God that shakes us to the core. If God alone can fulfill our longing, why does it feel as if God has hidden from us? Our body is like a lump of painful yearning, our soul like a land parched and lifeless. One gaze upon God's loveliness in the sanctuary of our inner temple is of more worth than the greatest treasure on earth.

The psalmist reminds us that the Israelites loved life, but greater than life itself was the love of God. We have lips not to waste words but to offer worship; minds not to command God's ways but to walk in obedience; hearts not to be hardened by pride but softened by humility. The essence of the spiritual life resides in this longing. There is no better way to pray.

SUGGESTION FOR MEDITATION: **Picture yourself in the desert alone.** *Where are you, O God? Why have you hidden yourself from me? Can't you hear my groaning?* **Imagine yourself growing more and more hungry and thirsty. Your body needs bread and water as much as your soul needs salvation. Just when you want to give up begging for God to come near, suddenly a new revelation occurs. Now is the time to stand before God in awe, in naked faith and pure worship, feeling without understanding the deepest intimacy between you and the Mystery.**

With the psalmist, we too have felt the pain of being forsaken by God. We long to reestablish our once intimate relationship. At such junctures of our journey, we face the razor's edge of deciding either to feel depreciated and abandoned by God or to feel so appreciated that we abandon ourselves to God.

We see that even our losses lead to more longing. Along the way we opt to plead for, never to presume upon, God's mercy. Our first goal is to bless the Lord at all times and to thank God for every favor. Rather than clench our fists in frustration, we lift up our hands in prayer. Rather than take God's name in vain, we call on the Most High for help. Spiritual transformation begins with compunction of heart; it moves from purification to illumination to transformation. Sleepless nights become vigilant watches. The bride-soul lights her lamp and awaits the coming of her Beloved. Fears disappear. Anxiety retreats in the face of trust.

A soul this in love with God has but one choice: to cling with all her might to the mightiest hand of all. The safe, protective canopy of God's sanctuary is where we want to dwell eternally.

PRAYER: Lord, amidst this parched land of longing for you, let there arise like incense from my lips prayers of praise and adoration. As I lie on my bed at night, let me lift up my soul and call upon your name, for you are my help and my salvation. Let me rest under the shadow of your wings. In moments of mystic wonder, let me cling to you, for your right hand holds me fast. Blessed be your name and the place wherein you dwell. Amen.

FRIDAY, MARCH 12 • Read 1 Corinthians 10:1-8

In his retelling of the story of the Israelites crossing the desert, Paul draws an important analogy for our spiritual life. As they left the Egypt of slavery, so must we leave the prison of our sinfulness and enter the promised land of our salvation.

The journey from infidelity to faithfulness is arduous, but we must ask God for the courage we need to make it. Paul recounts many details of this period of wandering. In his mind they prefigure lessons we Christians must learn. The first is not to become proud and overconfident. Even though God's plan of salvation was in place from the beginning, due to the weakness of our vision we may not have grasped its meaning. The Israelites ate manna; they drank water from the well that followed them. But more than that we have the privilege of partaking of Christ's own body and blood.

Despite these saving gifts, we still rebel against God. We practice subtle, if not overt, idolatry. We engage in immoral revelry and many forms of gluttony. No wonder God's wrath surges. We have a lot to learn from salvation history, so let us be on guard, lest we betray our covenant promises. The only rock on which we can afford to rest is Christ.

SUGGESTION FOR PRAYER: Picture the cloud by day and the fire by night that signaled God's presence amidst the nation of Israel. Pray for the courage to trust this divine leading. Then cross the desert of doubt and fear, of little faith and wanton sin, to the land of certitude and trust in the fullness of redemption. Taste and savor the freedom that awaits believers who glimpse the promised land and go there, thanks to God's grace.

How many times have we asked God not to test us beyond our strength to endure, while at the same time testing God by the childish antics of our forgetful, sinful, self-centered behavior? In their stubbornness the Israelites tried God's patience and received just punishment. They were bitten by poisonous snakes. Plagues were sent upon them by the Great Destroyer.

What happened to them in ancient times can serve as a warning to us today. We who witness to the death and resurrection of Jesus Christ are not superior people able on our own to pass the tests that besiege us. We are more vulnerable than we know. We think we stand on solid ground, but we must take care not to fall.

God's fidelity to us is not in question. What matters is whether we have the faith of warriors or only a weak set of beliefs that blow away with any ill wind. Happily for us, God permits us to be tested but not to the point where failure is inevitable. Hope springs eternal if we are sincere about reforming our lives and making God's ways our own.

PRAYER: God of power and might, save us in your mercy from the sin of complacency that draws forth your wrath. Forgive us for harboring the illusion of self-sufficiency that belies our baptismal call to faith, hope, and love. Let your only Begotten Son be for us a wellspring of living water from whence flows an endless stream of forgiveness. Let your Spirit help us to endure without complaint the suffering that leads us to the Cross. Above all, grant us, O Lord, the blessed grace of conversion so that we can turn over ourselves, body and soul, to you. Amen.

SUNDAY, MARCH 14 • Read Luke 13:1-9

THIRD SUNDAY IN LENT

In this passage Luke gives us at one and the same time a parable of compassion and the picture of the church. Many disciples try to be like Christ but fall short of this lofty ideal due to habitual sins like sloth, laziness, and procrastination. Jesus reminds those with ears to hear that no one knows the day or the hour when he or she will be accountable to God's judgment. Did the Galileans know that their blood would mingle with the bloody sacrifices they offered at the Temple? Did the construction workers know that a tower would fall and kill eighteen of them?

Jesus tells the parable of the fig tree to drive home his point. For three years it has borne no fruit, so the gardener is told that he might as well destroy it. He asks the orchard master for one last reprieve. The master agrees to give him a little more time. That is the way it is between us and God. We are given time to reform our lives before it is too late, but this state of merciful allowance will not last forever. Our day will come.

SUGGESTION FOR MEDITATION: Walk into any garden and pause before a plant that looks as if it is about to die. See it as a metaphor for the spiritual life. Are we healthy or diseased plants in God's garden? Do we presume upon God's patience? How much time do we think we have left? What matters is that we live now as if this were our final hour. Pause in the silence of the garden and hear the call to repentance. Vow to let God's ways become your own. Attune your whole being to the task of bearing fruit that will last.

Room at the Table for All

March 15–21, 2004 • Joyce Hollyday[‡]

MONDAY, MARCH 15 • Read Joshua 5:9-12

During one of the most memorable nights of my life, I awoke after three hours of sleep and rode a camel up Mount Sinai under the Big Dipper and an eyelash of a moon. The last part of the trip was on hands and knees, scrambling over rocks and boulders. I found a cleft in a cliff facing east and huddled there out of the wind and waited. Soon a tiny pinpoint of red light appeared on the horizon, and before long the entire wilderness before me was flooded with sunlight: a perfect moment for a profound insight into the meaning of life. But what came to me was, "I would have complained too."

The book of Exodus is filled with the murmurings and grumblings of the early Israelites, who wandered this wilderness for forty years. That wilderness time for our ancestors in the faith became a time of great blessing, for there they learned on a daily basis to trust God for all their needs. Justice prevailed as every family got exactly what was needed, and no one went without. In the wilderness everyone experienced God's sustenance, and everybody had a place at the table of plenty.

Guided by God and led by Joshua, the Israelites crossed the Jordan River into the Promised Land where "the manna ceased on the day they ate the produce of the land" (Josh. 5:12). This land "flowing with milk and honey" held new challenges: Would the lesson of the wilderness hold? Would justice prevail in this new land dripping with abundance?

PRAYER: God of justice, help us to cling to the lesson of the wilderness. Embolden us to work for a world in which your abundance is shared by all. Amen.

[‡]Associate Conference Minister for the Southeast Conference of the United Church of Christ and the author of several books, including *Then Shall Your Light Rise* (Upper Room Books, 1997); living in Pisgah Forest, North Carolina..

Clarence Jordan, founder of Koinonia Farm and author of the "cotton patch" version of the New Testament, preached about Jesus' entry into Jerusalem on a mule "whereon never man sat" (Mark 11:2, KJV). Jordan said he tried riding such a mule once, and when he got through, it was still a mule whereon no man had sat. Psalm 32 cautions, "Do not be like a horse or a mule, without understanding" (vs. 9). The mule will go its own way, oblivious to its own stubbornness. The psalmist understood that we human beings can sometimes be the same way.

Clarence Jordan said that one of the things we fail to understand is why scripture calls "taking the name of the Lord in vain" the unforgivable sin (Exod. 20:7). In his understanding, taking the name in vain has nothing to do with the usual interpretation of cursing, but with taking on the name of Christ—calling oneself a Christian—without living a transformed life. In other words, it means being a hypocrite.

When the Pharisee and the tax collector went to the Temple, they both got what they asked for, according to Jordan (Luke 18:9-14). The self-righteous, mule-headed Pharisee thanked God that he was not like other people and then subjected God to an accounting of his goodness. The tax collector pleaded for mercy. The Pharisee asked for nothing, and that's what he got.

Hypocrisy is unforgivable, according to Jordan, because it is the one condition of the soul in which a person does not ask for forgiveness. God won't grant a prayer that isn't uttered. To ask for forgiveness means to confess that we are sinners. At the moment that we confess our sin, hypocrisy disappears and God's grace flows. A prayer for mercy is always answered.

PRAYER: God of mercy, open our eyes to the ways in which we have failed to live up to your name. Forgive us our sins. Amen.

The sun was a mere glint of orange on the eastern horizon. I had just spent a short and restless night on the floor of a Baptist church in the Nicaraguan town of Ocotal. It was December 1983, and Nicaragua was at war. Forces known as contras were raiding vulnerable villages, terrorizing, kidnapping, and killing civilians. I was a member of the first U.S. delegation to journey to Nicaragua as part of Witness for Peace, a nonviolent, faith-based effort that established an ongoing prayerful and protective presence in that nation's war zones. We shared the church with refugees who had fled their homes. The night was filled with the sound of gunshots in the distance, and the cry of frightened children up close.

We awoke before dawn. The refugee women had risen even earlier. Firewood was stacked in the dome-shaped clay oven, and the women were already slapping out tortillas when the sun made its appearance. I was profoundly moved when they invited us to partake of their meager breakfast. These women shared literally everything they had with us, affluent strangers from a far-off country. Our sharing of tortillas and coffee at dawn was a Holy Communion. Those refugee women lived for each day, believing with the psalmist that God would provide. Even in distress they clung to the wilderness lessons of trust, generosity, and justice.

In this world where many people live on pennies a day and too many die of starvation; where most people in our nation fatten their bank accounts and too many die of problems related to obesity; where we in the United States consume six times more than our fair share of the world's resources—perhaps our confession needs to start with our inability to embrace trust, generosity, and justice; with our unwillingness to make room for everyone at the table.

PRAYER: God of generosity, we confess our transgressions and ask your forgiveness. Teach us to share with others as you have shared with us. Instruct us in the ways we should live. Amen.

When I was a child, my young ears heard the Twenty-third Psalm beginning this way: "The LORD is my shepherd; I shall not want." I was mystified. Why shouldn't I want him? Everyone around me was telling me I should. Eventually I understood the meaning of the psalm, and the image of Jesus as shepherd became a comforting one to me. I've prayed that psalm in many times of sorrow and fear.

I've occasionally thought back on my childhood musings and laughed, because sometimes I really haven't wanted to shoulder the cost of discipleship. Sometimes the gospel call to do justice and make peace is more than I want to bear. Discerning how to live faithfully in this land of plenty seems too mystifying.

I discarded Jesus the shepherd for a while. I was working with battered women and abused children. The image of the shepherd seemed too mild, too passive for a world as violent and unjust as ours. But I discovered that the shepherd was exactly the image they—and I—needed. Once again I found great comfort in the image of a tender shepherd who would climb down any cliff, venture into any ravine, follow any wilderness path to rescue one of the beloved sheep. These measures reflect the depth of God's love for us, the lengths to which God will go to keep us on the path of discipleship. When we stray or despair or become tempted to give up, God reaches out a loving hand. Always.

PRAYER: God of love, shepherd us on the path of faithfulness. Guide us into your ways of justice and peace. Amen.

Last year I gathered with other United Church of Christ clergy for a retreat in Chattanooga, Tennessee. During a Bible study, we reflected together on the fifteenth chapter of Paul's first letter to the Corinthians. Someone asked, "How do you think Paul would have defined death?" Dr. David Greenhaw, president of Eden Theological Seminary, replied that he could not speak for Paul, but that he turns to the parable of the prodigal son to find a definition. He pointed out that twice in the story the father pronounced that his son "was dead" but had come back to life (Luke 15:24, 32). Greenhaw said, "Death means not having a table at which to eat."

For millions of the world's people who are without family, without community, without a home for security and a table to share, life looks more like death. And for many of them, isolation and vulnerability lead to literal death. The prodigal son's journey from family table to life among the pigs and back home to a welcome feast is a tale of resurrection, one in which we participate whenever we offer an extravagant welcome.

Unfortunately, I often find myself identifying more with the older brother in the parable than any of the other characters—the one who tried to do everything right and sat on the sidelines grumbling when he didn't get the credit. In so doing, he only cut himself off from the party, missed out on all the fun, and failed to see his own sins and shortcomings. We don't get what we deserve. Thank God.

PRAYER: God of welcome, help us to be as extravagant in hospitality as you have been with us. Show us how to prepare the table for all. Amen.

During my fifteen years living with Sojourners Community in inner-city Washington, D.C., I often helped to give out food on Saturday mornings at our neighborhood center. Mrs. Mary Glover came through the line one bitterly cold morning when she couldn't afford to pay for food, rent, or a new pair of badly needed boots. Soon she volunteered regularly. Every week before we opened the line, Mrs. Glover offered a prayer that began with thanks for waking up that day to serve God. It always ended this way: "Lord, we know you're coming through this line today, so help us to treat you right." Mrs. Glover understood the end of the twenty-fifth chapter of Matthew, where Jesus says, "I was hungry and you gave me food, I was thirsty and you gave me something to drink, I was a stranger and you welcomed me...Just as you did it to one of the least of these who are members of my family, you did it to me" (Matt. 25:35, 40).

The parable of the prodigal son is one of many Bible stories about feasting. Jesus turns water into wine at a wedding banquet. Controversies swirl around him when he chooses to eat with prostitutes and tax collectors. His parable of the great banquet encourages listeners to open their tables to all in need. He shares a meal as a final act with his followers, and he comes to us today in Holy Communion as feast, host, and guest. Jesus welcomes us to the table with the same joy and generosity with which the father welcomed the lost son. May we so welcome others—and know as we do so that we welcome Jesus himself.

PRAYER: God of hope, help us to remember where you told us we would find you. Give us courage to extend the table and receive you in whatever guise you appear. Amen.

FOURTH SUNDAY IN LENT

I visited Maude in 1997 at a senior center outside Cape Town, South Africa. She told me about the police coming in the middle of the night, forcing her and her young children into a truck at gunpoint, and dropping them in isolated bush country, taking from them everything they owned. I asked her if she had forgiven them. She said, "I know that if I want God to forgive me, I must forgive them." I ventured that no sin Maude had ever committed came close to the violation done to her. But she—and millions of her comrades—didn't see it that way. They have been learning to see not with human eyes but with the eyes of Christ.

I was in South Africa to observe the unprecedented work of that nation's Truth and Reconciliation Commission. Again and again, I witnessed people who had suffered the most horrific tortures and tragedies offer forgiveness to their tormentors. With rare courage, they took seriously Christ's call to be ambassadors of reconciliation. As a result, South Africa is becoming a "new creation." The nation that arguably was the most brutally divided by racial hatred on the globe is now shining a beacon of hope for the world to see.

Apartheid declared that only a few people deserve a share of the world's abundance. Today South Africans are setting a new table with room enough for all to partake of its riches. They invite us to pull up our chairs and join them, to work for the day when all the world is a "new creation."

PRAYER: God of reconciliation, show us the way to be your ambassadors. Anoint us with your love and renew the face of the earth. Amen.

Reaping with Shouts of Joy

March 22–28, 2004 • Roberta Hestenes[‡]

MONDAY, MARCH 22 • Read Isaiah 43:18-19

In the midst of suffering, sorrow, and pain, any hopeful expectation of a better future is difficult to envision. The realities of brokenness and suffering can overwhelm us. We find ourselves drawn to rehearse the horror again and again until the mind is numb and the heart relinquishes hope as we fixate on the past. Such was Israel's experience during the period of captivity and exile. The nation had been shattered by war and suffering. Continuity between the past and the future had been ruptured. The people lost hope, just as we are tempted to do when suffering and evil enter our lives and threaten to overwhelm us.

Into this despair comes the word of the Lord bringing hope to a hopeless situation. This is not an empty word of superficial cheerfulness but a powerful word from the Lord who has already been revealed in human history as supreme over the forces of nature and sovereign over all human injustice and arrogance. This word is, in itself, a sign of divine mercy and power intended to stimulate confident anticipation. God is neither absent nor silent, as we might fear, but present and speaking into our lives, into our circumstances, and into our world. God can be trusted.

The prophet announces that the Lord is already active, doing something new and good for us because that is God's character and purpose. This good work of the Lord is already visible if we have the eyes to see it. Just as the tall grass first appears as a tiny blade of green, so our full realization of God's power and mercy does not happen all at once. But we can glimpse God at work even now, so we can live with courage and faith.

PRAYER: Lord, give me the eyes and ears of faith so that I may hear and trust your promise to do a new good thing. Amen.

[‡]Minister-at-large for World Vision International; pastor and educator, living in Tustin, California.

Exiled from the land of promise by the conquering armies of Babylon, Israel finds herself again in a place of barren wilderness and desperate need. Longing for help and direction, she receives a word of hope through the prophet. God will make a way in the wilderness. Not only will the Lord protect the people from their natural enemies, but God will provide everything they need including water to quench their thirst. God has done it before; God will do it again. We Christians experience much of life as those wandering in the wilderness, uncertain at times of our destination or how we will get there. Many times we find ourselves in hard and difficult situations feeling anxious, insecure, and needy. God does not abandon us in this condition but makes a way for us.

Life in the wilderness is a persistent theme in the scriptures as seen in the events of the Exodus and Exile and in the lives of people like Elijah, John the Baptist, and Jesus' forty days of temptation. Wilderness becomes more than a physical experience of survival in a dry and barren land; it becomes a place of spiritual formation and preparation for fulfilling God's purpose. In the wilderness, we learn to trust God's provision and guidance, discover satisfaction for our longings and needs. We receive God's protection and find our purpose. When we recognize God's presence with us in the wilderness, we discover who we are as loved and chosen by God. We also discover what we are meant to do: worship and witness, declare his praise among the nations.

Our witness in the world often emerges from our experience of discovering God with us even in the wilderness experiences of life.

SUGGESTION FOR MEDITATION: **When have you experienced life as a wilderness? How was God present in that situation? How might your experience shape the way you witness to God in the world?**

The psalmist remembers a time full of joy because of the Lord's goodness in bringing restoration from slavery in Egypt. Their delight in God's deliverance served as a powerful witness to the watching nations. Joy, attractive and contagious, gives impetus to the witness of God's people. The reality of joy changes the way we look and speak, influencing those around us. Not only do the Israelites shout and laugh in gladness as they celebrate God's goodness, but the nations around them join in recognizing the greatness of the transforming power of God on their behalf.

But that was then. This is now, and at this moment in the exile there seems little to celebrate. Hope comes hard. Living under the burdens and injustices of captivity, joy seems a distant memory and witness fades. Yet that good memory of abundant, overflowing joy can nourish our hope of God's willingness to change the future. Things can be different if God will hear our prayer and act on our behalf. So we also cry out: "Do it again, God. Restore us again."

Today there may be a surplus of weeping in our world and in our lives. Over time exuberant joy often turns into painful tears of regret and sorrow. But all is not lost. We can join the psalmist and cry out asking God to do a restoring work for us. Our God is a God of restoration, redemption, and healing. God's heart rejoices when we rejoice. So we can ask for restoration with awareness of God's mercy and good purposes for us: to mend what is broken and to make whole what is shattered or torn apart. God keeps promises. The challenges and circumstances beyond our control can be placed before God as we turn to the only One with the power and will to make things right.

PRAYER: Lord of restoration, we cry to you in hope for justice and mercy in the brokenness of the world, the brokenness of your church, and the brokenness within our lives. Amen.

Times of suffering and pain may tempt us to fear that our lives or our community of faith have lost their purpose and meaning, their sense of direction. Why should we go on in the face of painful loss or hardship? Why not give up, surrender our dreams, and settle for mere survival? This seductive temptation comes to individuals and to whole communities of the people of God. And some succumb. They turn inward and cease to move forward to do God's will. They become passive. Preoccupied and discouraged, they abandon the expansive purpose of God for something less. Witness ceases to matter.

The beautiful agricultural image of verses 5 and 6 powerfully motivates our perseverance in seeking to fulfill our God-given purpose of witness and worship. If we faithfully continue to invest our lives in God's will, even in times of testing and trial, God will, in due season, pour out a harvest of blessing and joy.

This harvest encourages us to be proactive rather than passive or reactive. The psalmist speaks of those who "go out." They may be sorrowful, but they still actively engage in carrying and sowing the seed, doing the necessary work to ensure the harvest. The church through the ages has often understood these words in light of Jesus' parable of the sower who goes out to share the word of God. We may go with tears but we go with something valuable to share: the good news of God's greatness and mercy. Our lives have significance and purpose as we are bound together with the purpose of God. The psalmist's prayer and promise is not simply about faithfulness but also about results. There will come a time when those who go out will come home again with their arms full of the sheaves of the harvest. They will have reason again to shout for joy.

PRAYER: God, use our tears to water a parched and thirsty world as we work to share your good news with those around us. Amen.

Many people experience the Christian faith as simply one ingredient in the swirling activities and commitments of an active, busy life, involving one arena of interest among many. Family, education, work, sports, hobbies, recreation, church, and shopping compete for time and attention as we decide how to focus limited time and resources. Our lives may feel fragmented and stressful as we seek to balance all our competing values in our search for ultimate purpose and meaning.

Paul made the amazing discovery that joyous, abundant life is found not in human credentials, achievements, or activities but in a new identity centered in a vital relationship with Christ Jesus as Lord. We see everything differently when we root and center our identity and life in this one who makes us righteous through faith in him. Our values change as he becomes more central in our lives.

Faith in Christ is not something we add to the mix of our lives. It is the foundation that shapes the whole building, the center that holds everything together. Jesus Christ is the one who takes all the pieces of our lives and reshapes us into persons pleasing to God and of significance in the plan of God. Other activities take on their appropriate significance as we realize how good and great Christ is. Even that which we once prized as of supreme importance can be set aside if it becomes a distraction or an obstacle to our knowledge of Christ who loves and gave himself that we might find newness of life in him, the one who is to be prized above all things.

PRAYER: Lord Jesus, I want to know you in your greatness and your goodness. Before you I lay down every prideful claim and acknowledge my need and desire to grow more and more in knowing and loving you. Amen.

Paul knows clearly what he wants out of life. He wholeheartedly, passionately wants to know Christ. He didn't start out with this passion, just the opposite, in fact. Christ Jesus had turned him around. Years of following Jesus, after meeting him on the Damascus road, has not dulled his desire but only heightened it. His experience of Jesus feeds his longing for a deeper knowledge, an even closer relationship, even as his life draws closer to its end. Paul's is not a naive yearning. His years of apostleship have been difficult and dangerous, bringing him to this prison cell from which he writes. He does not seek to know a Jesus of his own imagination but the resurrected Christ who came as God in human form and suffered, dying on a cross. This Christ who now owns him is the Christ that Paul wants to know in all of his fullness, including the fullness of suffering and resurrection life after death. Paul seeks total identification with Christ as his goal.

A man once asked with concern after many years of living as a Christian, "Am I closer to Jesus today than I was when I began? Do I love him more? Are other things occupying the place where Jesus should be in my life?" Many things distract us on our journey of faith. Like Martha we are "busy with many things." Our vision can become clouded, and we lose sight of what and who is most important as the center of our life. Spiritual activities can become substitutes for focusing our hearts and minds on our Lord himself, on his person, character, love, will and work in our lives and in our world. Jesus Christ has chosen to make us his own. We have the privilege of seeking to know him above all else.

PRAYER: Lord Jesus Christ, purify my heart that I may seek to know and serve you with passionate intensity. I praise and thank you for your suffering, death, and resurrection that make me your own. Amen.

FIFTH SUNDAY IN LENT

Mary keeps breaking the rules. First, she defies conventional expectations and sits at Jesus' feet as a disciple while Martha complains about her neglect of duties in the kitchen. In the last intense days before the Passover, Mary again experiences criticism as she takes her costly perfume and pours it extravagantly over Jesus' feet, using her hair as a towel in an act of deep devotion. This time Judas Iscariot voices the criticism. Although the text tells us that the motives behind his question are not sincere, nonetheless the question has some force. Clearly the followers of Jesus knew of his commitment to the poor. He announced it at the beginning of his public ministry. He demonstrated his concern for the poor in his teachings, his actions, and his own way of living. So Judas Iscariot expresses his attack on Mary about giving the cost of the perfume to the poor, assuming that he knows Jesus' priorities. But his assumption is wrong in two ways: He undervalues Mary's action, and he values money over Jesus.

Jesus comes strongly to Mary's defense. He sees the love and the depth of meaning in her action perhaps even more than she fully understands herself. The perfume belongs to Mary; it is hers to give. She chooses to give it to Jesus because she believes that he is worthy of it. Jesus affirms her gift, while at the same time reinforcing the ongoing obligation to the poor.

Mary sensed and responded to a unique moment in human history. Jesus will not be among them for much longer. She acts with sacrifice and devotion, which Jesus receives with gratitude. There is a time to give to the poor and a time to give to Jesus. May God help us discern the times.

SUGGESTION FOR MEDITATION: **Spend some time pondering this story and what each of the people in the room filled with the fragrance of perfume was thinking and feeling. What do you think your response to Mary's act would have been? What would Jesus say to you?**

Bridging the Gap

March 29–April 4, 2004 • Elizabeth L. Hinson-Hasty[‡]

MONDAY, MARCH 29 • Read Luke 19:28-36

Jesus' triumphal entry into Jerusalem is reminiscent of a war hero returning home after a victorious battle. Yet the familiar fanfare does not celebrate the use of force to conquer an enemy or divide territories. Jesus' entrance into the holy city may fit the pattern of ceremony for welcoming a king triumphant in battle, but Jesus' actions confirm that the power revealed in him is unlike any other. God's power does not set up territorial boundaries but bridges the gaps.

Some of Jesus' followers expect him to create a kingdom that will reflect prevailing social practices. They discover that Jesus announces a kingdom infused with God's love and peace. The people dancing in the streets are not those whom we expect but the undervalued of society: women, lepers, and other outcasts.

While our social context differs drastically from that of Jesus' first followers, this story can provide meaning for our lives and give cause for celebration. Our contemporary world evidences many different gaps: between rich and poor, individuals and families, animals and human beings, able bodied and differently abled, developed and developing nations.

We desperately need to identify and celebrate God's challenging presence in this context. The Lenten season invites us to think on a deeper level about our role in making God's transformational presence known in our world.

PRAYER: Powerful Peacemaker, create within me the desire to recognize the gaps between others and myself. Enliven my imagination so that I can see beyond my own needs and reach out to others, bridging the gaps. Amen.

[‡]Assistant Professor of Religious Studies, St. Andrews Presbyterian College, Laurinburg, North Carolina; clergy member of the Presbytery of Coastal Carolina PC (USA).

Embodying hope for the oppressed, Jesus enters the holy city not in comfort and style but plodding atop a borrowed colt. Traveling in this rather unexpected way, Jesus shows the gathered crowd that he is no ordinary king. He is the humble servant and symbolizes the possibility of God's kingdom entering their experience. What those in the crowd who watch Jesus misunderstand is that Jesus also calls them to be different.

Jesus' triumphal entry into Jerusalem provides the textual bridge to the rest of the story. The celebration is the climax but not the end. Jesus goes on to drive merchants out of the Temple, denounce corruption, and speak of a poor widow as a model of faith. As God's love and hope enters, change takes place. Tables are overturned, and the lowliest widow receives a position of honor. Though Jesus embodies the possibility that God's love might reign on earth, in the end his followers also must respond and embody God's creative love.

Christian theologian John Cobb thinks of this transformation in terms of the relationship between God's creative love and the world's responsiveness. God envisions the best possible reality that we might attain: a life where we experience justice, love, mercy, fairness, compassion, and equality. But ultimately a God so full of love and hope does not force us to accept these possibilities. Rather, God nurtures us to be part of bringing it about. We praise God for the opportunity to bring love into our world and to continue to write the story.

PRAYER: O God, challenge me to be different. Give me the strength and energy to respond to your love with hope-filled actions. Give me the courage to confront the needs of those in my community, my family, and the larger world. Amen.

It is easy to identify with the "spiritual high" of the crowd as we read about Jesus' triumphal entry as we sit in the comfort of our homes in nicely furnished rooms, perhaps with a steaming cup of hot tea. We may be tempted to praise God for our comfortable lifestyles. Luke's depiction of Jesus, however, challenges us to think and feel beyond our own experiences, to move out of our comfortable positions and to contemplate the world's needs.

In today's passage Jesus weeps over the people's inability to pursue ways of life that will "make for peace," to meet the world's needs by embodying God's love in the world: welcoming outcasts to the table, reconsidering rigid boundaries drawn to promote holiness, and rethinking relationships and views of wealth and prosperity.

This scripture may challenge us to move out of our comfortable positions and to contemplate the needs of our twenty-first century world. Where is God's love needed most? What can we provide here and now? Jesus exemplifies a way of life that illumines paths toward peace.

Doug Oldenburg, former moderator of the PC (USA), spoke at a community conference held at St. Andrews Presbyterian College. He encouraged the faculty to think of the role of teacher in terms of being the "primary text," which is studied more closely than the textbook.

All of us are called to live as the "primary text." What we do and say matters to God and to those we meet. As you think about your own role in addressing the world's needs, consider how your relationships and actions display God's love. How do you, or can you, play a role in making God's transformational presence real to others?

PRAYER: God, empower me to be an instrument of your peace. Enable me to live in such a way that my actions indicate my awareness that you matter to me. Amen.

Simon is an innocent bystander who shows up, unaware of what he will be forced to do. He is picked out of the crowd, seized, and made to carry Jesus' cross. Though he does not have a choice, here he enacts the role of a disciple by carrying a load too heavy to bear for one weakened by beatings and disappointment.

God does not force us to carry the burdens of others. We choose how we engage ourselves as disciples. One of the ways that we enact our role is by helping alleviate the strain that others feel.

While not a precise parallel to the scripture reading about Simon, the story of a pastor and his family whom I met in Guatemala comes to mind. Compelled by their beliefs, their concern for indigenous peoples, and the global economic situation, they have chosen to make an extraordinary commitment to share the burdens of others. They live and work in a hillside invasion community, a *barranca*, outside Guatemala City. The living conditions in this *barranca* are ghastly. Families of six to eight people live in one-room cement block homes with no toilet facilities, often without electricity. However, neither the pastor nor his wife is imprisoned in their home. They choose to play important roles in the community, choosing this hardscrabble life because they feel called to carry their cross in this place.

Soldiers *forced* Simon to carry Jesus' cross. The Guatemalan pastor *chose* to carry a cross of service. God invites us to see a bigger picture as we view ourselves as part of a larger web of relationships. God moves within us, calls us, and nudges us to live every single moment of our lives with authenticity and persuades us to bring love into the world. Ask yourself, How can I participate in God's redemptive love in the difficult situations as well as the gentle times of life?

PRAYER: Creative and loving God, nudge me, move within me, and stir my thoughts. Help me to contemplate the use of my talents in service to your larger vision for my life and the world in which I live. Amen.

None of us likes to recall painful moments. However, lamenting these moments can remind us of our common nature and need, which can motivate us to act.

The wails and sobs of the mourners who walk with Jesus as he makes his way to the site of his crucifixion offer great contrast to the shouts and celebration that accompanied his entry into Jerusalem. A rush of grief has overtaken the women and others surrounding Jesus. Jesus' statements to the mourners bring to mind his earlier lament over the coming destruction of Jerusalem. He has persistently called the people to repentance, and they have refused. Despite their resistance, Jesus laments with them again. Grieving over the lost possibilities, he cries out, "Do not weep for me, but weep for yourselves and your children."

Holocaust survivor Elie Wiesel, through the voice of a little boy, reminds us that we all witness suffering and must bear responsibility for acting out our memory of it: "We're present wherever you go; we are what you do. When you raise your eyes to Heaven we share in their sight; when you pat the head of a hungry child a thousand hands are laid on his head; when you give bread to a beggar we give him that taste of paradise which only the poor can savor."* By lamenting with those who suffer, we not only remember them; we convey our belief that God values all people. Their pain is not meaningless to us; it promotes our action.

PRAYER: God, make me a witness of your peace in a world in which I am surrounded by destruction. Heighten my awareness of others' pain and move me toward action. Amen.

---

*Elie Wiesel, *Dawn*. New York: Avon Books, 1970, 97.

God has not turned away from the people but is faithful, even in the face of their rejection. The psalmist's prayer of thanksgiving calls to our attention the constancy of God's steadfast love and faithfulness. As we confront hardship, distress, and alienation from God and others, God is revealed as the one who continually invites us into communion.

Isabella Baumfree had a special awareness of God's faithfulness and steadfast love. She was born a slave in a dark cellar where her parents were afforded a small corner in their master's house. She describes the beginning of her spiritual journey as a turning toward the inward spiritual life; she prayed private prayers in the cool shadows of the willows as she listened to the sounds of the nearby stream. In this safe haven Isabella could speak her mind and make her wishes known to God. Through that relationship she met a freedom of expression, creativity, and love that society had denied her.

This intimate friendship with God enabled Isabella to find her way through the formidable barriers of the world in which she lived. Unable to recall the chronological date of her birth, she remembered well the day of her spiritual rebirth—not found in the isolation and safety of the willow trees but through outward expression of her belief in Jesus as friend and traveling partner. That day she took on a new name: Sojourner Truth. She recognized her connectedness both to God and to others and celebrated God's steadfast love by exposing injustice, working for reform, and preaching peace.

Centering on our connection with God and others can enable us to recognize God's steadfast love in the world. When we turn away, God's faithfulness and love will draw us back into relationship with one another.

PRAYER: Loving God, increase my awareness of the circle that extends beyond familiar boundaries. Help me wade out into the world's stormy seas without fear that the undertow will pull me down. Amen.

PALM/PASSION SUNDAY

The Christian life is not about quick, easy solutions to problems nor is it about spiritual or economic highs. Contemplating the meaning of Jesus' triumphal entry into Jerusalem can do more than simply bridge the gap between Lent and Easter; it can challenge us to become bridge builders.

If we choose to celebrate with the crowd, then we must also choose to continue the journey. Our journey continues as we receive the invitation to respond and participate in God's creative love. We have the opportunity to confront the world's needs, using our talents to bridge the gaps between poverty and wealth, hunger and satisfaction, exclusiveness and fairness.

Hearing the difficult and challenging stories is the first step. To bridge the gaps we have to know where the gaps are, to understand why and how suffering takes place. The world will not change in a day or even in a short period of time. But we can wear away at injustice by entering the lives of others, lamenting with them, sharing their burdens, and grieving over lost possibilities. We can raise our voices in celebration of the opportunity to play a role in living out this most powerful story.

PRAYER: God, draw me closer to you so that I can more clearly see how to participate in bridging the gaps. Give me the patience to listen carefully to others, to lament with them over their losses, and to help them carry their burdens. Provide the tools to build a way out of no way, so that together we can cross over to a better way of life. Amen.

The Unexpected Messiah

April 5–11, 2004 • *Barbara Brown Taylor*[‡]

MONDAY, APRIL 5 • **Read Isaiah 42:1-9**

The first Servant Song of Isaiah is as dear to Jews as it is to Christians, although the identity of said servant remains a point of disagreement. While many Christians see Jesus in this passage, Jews do not. Instead some see the nation of Israel, whom God called in righteousness centuries before Jesus' birth, while others see the Messiah yet to come. Either way, the servant's job is to bring justice to the nations. An unjust world is proof that the Messiah has not come.

While Christians look for the same promise to come true, they expect it to happen when the Messiah comes again. Thus two ancient communities wait faithfully for the same event, but their different convictions prevent them from waiting in the same room. Historically, Jews have paid dearly for disagreement with Christians on this point. From twelfth-century England to twentieth-century Poland, Jews have been evicted, tormented, damned, and killed by Jesus' furious defenders; Holy Week has traditionally been the worst week of all.

In recent years, groups of Jews and Christians have decided to change history by changing the ways that they regard one another. This has involved significant changes in traditional readings of scripture as well as in how each group distinguishes itself from the other. While these peacemakers risk suffering at the hands of their respective religious communities for their unorthodox attempts at reconciliation, they are driven by the same vision that consumed Isaiah: a just world united under the mercy of one God.

PRAYER: Whether we await your Messiah's coming or coming again, O God, make us servants of your peace. Amen.

[‡]Teacher of religion, Piedmont College, Demorest, Georgia, and Columbia Theological Seminary, Decatur, Georgia.

In your righteousness deliver me and rescue me; incline your ear to me and save me.

This week the psalmist speaks in the first person. "Do not let the foot of the arrogant tread on me," the ancient voice begs God, "or the hand of the wicked drive me away" (36:11). "Be pleased, O God, to deliver me. O LORD, make haste to help me!" (70:1). If the book of Psalms is the hymnbook of the Bible, then these are the songs of surrounded soldiers in trenches, of mothers with children in houses on fire.

In the context of Holy Week, they sound like laments that Jesus himself might have sung once it became clear where his life's work was leading him. This makes the songs unbearably sad, since we know that his prayers will not be answered. He will *not* be delivered. The feet of the arrogant *will* tread on him, and the last hymn he sings will confront the barren truth. "My God, my God, why have you forsaken me?" (22:1).

So why do these psalms continue to comfort us, and why do we pray similar prayers even when we know that divine rescue is unlikely? Perhaps we believe that God *does* come through in the end—or *after* the end, to be more precise—and that the hope of resurrection makes all of these songs singable.

But some of us are not so strong. We look for help this side of the grave, where the comfort of these psalms lies not in God's answering but in our asking. It is good to ask God for what we want, whether or not things turn out that way. It is good to bare our hearts, to stop being brave, to drop all pretense that we can manage our worst fears without yelling for help. The comfort in yelling, after all, is the audacious faith that Someone hears.

PRAYER: **Whether or not we hear you, O God, we rest in the assurance that you hear us. Amen.**

Let us run with perseverance the race that is set before us, looking to Jesus the pioneer and perfecter of our faith.

As familiar as this passage may be, it contains some unusual ideas as far as the rest of the New Testament is concerned. In the first place, we have a race to run. While Jesus ran it *before* us, he did not run it *for* us. His grace enables our exertion.

In the second place, the passage refers to "Jesus" and not to "Christ," which is the author's way of naming the earthling Messiah who woke up hungry and stubbed his toe on the bed frame, just as the rest of us are likely to do. Paul never tells one story from Jesus' life in all his letters, and the creeds of the church skip from Jesus' birth to his death without one word about the years in between. But the writer of Hebrews believes that honoring the son of man is as important as worshiping the Son of God.

Jesus was more than a trussed-up sacrifice for our sins, whose only purpose on earth was to die. He, the pioneer and perfecter of our faith, not only explored unknown territory in his full-bodied trust of God but also left a map for the rest of us to follow. Once he had taken his seat in the bleachers at the right hand of God, he became the loudest voice in the crowd of those cheering us on.

As Jesus nears the end of his marathon this week, many of us will desert him. The sight of his pinched face and the sound of his sucking for air will be too much for us. We will drift off to wait for him at the finish line instead, missing what we most need to know: *Human beings can run like this.* He came to show us how.

PRAYER: As you are present with us in our races, Lord Jesus, may we remain present to you in yours. Amen.

MAUNDY THURSDAY

So if I, your Lord and Teacher, have washed your feet, you also ought to wash one another's feet.

The Fourth Gospel mentions no Holy Communion on the night before Jesus' death. Instead, John says that Jesus rises in the middle of supper, trades his robe for a knotted towel, and washes his disciples' feet. This sacrament involves no bread, no wine, just feet—twenty-four of them at least, with ruined toenails, burst blisters, yellow corns where the hand-me-down sandals rub and thick calluses underneath. When Jesus finishes washing them, he leans close to dry them since his only towel is around his waist. Trust me, that towel is not something you want near your food when the foot washing is over.

On the next to last day of his life, Jesus gives his disciples this example to follow once he is gone, the lesson that he hopes will continue to teach them forever. This lesson is not in words either. It is a lesson in bodies, which the church has always cut a wide swath around. On the whole, we prefer sacraments with inanimate objects: a nice loaf of bread that does not move, a cup of wine or grape juice that will not talk back. These things are much easier to spiritualize than a bunch of smelly feet, each one attached to a singular human being with real warmth, real dirt, real faith, real doubts. Jesus understood how it worked. You cannot take a foot in your hands without getting really close to another person; once that happens God's word becomes flesh.

Whether or not we celebrate this sacrament on a regular basis, it is there to remind us that Jesus does not live inside a cross, an altar, a loaf, or a cup. Until we recognize him in one another, he is not here. Once we meet him in one another, there is no place he is not.

PRAYER: Risen Lord, be known to us in the washing of the feet. Amen.

GOOD FRIDAY

From then on Pilate tried to release him, but the Jews cried out, "If you release this man, you are no friend of the emperor. Everyone who claims to be a king sets himself against the emperor."

According to the first-century historian Josephus, Pontius Pilate was a brutal but effective Roman prefect who ruled Judea for ten years. During his tenure he faced a massive protest when his troops carried Roman images into Jerusalem. He spent Temple funds on a city aqueduct, and when the people revolted he sent soldiers dressed as Jewish civilians into the crowd to beat them with clubs. When he presided over the slaughter of Samaritan pilgrims in 35 C.E., he was finally recalled to Rome.

This history makes Pilate's performance in the Fourth Gospel all the more peculiar. In John's narrative, Pilate tries repeatedly to release Jesus, while "the Jews" demand his blood. They finally win, John says, by suggesting that they are on the emperor's side (since when do conquered Jews side with Caesar?).

While Pilate failed to protect Jesus, later Christians rehabilitated him into one of their own martyrs. By the sixth century, Saint Pilate had his own day on the Coptic Church calendar. Thus the Roman prefect who handed Jesus over for crucifixion received exoneration, while Jesus' own people were assigned guilt for his death. In centuries to come, this telling of the story would result in the persecution of Jews by Christians around the world.

Whatever else Christians grieve today, that Jesus' death on the cross should become a source of enmity instead of its end is high on the list. "It is finished," he said, giving his life for love of the world. May those who follow him devote their lives to making his last words come true.

PRAYER: God of the killers and the killed, break our blaming hearts today, so that we are defenseless before your redeeming love. Amen.

HOLY SATURDAY

Pilate said to them, "You have a guard of soldiers; go, make it as secure as you can." So they went with the guard and made the tomb secure by sealing the stone.

Today's narrative involves a great deal of human activity, but the central character is not a person but a stone. If it was a typical tombstone, then it was round and flat, about three feet across and six inches thick. It was set into a groove in front of a rock face that had a low door carved in it, so that the stone could be rolled back and forth in front of the opening. The door led to a small, hewn cavern with one or more ledges in it, where dead bodies rested until they decomposed. Then family members gathered the bones for secondary burial in a small stone box, or ossuary, so that the ledge was freed up for its next occupant.

According to Matthew, Jesus' body is carried to a brand new tomb donated by a rich man named Joseph of Arimathea, a disciple who remains when all the other men have fled. Joseph not only has the guts to claim Jesus before Pilate; he also has the humility to join the women disciples in tending Jesus' body. Then he rolls the stone in front of the tomb and goes away, leaving the two Marys in charge.

On Saturday, the Passover Sabbath, the women may still be there when the guard of soldiers shows up to fix the stone in place. Some national security advisors accompany them, doing all in their power to ensure that no one else's idea upsets their idea of what is good for the people. After sealing the stone, they have only to sit down and watch it. They have, after all, done everything in their power.

PRAYER: Nothing stays buried in your presence, O God. Save us from placing our confidence in stones. Amen.

EASTER SUNDAY

On Sunday the stone is not where it should be. The tomb gapes open and Jesus is not in it; rumors fly. He has only seemed to be dead. His body has been stolen. He has been raised by God. Then he appears to some but not to all, so that faith matters more than ever. What can be believed depends on whom can be trusted, and not even his disciples all believe the same thing.

By the time of Peter's preaching on a regular basis, two schools of thought existed about what it meant to follow Jesus. According to one, it meant keeping the same covenant that Jesus had kept, with continuing reliance on Torah as the revealed word of God. According to the other, it meant entering a new form of the covenant, with reliance on Jesus as the living word of God.

Peter started out in the former school but ended up in the latter, as God opened his eyes to just how big Easter really was. God's presence in the life, death, and resurrection of Jesus Christ was not a gift to a single nation but to every nation, Peter said. God showed no partiality. Anyone transformed by those events was acceptable to God, whether she or he said thank-you in Hebrew, Latin, or Greek. To believe in the possibility of asking God's forgiveness in Jesus' name was to receive it. Easter was that big.

Within a few centuries it grew smaller as Christians worked out complex systems of belief. Easter was only for those who believed in the Virgin Birth, the Trinity, the Nicene Creed. It belonged only to baptized members of the Christian church who believed in God's partiality toward them. What would Peter have said?

He is risen. Believe that, and the rest will take care of itself.

PRAYER: Every time we think we have you cornered, O God, we trust you to escape. Amen.

God's Power Working in Us

April 12–18, 2004 • Ruth L. Clemmons[‡]

MONDAY, APRIL 12 • Read John 20:19-31

In July 1969, what was appearing on the TV screen mesmerized America. I remember feeling almost suffocated with tension as I watched Neil Armstrong step off the bottom rung of a ladder onto—who knew what? And then I saw him actually walking on the moon! Incredible! Even today some people refuse to believe that this event actually happened.

Picture the excitement of the disciples as they behold the risen Lord for the first time. Even though he had told them he would rise again and had sent them word after the Resurrection, they are unprepared for the reality. As they meet fearfully behind locked doors, Jesus appears in their midst saying, "Peace be with you." Yet there is still uncertainty until he shows them the marks on his hands and feet. Then comes assurance and jubilation. From that moment, enabled by a living Presence and a compelling faith, they are qualified to be true witnesses. They can declare the risen Christ based on firsthand knowledge.

But what about us? Jesus must have been thinking about us when he told Thomas, "Blessed are those who have not seen and yet have believed" (v. 29, NIV).

I was not actually there to see Neil Armstrong's moon walk, but I really believe it occurred. I was not present with the apostles in that upper room, but I believe that Jesus died and rose again and lives today. This faith gives me the blessed hope that I must share with others.

PRAYER: Lord of miracles, move me beyond mere belief to an experience and ongoing relationship with Christ that will give me boldness in witnessing. Amen.

[‡]Retired teacher; Volunteer in Mission; member, Bay Street Baptist Church, Eustis, Florida.

Seeing is believing. Thomas was so like me! He couldn't go beyond what his eyes could see. Not that he was a halfhearted follower of Jesus. Just a few days earlier, when the other disciples were urging Jesus to stay away from Jerusalem, Thomas had said, "Let us also go, that we may die with him" (John 11:16, NIV). Now his friends tell him that Jesus is alive, but Thomas hasn't seen for himself; he demands a sign.

When Jesus returns to show himself to Thomas, he doesn't reprimand the doubter. He simply sees a need and offers to fill it. Thomas responds with the strongest confession of faith recorded in the Gospels: "My Lord and my God!" Here is the purpose of John's Gospel, according to John 20:30-31—to move Christ's followers from a sign faith to a truly life-giving faith.

The Greek word for "believe" is *pisteuo*, which includes these meanings: 1) acceptance of an assertion as true; 2) an attitude of patient confidence; 3) active obedience. Thomas fulfilled all three of these aspects of belief; he acknowledged with his head, surrendered with his heart, and followed through with his life.

Yes, seeing is believing. *But believing is also seeing.* When we believe, we begin to see what God is doing in our lives. In Solzhenitsyn's novel *One Day in the Life of Ivan Denisovich*, Ivan mocks the faith and prayers of his Christian friend Alyosha, noting that prayers won't help him get out of prison any earlier. Alyosha explains that he doesn't pray to get out—he prays to do the will of God every day, right where he is. He sees meaning for his life in the middle of suffering, for he sees Jesus there.

PRAYER: Lord of compassion, I thank you for your patience with my doubts. Help me to trust you even when I can't see what you are doing. Amen.

The religious and political leaders are furious. Jesus' followers have filled Jerusalem with their message, even after strict warnings to cease and desist. And then they have had the audacity to escape from jail and return to the Temple courts to continue their teaching. The same Peter who so recently denied Christ speaks now for all of them: They are witnesses to incredible events; they have a commission from God; and they have made their decision. A few days earlier they were fearful, but now they have seen the risen Christ and have been empowered by the Holy Spirit.

Jesus did not seek vengeance on those who killed him; he offered forgiveness. The religious and secular leaders didn't want forgiveness; they wanted exoneration, and that meant silencing those who told of Jesus' love and his death for them.

Such persecution is not just ancient history. Today thousands, even millions, who in the face of violence continue to tell about Jesus Christ, just as the apostles in Jerusalem did. Many suffer harassment, loss of employment, imprisonment, unspeakable torture, and even death for their faith. Church buildings are destroyed. Yet instead of being weakened by persecution, the body of Christ continues to grow.

Many see the conflict between God's authority and the world's opposition as a danger. God would have us see this conflict as a challenge that should prove healthy to our relationship with God. "These things I have spoken unto you, that in me ye might have peace. In the world ye shall have tribulation: but be of good cheer; I have overcome the world" (John 16:33, KJV).

PRAYER: Lord, our Defender, protect our brothers and sisters in Christ who are targeted for attack because they proclaim a resurrected Jesus Christ as Lord and Savior. Give them courage and comfort and the power of the Holy Spirit as they suffer for their obedience. Amen.

Larry Pepper's dream was about to come true. As a NASA flight surgeon, he had been involved in America's space program for several years. Now at last he was among those actually in line for space travel. But it wasn't to be. Larry had become aware that God wanted him somewhere else—at a hospital in Uganda, of all places. To his shocked friends he explained, "It was simple obedience to God."

So too would the early apostles, Peter and John, have responded. Still imperfect men, but now filled with courage, a gift of the Holy Spirit, they have a daring new faith. Warned not to speak in the name of Jesus, they explain that they must. Having been jailed yet again, they had no sooner been miraculously released than they were back in the Temple teaching, risking everything.

Persecuted even to death, Peter and John don't have the benefit of seeing ahead to the church that will venerate and honor them. They only know that Christ has risen, and they can recall his words, "Whoever wants to save his life will lose it, but whoever loses his life for me will save it" (Luke 9:24, NIV).

Today this challenge is always before me: to surrender my will to God's design. I have my own plans, hopes, aspirations, and fears. There may be difficulties in going God's way that are not part of my blueprint—rough spots, sacrifice, even rejection. But I am reminded that surrendering my life to God is not done in a moment or by my power. It is a daily, continuing, lifelong process; and the strength must be on God's side, not mine.

PRAYER: Lord, my Redeemer, you have gone before me and shown the way. Holy Spirit, give me the courage to leave my comfortable niche and the insight to see the opportunities before me today. Amen.

On the picturesque volcanic island of Patmos, my husband and I followed a road up the steep hillside to the venerated St. John's Grotto, lovingly cared for by monks from the monastery of St. John. Nearby is a theological school. To me, this was an ideal, peaceful setting in which to commune with God.

However, in John's day, Patmos was anything but a place for retreat and meditation. It was a kind of Alcatraz, a dumping ground for criminals, perhaps even the criminally insane. The Aegean Sea served as an effective, unbreachable wall. What a horrid, frightening place for the gentle apostle of love and forgiveness to find himself in at the age of ninety!

Isolated, separated from family and friends, banished to a tiny piece of rock surrounded by the sea, John could give in to loneliness and despair. But he knows nothing can separate him from the love of God, and he has Jesus' promise, "Peace I leave with you, my peace I give you" (John 14:27, NIV). So even in this most difficult setting, John has a tremendous worship experience. As he prays, the Holy Spirit gives him an astonishing message that has remained tidings of hope to Christians through the ages.

Sometimes I feel that I am on my own island of Patmos, surrounded by problems, sorrows, or physical trials. John demonstrates that it's not *where* you are but *whose* you are that determines your outlook. In spite of outward circumstances, he can still hold to Jesus' promises; through the clamor he can hear God's voice; despite the evil around him he can see God's beautiful plan for the future.

PRAYER: Lord of perfect peace, I pray that my reactions may not be controlled by the situations in which I find myself but by my relationship with you. May I always be aware that you are greater than my circumstances. Amen.

Exiled to a desolate, remote, windswept island in the Aegean Sea, John is not concerned about himself but about Christians in the Roman province of Asia. Most of the apostles, as well as many other followers of Christ, have been put to death. John sees more trials ahead, because Domitian, on the throne in Rome, claims deity and demands to be worshiped as a god.

John writes to give believers new hope. He has received a message from God giving admonition and encouragement, and telling of a wonderful future. He records his vision and apparently intends that it be circulated from city to city, as he lists seven churches (v. 11) in the sequence in which they appeared on a circular road, beginning in Ephesus.

This short passage reveals the whole gospel as it speaks of God, the Eternal One, and God's incredible grace. It reminds us of Christ, whose love led him to the cross, and tells of the Resurrection and the exalted position to which Christ was raised. Repeating the assurance of forgiveness and of a special standing before God, it envisions Jesus coming again, when everyone, friend and enemy, must acknowledge him as Lord.

Finally, this passage asserts God's claim to total sovereignty. "I am the Alpha and the Omega, who is, and who was, and who is to come, the Almighty" (NIV). God began history and will end it as God wills. Because we fit in somewhere between the beginning and the end, God supremely rules over all our days.

PRAYER: Lord of all hope, give me the love that will impel me to share the good news with others and the faith that will allow me to leave the future to you. Amen.

Rather than fear or dread, our God evokes extravagantly joyful praise. Here, in the "Hallelujah Chorus" of the book of Psalms, is a climax, a paean of praise—not to a benevolent father figure, not to a deity who can be put into a denominational box, but to the Sovereign of the universe. This is the kind of hallelujah we will find in heaven. The psalmist pays homage not for what God has done but for the glory and majesty of God's being. Overwhelmed as he comprehends the honor due God, he bursts forth with the call to "praise" thirteen times in this short passage.

"Praise God in his sanctuary; praise him in his mighty heavens" (NIV). What can contain such acclamation? We may have this experience in a prayer closet or in a cathedral. Some honor the Lord to the thunder of great organs; some sing and clap to guitars and trumpets; some sway and dance to drums and tambourines; others praise with lowered voices and with lookouts at the doors. Whatever the medium or setting, we acknowledge that God is deserving of honor and adoration from us, God's created beings. When we have some understanding of how big our God is, we realize how small we are. Yet we can approach God with the assurance that we don't have to make ourselves worthy to worship, because Jesus is our righteousness.

Surely glorifying God with the heavenly host in Christ's kingdom will be easy. Today as I gather with God's children in corporate worship, the holy awe that leads to true praise is sometimes elusive. And living each day here and now in a spirit that honors God's name and speaks of God's holiness—that's hard!

PRAYER: Almighty God, I pray that my everyday life may be an offering of praise to you. Amen.

God's Transforming Presence

April 19–25, 2004 • David Miller[‡]

MONDAY, APRIL 19 • Read Psalm 30

Words only have power in context. An impatient husband greets his wife, "Thank God, you are finally here!" A worried parent greets a child on a snowy afternoon at the school bus stop, "Thank God, you are finally here." Same words, differing contexts.

The context of Psalm 30, one of the great psalms of thanksgiving, gives its words great power. The psalmist borrows the words from the corporate worship of God's people to form a very personal prayer of thanksgiving. Ill with a sickness unto death, the psalmist has given up because death is certain. In a situation that appears hopeless, the psalmist likely has put his worldly affairs in order and resigned himself to death. However, he does not die. The anticipation does not become reality. Despair turns into the laughter of wholeness. Depression becomes the joy of healing. Discouragement grows into the happiness of new life.

This unknown psalmist thanks God from a heart overflowing with gratitude. Healing emanates from no physicians, no miracle drug, no positive thinking, no mere luck—but from God. God has healed the psalmist.

> O Lord, my God, I cried to thee for help, and thou
>   hast healed me.
>
> . . . .
>
> Sing praises to the Lord, O you his saints and give
>   thanks to his holy name. (RSV)

How refreshing to hear one so sure, so certain, so straightforward praise God.

SUGGESTION FOR MEDITATION: The psalmist troubles and humbles us! Each of us has been touched by the loving, purposeful, and healing Presence. How do we express our gratitude?

[‡]Financial planner with AXA Advisors, Nashville, Tennessee.

Summer in South Carolina hates to give up to fall. The month of August burns like a fiery furnace, and the last week of August 1948 was brutally hot.

Julian and Olivene had been married two years and were about to make their first contribution to the Baby Boomer generation. They had already made two false-alarm trips to the Divine Savior Hospital in York. The third trip promised to be the real thing. The expectant father stood in the door of the delivery area, which doubled as the emergency room, in order to keep out two drunks who wanted immediate attention.

Olivene, heavily sedated, gave birth to their first child. When Julian saw the baby—a boy!—his heart raced with excitement. But the doctor turned and said, "I'm sorry, Julian; the child is stillborn." From joy to desolation. Tears filled his eyes as he considered how Olivene might cope with the news that her child was born dead. Through tears he watched a nun pick up the body of his lifeless son. She looked at the baby and cleared his mouth with her fingers, then she bent down and breathed into the lifeless body. I took my first breath.

My father's mourning turned to dancing with joy. The psalmist understood what my father experienced at my birth. The psalmist wrote,

> You have turned my mourning into dancing;
>   you have taken off my sackcloth
>   and clothed me with joy,
> so that my soul may praise you and not be silent.
>   O LORD my God, I will give thanks to you forever.

SUGGESTION FOR MEDITATION: **Consider the times that God has entered your life and brought joy from sorrow, light from darkness, hope from despair, and dancing from mourning.**

I must confess that the story of Paul's conversion on the Damascus road has always troubled me. I know what others have told me; but, when I read the text, Paul's conversion disappears like a morning fog.

I do find in the text a man named Saul headed for Damascus with the desire to arrest the followers of The Way and bring them back to Jerusalem. This Saul sees a light from heaven, falls to the ground, and hears a voice that asks, "Saul, Saul, why do you persecute me?" The stunned Saul responds with a question of his own, "Who are you, Lord?" The voice replies, "I am Jesus, whom you are persecuting. But get up and enter the city, and you will be told what you are to do."

I hear no confession of faith from Saul, now blind. Those accompanying Saul lead him into Damascus.

The instructions Paul receives from the voice of Jesus are worthy of deeper meditation: "Get up and enter the city, and you will be told what to do." *The voice tells Saul only the next step.* It does not tell him that he will become a follower of The Way, that he will be known as Paul, that he will make three great missionary journeys, that he will suffer great hardships, that his letters will be considered sacred scripture, and that he will die in Rome.

Certainly Saul wanted to know more, just as we want to know more. But the Damascus road story teaches us that we, like Saul, often find ourselves at a place in our faith where we can only know the next step. We are not privy to the whole story of what unfolds ahead, only the next step. However, though physically and spiritually in the dark, Saul allowed himself to be led. He becomes a model of the life of faith for us. Faith emerges as the courage to take the next step even though sometimes our path appears to be a journey into darkness.

SUGGESTION FOR MEDITATION: Recall a time when God pointed you in a direction that seemed a journey into darkness. How did you respond?

Yesterday I confessed that I find it difficult from the story recorded in Acts to see that Saul was converted to The Way on the Damascus road. However, much more of the story remains.

The Lord speaks to a resident of Damascus named Ananias, telling him to find a man from Tarsus named Saul and to lay hands on him so that he might receive his sight. Fearfully Ananias answers, "Lord, I have heard from many about this man, how much evil he has done to your saints in Jerusalem."

This reasonable response articulated Ananias's vulnerability to the very person known as an enemy of The Way. Yet the Lord asks Ananias to move far beyond his comfort zone and to give aid and comfort to the enemy. Ananias obeys. After finding Saul, he lays his hands upon him. Saul rises with his sight restored and is baptized.

Because Ananias's faith overcame his fear, Saul and the world were never the same. Once long ago, something happened in Damascus to and through two unlikely men, and the world was changed for the better. Who knows? It could happen again!

SUGGESTION FOR MEDITATION: **Recall a time when you moved beyond your comfort zone and began to see those in need as your sisters and brothers. Whom do you know who desperately needs to hear you call her or him "sister" or "brother"?**

The picture of Simon Peter in the Gospels always evokes within me a sigh of relief. Simon Peter embodies humanity's contradictions: He is faithful and faithless. He is fearsome and fearful. He is any one of us.

When Jesus calls this fisherman to cast his net for the kingdom, Simon Peter has fished all night and not caught a single fish. One of the last scenes in the Gospel of John captures Simon Peter and some of the other disciples fishing. Guess what? They have fished all night and not caught a single fish.

Jesus tells the professional fishermen what to do in order to get a net full of fish, just as he had done when he summoned Simon Peter a few years earlier. Someone in the group recognizes Jesus, and Simon Peter, stripped for work, pulls on his clothes and jumps into the cold lake. He has always wanted to make a big splash in front of the disciples and Jesus.

I've always felt that Simon Peter probably has reminded the other disciples upon more than one occasion that none of them has ever walked on water. And on this morning he probably sinks like a rock at first trying to do so. But somehow in his waterlogged clothes he splashes and sloshes his way to shore, leaving the other disciples to struggle with a net full of fish and a boat needing to be rowed to shore.

If there were such a thing as spiritual DNA, Simon Peter and I would be found to be related. Our kinship reveals itself when I am at my best and when I am at my worst as a follower of Jesus. Sometimes I have wanted to make a big splash when I should have been hauling in the nets.

SUGGESTION FOR MEDITATION: When have you made a big splash? Who was left in your wake?

The disciples have labored through the night. Their net has come up empty time after time. Then, upon the advice of a stranger on shore, they cast their net on the other side of the boat and their net fills with fish. Disciples "0," Stranger "153."

When the disciples row their boat, pulling the net filled with fish, to the shore, their conjecture that the stranger is their Lord proves to be true. The Lord has prepared a hot meal for them. Because he cares about their physical needs, he feeds them.

Once again the Lord demonstrates what he expects from the disciples and from each of us. His followers are to feed the hungry, give water to the thirsty, welcome the stranger, clothe the naked, and visit the sick and the prisoners. We do these things in his name, not our own, and for his glory, not our own.

The conversation between Simon Peter and Jesus clarifies the thrust and the direction of our discipleship. Three times our Lord puts the question to Simon Peter: "Simon, son of John, do you love me?" Simon answers the question in the only way that he knows, with emotion: "Yes, Lord; you know that I love you." Yes, Jesus does know that Simon loves him. The question is whether Simon knows what it means to love Jesus. In Jesus' response to each of Simon's three affirmations of love, Simon receives a commission: "Feed my lambs." "Tend my sheep." "Feed my sheep."

Jesus Christ calls us, like Simon, to demonstrate our love by acting benevolently. We prove our love for him not by the sincerity of our emotions or our intentions but by our actions.

SUGGESTION FOR MEDITATION: **Recall a time when you made an emotional statement or commitment, only to realize later you were not prepared to follow through on your vow.**

The body of Christ in the last decades of the first century had been beaten and brutalized, torn and tortured, subdued and savaged, ripped and raped. The hand of Rome intensely persecuted Christians, throwing some to the lions in the coliseum, dipping others in pitch and burning them alive to furnish light for the emperor's evening parties. Most early Christians understandably experienced waves of despair and hopelessness. In the midst of this great persecution God spoke to a man named John by revelation. This revelation to John circulated among the churches. John wrote the letter in a special code easily deciphered by Christians of the first century, but unintelligible to those outside the faith.

The message of the Revelation to John can be summed up in one word, *hope*. This word of hope proclaims that the followers of Jesus Christ are not alone. God still remains God, and in the end God will be victorious.

Unfortunately many have interpreted the Revelation of John as a playground for creating fear, while others have made fortunes selling books that reveal the key to unlock its mystery. Yet today's passage from Revelation portrays a feast for eyes and ears. Gathered around the throne of heaven John sees the living creatures, the elders, and the angels, all joined in a chorus of praise for the Lamb. Who is this slain Lamb worthy of all the praise of heaven and earth? He is the one we need to know in times of trial and tribulation and in times of joy and exaltation. He is our hope everlasting.

SUGGESTION FOR MEDITATION: **Where do you turn for hope in times of despair and hopelessness? How can you share the hope of Revelation with others who despair?**

Deeper into God

April 26–May 2, 2004 • *Michael Battle*[‡]

MONDAY, APRIL 26 • **Read Acts 9:36-43**

Peter put all of them outside, and then he knelt down and prayed.

What a strange way to think of God, that you have to kneel down to sense God's presence. Is God somehow hiding downward awaiting our discovery? While instructing junior faculty members in theological education I discovered a common concern, that of fear: fear of not getting tenure, fear of not living out their passion for teaching, fear of imbalance between career and family and between God's call and actual faithfulness.

During a visit to the Indianapolis Museum of Art I was enlightened by a piece of art that the guide never showed us, a work off the beaten path and without so much as a title. Written below the work were these words: *Untitled no. 9, 1994.* It depicted a flower deep in the middle of blackberries. The work was held together by hair oil, mayonnaise, and some other common substances. The artist Helen Chadwick described her work: "The living integrates with the other in an infinite continuity of matter and welcomes difference not as damage but potential."

"The living integrates with the other." In this way we might think of God and know God who loves us and treats us as potential and never as damage. I thought to myself, *This is why Peter had to kneel down to pray.* Knowing God requires a search downward, deeper than ourselves, deeper than our fears. Knowing God requires integration into the other, the greatest other—God.

PRAYER: Miraculous God, bring us more and more into the potential of our humanity. Help us to see how wonderfully we are created. Amen.

[‡]Assistant Professor of Spirituality and Black Church Studies, Duke University Divinity School, Durham, North Carolina; priest, St. Ambrose Episcopal Church.

How long will you keep us in suspense? If you are the Messiah, tell us plainly.

Jesus' response to the question leaves those still searching for superficial answers, those not willing to go deeper, wanting. Jesus responds that we can know that he is the Messiah through the works of his life. But to know these works requires a relationship to Jesus in which love becomes synonymous with knowledge. In other words, as Saint Augustine taught us, to know God is to love God. We can't know God without loving God. Jesus responds with the metaphor of a shepherd and his sheep.

As we draw closer to God our initial perceptions change. On the third floor of the Indianapolis Museum of Art the guide instructed my group to look at a grey rectangle on the wall, "Stand back and simply look at it." So we stood there in an enclosed space, dark except for the grey rectangle on the wall. "Now, go and touch the painting," she said. As I came closer to the wall, it gave way to empty, deeper space. The grey rectangle wasn't a picture after all, but something beyond my earlier perception. It was really a hole in the wall.

I finally got close enough to the "painting" on the wall to see see what was really there. When Jesus says, "I have told you, and you do not believe," he knows we cannot understand our faith until we get closer to him and understand the imperishable nature of our relationship with him. God does not wish to scare us or intimidate us but in fact to invite us into a deeper life in which we see more clearly how to live. Jesus' words are a warning to those who would rather get the religious words right instead of living right.

PRAYER: Almighty God, let us move deeper into you. Let us increase our reach toward you through daily prayer, acts of kindness, and faith even in the midst of fear and despair. Amen.

What is apparent about God is not the deeper reality.

Walter Wangerin, one of my favorite storytellers, has evidently passed along his gift to his children, especially to his daughter Talitha. She is the youngest of four children. Her mom, dad, sister, and brother are white, but her other brother and she are black. They were adopted as babies. Talitha tells the following story to illustrate the difficulty people have in understanding how two different races can be part of the same family.

When Talitha was four years old, her family stopped for lunch at a diner. Staring at the family's odd assortment of black and white members, the waitress asked if they were on a field trip. When Talitha's father replied no, the waitress asked, "These ain't your students?" Wangerin again responded no. "Your kids?" she asked. Wangerin finally answered affirmatively. The waitress thought for a moment and said, "Adopted!" Pointing her pencil at Talitha and her brother, she said, "That one and that one, right?" "Right," Wangerin said. Pleased with herself, she finally took the family's order.

In Talitha's story, an apparent group of students is found to be, upon deeper investigation, a family. In the story of Peter, who raises Tabitha from the dead, everyone believes the loved one is lost to them forever. But the apparent reality of the power of death over life is overcome by the deeper reality of God's power over death. Like the waitress, the people of Joppa learn a new thing this day—that new human identities are constantly being formed by the miracles of God.

PRAYER: Almighty God, you are more ready to believe in us than we in ourselves. Give us that vision to see beyond our surface until we see your presence in our midst. Amen.

Jesus, who said that he came to bring an apocalyptic sword, died on a cross rather than retaliate with the wrath of heaven. When we get closer to Jesus' vision of God through the revelation to John, we see that the God we want to hide from actually desires the safety of all creation. We discover the strange and paradoxical imagery of "the Lamb at the center of the throne" who will protect us and be our shepherd. In John's revelation we also see the new vision of Jesus.

We human beings tend to separate word and action, often failing to do what we say we will do. In John's vision, every nation must learn to see God as both Lamb and Shepherd, as both the word and the action. Going deeper into God enables us to glimpse this paradoxical power and redemption.

The passive Lamb that was slain becomes the shepherd who guides. Here true power resides. As Jesus reminded us earlier this week, he knows his sheep; he protects his sheep; and he gives his sheep eternal life (John 10:8-30). Today's passage reminds us that God has not forgotten God's own. The shepherd who guides the sheep to the waters of life is the one who wipes away every tear—what an amazingly tender and gentle God!

The revelation to John shows us a new reality, a reality that assures us of salvation in the Lamb and the protection of the Shepherd as we move deeper into God. As we move into that deeper communion with God, we also gain a clearer sense of God's vision: the numberless multitude from every tribe and language, every ethnic group and nation, standing in the presence of the Lamb who sanctifies all. Today use the eyes of your spirit to see your brothers and sisters surrounding the Lamb. Sing the praise to God that we read in Revelation 7:12.

PRAYER: Dear heavenly Father, pray in us so that we can believe in more than ourselves. Amen.

Miracles still occur today. In South Africa both Afrikaners and black people adhered to the belief that God chooses one people, a belief that led to years of violent division and to a separation of races and cultures. Despite this history, the miracle in South Africa is Pentecost when a diversity of languages, people, and cultures bound by the Holy Spirit are led beside still waters.

Psalm 23 is a movingly personal expression of one individual's experience of the bond between the Shepherd and his sheep. Yet if we look more deeply into the psalm, we find that the experience of eternal love and assurance is available to all, including both Afrikaner and black.

The Spirit will always stand by us to lead us to still and deeper waters. When the Afrikaners rose to power in apartheid, their interpretation of "the Lord is my shepherd" changed from that of identification with the least and the lost to God's election only of themselves. Often those in the world cannot accept the Spirit Shepherd because they neither see such presence nor know such presence; they settle for war or competition. This psalm reminds us that God is with us "all the days of [our] life" a miraculous presence even in the midst of violent reality. South Africans currently walk beside still waters because they have finally heard the Shepherd's voice for all people.

PRAYER: Gracious God, when we find ourselves more tempted to curse than to bless, give us an awareness of your grace that we may see you and your intention to save all of the world. Amen.

"How long will you keep us in suspense? If you are the Messiah, tell us plainly." The question asked by those around Jesus rings true today. We ask, "How long?" We hear preachers and teachers try to answer the question. We write and read books that focus on the question. We want to know how we will recognize the Messiah.

Jesus answers with clarity and with mystery. "My sheep hear my voice, and they follow me." We think, *Of course, the sheep respond to the voice of the shepherd. That's the nature of sheep.* Or do sheep learn to respond to shepherds? Maybe our relationship should mirror the relations of sheep and shepherds. Consider this English noun *sheep*. It represents a single animal and a multitude of animals. Imagine an individual sheep grazing in a field. The sheep is content. For us, the image of a solitary sheep corresponds to the ways in which we read and meditate on scripture. Like that grazing individual sheep, we feel a contentment as we reflect on scripture and allow the Word to move deep within us.

Sheep live in flocks or in a community of sheep. We also hear the voice of the Shepherd as we live in the community of faith. The community challenges us to use our gifts for mission and ministry. It comforts us when we need solace. In community we learn peace. In community we learn accountability. In community we discover the ever-deepening love of God.

"How long will you keep us in suspense?...tell us plainly." Where is the Messiah, the Shepherd, today? The Messiah is found as we live deeply in scripture.

PRAYER: Come community of God, Father, Son, and Holy Spirit. Make your home among us. Amen.

The reign of Christ is primarily about the creation of an environment in which we truly become human. The revelation to John attests to the reign of Christ in which a new authority is established (the Rule of the Lamb) in order for us to fulfill our human potential. Christ, as king of this new order, sends out a platoon of disciples, not to kill but to reshape violent reality, aware that his kind of reign carries a price: "See, I am sending you out like lambs into the midst of wolves" (Luke 10:3). Those who follow Christ, must now be a different kind of people in world. No longer can we live capriciously or aimlessly, following our every whim and addiction. Christ's kingdom has defined all of us differently, as the kind of people who create environments conducive to the interaction of diverse personalities and cultures. We need only look at the world's obsession with violence to see how different is Christ's kingdom.

I observe this difference between Christ's kingdom and our cultural environment when I watch television programs. So many shows present protagonists who are attractive and violent. Violence rules. We learn from television that domains and kingdoms, whether a nuclear family or a criminal gang or a city, operate smoothly through threats of violence.

Jesus' reign is different from those portrayed on television. One way to think of Jesus' reign comes from the African concept of *ubuntu*, an environment of vulnerability in which persons recognize that their humanity is bound together with the humanity of another. All peoples are bound to the Shepherd by their common fears and vulnerabilities, and in their need to find their human identity in the eternal love and assurance of Christ's kingdom.

PRAYER: God, help us to accept your invitation to come ever deeper into your divine life. Help us to anticipate the fullness of your reign. Amen.

In and through Us

May 3–9, 2004 • Bradford L. Motta[‡]

MONDAY, MAY 3 • Read Revelation 21:1-4

I have done many weddings during my ministry. Some brides and grooms are quite calm, while others make me wonder if they will get through the ceremony. When I see a nervous bride or groom, I immediately give a lot of attention and instruction to the person who will stand next to her or him during the ceremony. I have learned that people take great comfort during stressful times from the people who stand with them.

Verse 3 of today's reading contains three affirmations that God will be with God's people: "God is among mortals"; God "will dwell with them"; and God "will be with them." While much about the book of Revelation is confusing and sometimes upsetting, this repetition of God's presence with us is an incredible assurance.

Many situations we face in life cannot be predicted. The reactions of people around us to what may be happening in our lives cannot be predicted. Our own ability to cope with the unknown cannot be predicted. But today's scripture assures us of one thing that is always predictable: God will be with us.

Jesus faced new challenges and obstacles every day. He found himself in direct opposition with people who should have been his allies. Jesus' strength lay in his knowledge that God was with him no matter what he faced. That same knowledge can get any one of us through any situation.

PRAYER: God of power and might, give us the knowledge of your presence that Jesus relied on that we might be faithful in living as his disciples in the world. Amen.

[‡]Senior pastor, Morristown United Methodist Church, Morristown, New Jersey; past president of Christian Educators Fellowship; national trainer for the Disciple Bible Study program.

TUESDAY, MAY 4 • Read Acts 11:1-10

"Why did you go and have dinner with them?" That is the question posed by the apostles to Peter. Sometimes we find it hard to believe that Jesus' followers had really listened to and heard what he taught them. While these apostles raise a question about sharing a meal with Gentiles, they clearly are upset about more than that. Jesus and the presence of the Holy Spirit are *theirs.* The idea of sharing this new spiritual food is more than they can comprehend. The early Christian movement was plagued by a "them and us" thinking that exists in the church and in the world today.

The church I serve has a number of homeless people who arrive after the worship service for the fellowship hour and immediately head for the table of coffee and bagels. Many members get upset about the situation. The homeless people who frequent "our" fellowship time are not the cleanest of people; in fact, one is referred to (less than affectionately) as the "mud lady." Much time has been spent dealing with her unsettling presence, with some members wondering how I can allow her to eat with us. I understand their feelings, but I cannot find one bit of scripture or any example of Jesus that will let me exclude her from "our" fellowship hour.

Jesus invited us to a life of inclusiveness and compassion. Too often Jesus' early followers resorted to the exclusive behavior that they enjoyed before Jesus broke down the barriers between people and cultures. I am sure that it was difficult for them. I know that it is difficult for us. May God give us the eyes of Jesus that we might see people the way he does.

PRAYER: God of loving eyes, help us to see what human eyes often don't see: the hope and promise that is in every one of your children. Help us to live in fellowship and peace. Amen.

In and through Us 137

Today's reading continues the story from yesterday. As soon as Peter finishes telling the apostles about his dream, three men arrive. The Spirit tells Peter to follow the men, who take him to the house of a man who has been told by an angel to send for Peter because Peter has a message for him, and indeed he does. As soon as Peter arrives, the Holy Spirit comes upon this Gentile household.

Peter allows his feet to take him to a place where the Spirit leads. The scripture says that "the Spirit told me to go with them...." Peter, who had denied knowing Jesus three times to save his own skin, now follows the guidance of an inner voice that leads him to new places and encourages him to try new things. Peter has not only listened to Jesus; he has allowed his feet to follow the Spirit's leading to bring good news to the Gentiles.

Every one of us can learn from Peter's faith and actions. Not only does Peter feel the Spirit leading him, but he also follows though he has no idea of his destination. The easy road in life follows a familiar and comfortable path. But faith in God sets us on paths that are not quite so well-traveled or smooth.

A friend of mine confessed that when she heard that her neighbor had just come home from the hospital, her first thought was to go visit her. Then she began to think about it. *I don't really know her that well,* she thought. *I am sure she will have enough visitors.* But my friend couldn't rest and she finally, nervously, went to visit the woman. That visit resulted in a deep friendship. The still small voice spoke and her feet followed.

PRAYER: Dear Lord, help me to have the feet of faith that lead me to places you have called me to go. Amen.

Psalm 148 is a song of praise that is "over the top." The writer cannot say enough about the infinite ways all creation can praise God. Believers have so much to be thankful for that praising God is not just an obligation; it is something we have to do because of the very greatness of God.

Take a few moments to read the creation story in Genesis 1:1–2:4, taking note of all the things God created. Now look again at Psalm 148 and see how all of the creation is included in this song of praise. Not only are we as human beings responsible for taking care of creation, but we are partnered with creation in praising God. Understandably this psalm inspired Saint Francis of Assisi to write his "Canticle of the Sun."

Throughout the Gospels we hear and see Jesus celebrating the creation around him. He speaks of God's care for every little creature, of the lilies of the field and the birds of the air. By living in partnership with creation, Jesus experienced the presence and love of God.

During the past year I have found a wonderfully relaxing time in going for a leisurely stroll before going to bed for the night. I walk the downtown streets and look around at trees, stars, the moon, and the beauty of the dark night. Almost always the walk turns into a spiritual experience. I savor the beauty that surrounds me and feel close to God. Even the shortest strolls result in praise of God and God's creation. The spirit of Psalm 148 fills my soul.

PRAYER: Gracious God, worthy of all praise, give to us that sense of celebration Jesus found in the creation around him. May that celebration draw us closer to you and one another. Amen.

Most of us are familiar with the Ten Commandments, the ten conditions that God laid out for the people. Four of the commandments have to do with our relationship with God, and the remaining six deal with our relationships with one another. In John 13:34 Jesus gives a new commandment. He tells his followers that not only should they love one another, but they should treat one another in the same way he has treated them, with love. The eleventh commandment links God's love for us in Christ with our love for one another.

The challenge of the commandment is beyond our comprehension. Jesus' love for his disciples and followers did not rely on his mood or on how well things were going. It did not depend on the faithfulness of the disciples or on their understanding of what he taught. Jesus loved. There were no rules. Jesus loved.

As human beings we often find reasons not to love. Perhaps someone "is not a very nice person" or "has hurt a lot of people." Maybe we give up a friendship because a divorce has forced us to choose sides. We find reasons to separate ourselves from one another. Jesus loved. His commandment to us is to love, not in the way people love but in the way he loves us.

PRAYER: Loving and gracious God, give me the heart of Jesus that I might love others with the same care and forgiveness with which he loves me. Amen.

I was asked to chaperone a school field trip with one of my children. Each chaperone was to keep his or her eyes on eight third graders and ensure their safety. My biggest fear about the field trip to the science museum was that I would not be able to tell which children in the museum were with us and which were with another group. My fears subsided when I arrived at the school and discovered that the children would wear colorful T-shirts for the trip. My red group was easy to spot, and I could always see them.

Identifying Christians is not quite so easy as putting on a T-shirt. We do not all wear the same outfit, and we certainly do not all look alike. Jesus says that what distinguishes us as his followers is our love for one another. Others will know us by our love. Loving one another is not only a commandment to follow; it is our "mark."

I remember a children's message that I gave one Sunday morning in which I talked about how Jesus calls us to reach out in love to people. One child responded, "I love people even when no one is looking." Out of the mouth of a child came an important truth. The love we have been called to share is more than just a rule; it is a way of life we practice even when no one else is looking.

PRAYER: Loving and gracious God, give me the mind of Christ that allows me to love without trying. May others know me by my love. Amen.

We began the week and now complete it with a reading from Revelation. Today's reading assures us that God who "[sits] on the throne" can make all things new. This regal image depicts a very present God who gives guidance and a wonderful future to all who believe. Through God all things will be made new, and we are assured that God was there at the beginning of everything and will be there at the end. God always was and always will be. What a powerful message for us to claim and live.

I was teaching a fifth-grade Sunday school class, and the children had a drawing project as part of the lesson. Because I am not an artist, I usually do simple stick figures and hope that others can get an idea of what I am trying to represent. So I was sympathetic when one boy, completely flustered by the drawing task, kept grabbing a new piece of paper and starting over. After the third try he said, "I keeping making mistakes; and when I erase, it makes my paper look old. I want it to look new."

God's promise to make all things new is a promise for our similarly frustrated hearts. God does not erase over and over again the things that are bad, covering each erasure with another try. God makes things new. God's power to make a new creation out of a broken world is a promise that we can count on. Like Jesus, we can live knowing that God promises to be with us no matter what we face. God has the power to make all things new, in us and through us.

PRAYER: Creating God, give us the faith of Christ that we need to help us live with the possibility of all things being made new. Create in us. Create through us. Amen.

All People Are God's People

May 10–16, 2004 • Frank Ramirez[‡]

MONDAY, MAY 10 • Read Acts 16:9-12

During our sabbatical my wife and I spent some time at Chaco Culture National Historical Park in northwest New Mexico, the cultural, religious, and trading center of the Anasazi civilization a thousand years ago. Copper bells and macaws from Mexico; shells from California; pottery, turquoise, talismans, and precious corn from throughout the Anasazi world made their way through Chaco. The peoples of the smaller surrounding towns who never left the vicinity of their villages nevertheless knew of Chaco.

The great Chacoan roads spread out in all directions for hundreds of miles. Some led to other Anasazi cities. Others seemed to go nowhere. But whatever might lie at the end of the highway, there was no question that ultimately all roads led to Chaco.

The cosmopolitan city of Philippi was on a major road as well, the Via Egnatia. Named after Philip II, the father of Alexander the Great, this Macedonian city observed Roman law and principles even though it was only legally and not geographically a part of Italy.

Because Philippi was considered a Roman city, many military families retired there. Military retirees often received Roman citizenship for their service without ever having actually been to Rome. Like the scattered ancient Americans who considered themselves part of the Chaco culture, so too the Philippians understood the concept of citizenship in a place they'd never seen. Identifying with something larger than their local ethnic identity, they understood that all peoples are part of the greater family of God.

PRAYER: Lord, I am yours, and everyone I meet, friend or stranger, is yours as well. I praise you for the diversity of your family. Amen.

[‡]Pastor, Everett Church of the Brethren, Everett, Pennsylvania.

When the Chaco civilization began to fade in the twelfth century C.E., the leadership seems to have traveled fifty miles north to the misnamed Aztec ruins near Aztec, New Mexico. There, next to a gentle, life-giving river, the culture had a fresh start.

When the apostle Paul arrives at Philippi, a city with many legionnaires but few people of Jewish background, he does not go first to a synagogue, as is his practice. Instead he seeks out a life-giving river, where he discovers a prayer group. This prayer group consists of people known as God-fearers, Gentiles who believe in the God of Israel but who, for one reason or another, are not able to become part of God's covenant. Whether they are men who do not wish to undergo circumcision or women who are unattached to a male convert, these individuals would be fairly familiar with the scriptures and the practices of the faith.

In this instance the prayer group consists entirely of women, including the worship leader. Lydia is a wealthy individual who deals in purple, highly prized in the ancient world. As head of her own household Lydia probably has become the worship leader for this house church, and her home served as a base of operations for Paul's visit to Philippi. These ministries came about because the women who gathered at the life-giving river had open and faithful hearts, ready to receive Paul's message of God's inclusive love and grace.

PRAYER: Lord, you have potential servants whom no one seeks out because they are in unlikely places. If it is your will, help me be the one who reaches out to such people. Amen.

During our travels through the American Southwest studying the lives of ancient peoples, my wife and I were astonished that they could have flourished in a land of intermittent, even rare, rainfall. Yet these people came to know the properties of every plant and the use of each to bless their lives.

The yucca, for instance, with its sharp fronds and purple fruit, provided for a variety of needs. The fronds themselves could be chewed until they were broken down, then woven and plaited into sandals. The yucca's starchy fruit could be harvested in its time; its roots could also be eaten. Soap was another product of the plant.

In Psalm 67 the blessing of God, like the yucca, is expected to do many things, While nationalistic tensions divide people today, and natural resources such as the rain forest are destroyed, the psalm reminds us that God's plan of justice and salvation includes all the nations as well as the good harvest. To be one with God's purpose includes the increase and yield. Life and the benefits of life are the immediate result of God's blessing. The phrase, "Then the land will yield its harvest, and God, our God will bless us" (NIV) seems to suggest that the effect of praise from God's people is beneficent increase, to God's glory.

SUGGESTION FOR MEDITATION: **Whether you live in a temperate, cold, or warm climate; an urban, suburban, or rural setting, you may have opportunities to nurture plants on farms, in gardens, or in flower beds. In what way today can you perform God's will through the care and maintenance of the plant kingdom?**

While studying the ancient Americans who lived a thousand years ago, my wife and I were surprised by the way the juniper tree tied generations together. The Anasazi made a tea from the purplish-gray juniper berry that they used for medicinal purposes. My wife, Jennie, recalled that her hundred-year-old grandmother made that same tea to cure ailments.

Psalm 67 reminds us that all people are God's people, from the ancestors of the contemporary Puebloans separated from us by a gulf of centuries, to the nations that shared and still share the crowded world of the ancient Middle East. This psalm in any translation is addressed directly to God with the wish that "your saving power [be known] among all nations." This universal perspective is built upon the recognition of God's sovereignty over all nations and churches, not just a special few.

The psalmist implores God to "make his face to shine upon us." This call for face contact with God suggests a desire for personal relationship and blessing. Nations also develop healthy, blessed relationships when God's face shines upon them.

The Bible's universal outlook, especially in this week's texts, calls us to break away from narrow perspectives and nationalistic concerns and to embrace the blessings of earth and heaven that follow our obedience to God's plan for all peoples. "May God continue to bless us."

SUGGESTION FOR MEDITATION: **Reflect on stories and photos in your local newspaper of people in your community. How are these people a part of your life? In what way today can you widen the circle of your acquaintance? Reflect on ways in which you can make yourself a part of the lives and the needs within those lives.**

While on sabbatical my wife and I stopped at the Ute Tribal Park in Colorado, where a member of the Ute people took us on a tour of various ancient pottery sites and Pueblo ruins on tribal land. The guide identified many of the plants near at hand and described their medicinal qualities, many of which he had learned from the elders of his tribe when he was a boy.

I doubt if any of us in our tour group thought of the guide as our personal healer. Later, however, two teenaged girls in our party uncovered a piece of a human skull underneath an unbroken pot buried in the earth, indicating a burial site. Our guide supervised our reburial of the artifact, then selected a special sort of sage, which he had earlier recommended for its calming effect, to prevent the young girls from having bad dreams.

I don't know if the invalid at the pool at Beth-zatha thinks of Jesus as a healer either. The disabled man has placed his hopes on one method of healing, on the moment when the water of the pool is stirred. Yet his own disability prevents him from taking advantage of the healing waters. He evidently has no community of family or friends to be his advocate, to put him in the pool at the right moment. Jesus stands in the gap, becoming the agent of healing and bypassing the regular means.

When accommodations for those who need healing are inadequate, then it is up to us as the body of Christ also to stand in the gap and to advocate for the healing. Though we are unlikely healers, we are called to fill needs where we meet them.

PRAYER: Dear Lord, sometimes I feel like a wounded healer, unworthy of the tasks of the gospel you have set before me. Support me and guide me in those moments. Stay with me always. Amen.

SATURDAY, MAY 15 • Read Revelation 21:10, 22–27

The ancestral Puebloans built Pueblo Bonito in Chaco Canyon between 850 and 1150 C.E. With over six hundred rooms and five stories tall, it was the largest structure in North America until the late nineteenth century. Some of the rooms doubled as calendars. A specific window, for instance, might allow the sun in only on the winter solstice.

Yet all of that ancient glory pales in comparison to the holy city of God's reign. Innumerable attempts have been made to use the book of Revelation as a calendar of sorts, supposedly to detail the future. But in his book *The Most Revealing Book of the Bible* Vennard Eller suggests instead that the key to understanding Revelation is recognizing its graphic, image-filled content as consistent with the rest of the New Testament and meant to be understood by all people at all times.

A professor of mine back in college days, Eller said of today's scripture text that despite the fact that God's just judgment has already taken place, the doors to the holy city are wide open, and traffic streams into the new Jerusalem. Gates, previously closed for protection, are thrown open in perfect safety. Who could still be coming in? God's action of purification and justification continues, and those who are condemned are now redeemed!

In Revelation's vision of the new Jerusalem, there is no need for calendars. There is no need of a temple, for God's glory is everywhere. There is no night, nor sun or moon to mark the passage of time. The new Jerusalem is eternal. It is its own light and a light to all nations.

PRAYER: Shine in our lives, gracious and forgiving God. Fill our lives and our futures with hope for all of your creation. Amen.

All around the modern city of Phoenix, Arizona, are the remains of a sophisticated system of canals that channeled water from the Salado River to fields and farms, blessing the area with life-giving water despite the arid climate. This thousand-year-old system is so well designed that when Euro-Americans arrived on the scene they built canals that run along the same courses.

People who live in arid regions can appreciate the life-giving qualities of a river. Like Ezekiel (47:1) and Zechariah (14:8-9), John the Revelator includes a river in his description of the New Jerusalem. Because the Lamb who was slain, the perfect sacrifice, is at the center of things, the river in the New Jerusalem flows from the Lamb's throne.

The wish expressed in Psalm 67 finally comes to pass. All the nations gather to praise God. The river irrigates the tree of life, whose leaves are "for the healing of the nations." Some great rifts between nations may be beyond human efforts to heal. The final healing may only come when God's authority is recognized. Without any one of these nations the healing is not complete.

In the New Jerusalem, irrigated by the river of the water of life, healed nations retain their identities. But the citizens of the holy city now bear the name of God the Lamb on their foreheads. Where once, by accident of birth, they were identified as citizens of nations, they now rejoice in their new identity as the people of God.

PRAYER: Lord, instill in us the desire to bring about your peace in the midst of all peoples in all places. Amen.

Seeds of Transformation

May 17–23, 2004 • *Susan Cartmell*[‡]

MONDAY, MAY 17 • Read Acts 16:16–25

In South Africa's freedom struggle, the worst of times were also the best of times. When Nelson Mandela was sentenced as a political prisoner to twenty-seven years in Roben Island, a maximum-security facility, he turned the prison into a school for revolutionaries, recruiting people from his cell for the African National Congress. Throughout the cell blocks other prisoners followed Mandela's example, one freedom fighter giving thanks that the time of persecution in jail had invigorated the revolutionaries and their movement. No amount of persecution could ultimately stop the Black Nationalists because the liberation fighters were already free. They could be put behind bars, but their hearts and minds had been liberated.

What sets Paul and Silas apart from so many people in their day and in ours is that they are free. No adversity they face can compromise their freedom. They can be beaten, thrown in jail, and clamped in stocks, but still they sing hymns of praise to God. They may be persecuted but their hope and trust in God's providence cannot be eliminated. Even in prison the apostles inspire the other inmates with their faith.

Freedom is a state of mind, a voice that refuses to be silenced, a reluctance to let others define our mission. It is the willingness to see the creative options in each struggle we face, to minister to others though we find ourselves in chains.

PRAYER: Holy One, come into the places where I feel most trapped and help me to see new possibilities. Help me to find my voice and sing. Help me to let go of all that binds me and to let you work through me. Amen.

[‡]Senior minister, Congregational Church, Needham, Massachusetts.

Last summer a woman in my congregation was furious at me, which happens occasionally to a minister. I could not think of anything to say to calm her down. I felt defensive and was tempted to get angry myself, but I had been down that road too many times and knew it was a dead end. So I said nothing, and I waited. I later discovered that the woman was experiencing a terrible crisis in her family, and although she needed my help, she did not know how to ask for it.

Perhaps the greatest miracle in Paul's jail cell was not the earthquake but Paul's patience with his jailer, his compassion for his guard. Paul did not write this man off or treat him as the enemy. He saw his jailer as a child of God.

Most of us assume that people fall into two categories, those who are with us or those who are against us. Not many of us realize that we always have a third choice, to accept human foibles in our friends and to find human needs in our adversaries. We may assume that the only two possible outcomes of our actions are winning the game or losing. But we always have a third way, to stay in the game and change the rules. If we can break the chains of success or defeat, we will discover that we possess the power, with God's help, to transform relationships and circumstances. That is our challenge.

Surrounded by enemies, Paul refused to forfeit his compassion. Faced with one set of adversities after another, he found the transforming gift in every situation.

PRAYER: God, grant me the humility to wait when things are tense. Grant me the wisdom to put my adversity in your hands and the faith to believe you will show me the transforming gift in every situation. Amen.

One of the cruelest ways to destroy a civilization is to deport its people. Ancient empires practiced deportation to destroy an enemy's culture and religion and to prevent a nation from posing any future challenge. When the Babylonians destroyed the city of Jerusalem, leaving the Temple in a pile of dust and rubble, they struck at the soul of the Israelites. But to complete their devastation, the Babylonians turned the survivors into refugees. Forced to march to Babylon, Hebrew families endured a harrowing journey, and stragglers were left to die in the sun. Once in Babylon, the Hebrew people were lost, far from home and all that had supported their families and their faith.

In that foreign land, the Israelites faced a big decision. Would they give up on the faith that had sustained them or try to refashion Judaism? Without the Temple, they wondered how to worship. Without their homes, they wondered how to observe the Sabbath. Without their own lawgivers, they wondered how to live by the Ten Commandments. But it was in Babylon that the Hebrews rewrote the early books of the Bible and refined Jewish law. It was in exile that Jewish religion was codified.

After several generations had passed, the Israelites returned to Jerusalem to rebuild their beloved house of prayer. Our psalm is associated with those days. Carrying no hint of defeat, no whisper of despair, it reminds us that we cannot control what others will do to us. We can only control our response.

Often the difference between victory and defeat rests in a decision we make at the outset of a struggle not to allow ourselves to be defeated. Our success depends on our ability to uphold our faith, no matter what, trusting that God "guards the lives of [God's] faithful."

PRAYER: O God, as I remember the many people who have found faith in adversity, help me to persevere. Amen.

ASCENSION DAY

Ironically some of life's most beautiful experiences come out of life's most difficult circumstances. Pearls, for example, are the product of an oyster making the best of a bad situation. When a grain of sand gets under the oyster's shell, it grates against the soft tissue of the mollusk. The oyster covers the sand with layers of calcium carbonate to smooth over the roughness, and a beautiful pearl results.

Unanswered prayer is the sand in our souls that rubs against our soft underbellies and drives us crazy. That nasty hard fragment wedged into our most vulnerable recesses scrapes at our souls like a grain of sand. Yet, by working with these aberrations, we can transform them into pearls of wisdom and great faith.

The disciples had prayed that God would restore Israel to its former glory. For generations the people of Israel had prayed to be rid of a succession of occupying armies. When Jesus made his way around the countryside, people had begun to hope God would hear their prayers and grant them the justice they deserved. Thus before Jesus ascends into heaven, it seems the right time to ask him when they should anticipate God's answer to their prayers in the way that they expected.

Jesus responds that we cannot ever understand the mystery of unanswered prayer. It is God's place to know why things fail to meet our expectations, and our only consolation is to trust that the Holy Spirit will enter our souls and work with the hard fragments of deep disappointment to bring forth pearls of great faith. Working through their disappointments, the disciples will build the Christian church, a stunning pearl. May we also trust the Holy Spirit to bring something precious from the hardest experiences we face.

PRAYER: God, help me hand over my soul's hard defeats to your creative touch. Amen.

The movie *The Last Temptation of Christ* features an unforgettable scene in which Jesus runs on the beach by the Sea of Galilee. He is just beginning to see that God has a plan for his life, but he is not sure he wants any part of it. As the film portrays this confused young man's gradual reconciliation of himself to the divine call, we begin to appreciate what may have been Jesus' initial ambivalence about this anointing, his summons by God to be the Christ, the son of the living God, the Messiah. Perhaps because he is terrified by the weight of all that lies ahead, Jesus' run on the beach is almost a running away.

God's call can be a mixed blessing. Any sensible person might be tempted to look for an escape clause. After all, Moses, Jonah, and Esther all tried to flee before they reconciled themselves to their fate and accepted the summons to become great prophets. In today's passage Jesus prays for each of us. His fervent hope is that we who follow him might find the same relationship with God that he has come to know and trust. Jesus asks God to grant to each of us all the intimacy of his own relationship with the Father. Though we may feel ambivalent about the challenges and the terror that may lie ahead, our bond with God in Jesus will free us to experience the exquisite joy of the call to discipleship.

A monk startled me once when he said, "I pray that Jesus will bring you to the One he called 'Abba.'" It seemed a nerve-wracking but incredibly compelling notion.

SUGGESTION FOR MEDITATION: As you meditate today, use the monk's prayer and ask Jesus to bring you to the One he called "Abba."

On the cross, one of the robbers next to Jesus beseeched him, "Remember me when you come into your kingdom" (Luke 23:42). The criminal's plea mirrors a question that burns in each of our hearts: "Will Jesus remember me?" Will God in Christ take note of little me, whose only claim to fame may be that I, like the robber, ask Jesus to know me as I am?

The last words in the Bible answer this burning question with words of reassurance. We are not alone, because Jesus promises that he will never be too far away. He has not abandoned us for some heavenly plateau. He is not like a sports anchorman gazing at our lives on the field of play with running commentary or aloof disdain. Jesus is rather like a doting parent who has sent an angel to watch over us.

Perhaps it is true, as some believe, that the Second Coming will be a rapturous event in which some will be lifted on eagles' wings while others will be left bereft of hope. Anything is possible. But these last words in scripture do not suggest that scenario. Instead, they tell us that Jesus will not forget that we struggle to live in faith each day. When he returns he will bring a heavenly reward for those who have striven to live with integrity even in the face of evil. Yet he promises that any who call on his name may "take the water of life as a gift" and enter the gates of the holy city.

PRAYER: Help me, O Christ, to put my faith in you, and to let go of every doubt that would separate me from your grace and love. Amen.

In 1806 students at Williams College were overtaken in a thunderstorm and were forced to seek refuge in a haystack. As they prayed in that haystack shelter, they believed that God told them to begin the American Missionary movement, which they established four years later. In successive decades, hundreds of men and women of faith left New England and traveled to Africa, Asia, the Middle East, and Latin America to share their convictions and to start new Christian communities. Sharing their experiences of God in Christ, they ministered to folks hungry for the gospel. They sowed the seeds of new faith. Over time God nurtured those seeds and brought forth the fruits of new faith. Now we find that the Christian church is blossoming in places like Africa and Asia.

Before Jesus ascends to heaven, he strives to make his disciples understand that he is the fulfillment of their ancient scripture. As witnesses to his life, death, and resurrection, they are authorized to proclaim repentance and forgiveness in his name "to all nations."

Inspired by Jesus' words and the strength of his will, the first disciples told others what they knew about God because of Christ Jesus. Bit by bit the stories planted seeds, and God nurtured new churches all over the Mediterranean. The church of Jesus Christ was born out of the efforts of a ragtag crew of followers in a religious backwater region, in a captured nation at the far end of the Roman Empire. There, laboring in obscurity day after day, followers of Jesus shared their faith and witnessed to the work and word of Jesus Christ.

When we ask, "What can I do to change this world?" Jesus says, "Tell your story. I will do the rest."

PRAYER: It is strange to think that you might need me, O God. Open new doors and draw me to places where my witness may fall on fertile and receptive soil. Amen.

Created and Renewed by God's Spirit

May 24–30, 2004 • *Kenneth L. Carder*[‡]

MONDAY, MAY 24 • Read Psalm 104:24-34, 35*b*

Psalm 104 eloquently affirms God's sovereignty expressed in the bringing of the world into being and the constant renewal of it by the divine Spirit. The psalmist acknowledges the interdependency of all creation, as each creature and object has a role to play in God's order. All components of the creation bless God simply by fulfilling their rightful place in the complex and interconnected universe.

The Bible affirms that creation is brought into being by God's spirit. Genesis 1:2 declares that "the earth was a formless void and darkness covered the face of the deep, while a wind from God [or while the spirit of God] swept over the face of the waters." The universe came into being as God's spirit brought order from chaos, light from darkness, form out of formlessness, and finally Adam from a clump of clay. The psalmist breaks forth into singing as he meditates on this splendid intricacy and wonder of God's creation: "When you send forth your spirit, they are created; and you renew the face of the ground."

All creation blesses God when creation is seen and treated as a precious gift from God and a revelation of God's sovereign goodness. All around us are signs of the creating and renewing work of God's spirit. Our own spirits can be renewed by reflection upon and celebration of God's magnificently beautiful and wonderfully interrelated world.

PRAYER: **"Bless the LORD, O my soul. O LORD my God, you are very great. You are clothed with honor and majesty, wrapped in light as with a garment. May the glory of the LORD endure forever; may the LORD rejoice in his works." Amen.** (Ps. 104:1-2, 31)

[‡]Bishop, The Mississippi Area, The United Methodist Church, Jackson, Mississippi; president of the General Board of Discipleship.

God's spirit creates the cosmos, binds its intricate parts together, and persistently renews the earth. But there is more! God's spirit gives humans their very life, identity, and worth. "Then the Lord God formed man from the dust of the ground, and breathed into his nostrils the breath of life, and the man became a living being" (Gen. 2:7). The same Spirit that moved over the watery chaos and brought the world into existence created humankind in the divine image and breathed into the lifeless dust the breath (spirit) of God.

Therein lies our identity and worth. Although we share kinship with the animals and share in the interdependency of the universe, God has given us special identity, worth, and purpose. We are made in the divine image and are creatures on whom God has bestowed God's own spirit.

However, we know all too well that human beings have distorted the divine image and quenched the divine spirit. We define ourselves by our biological drives and characteristics. Searching for a sense of worth in such externals as appearance, titles, possessions, position, or academic degrees, we have forsaken our true identity and discounted our authentic worth. We are sinners!

God does not leave us to our own devices. God acts decisively in Jesus Christ to renew humankind and to restore the divine image. God's spirit leads us back to our true identity as children of God. "When we cry, 'Abba! Father!' it is that very Spirit bearing witness with our spirit that we are children of God...and joint heirs with Christ."

The same Spirit that brings creation into existence and renews it bestows upon us our identity as beloved and redeemed children of God.

PRAYER: Creating and renewing God, you created us in your own image and redeemed us as your children; through your Spirit continue to recreate us and restore your image within us; through Jesus Christ our redeemer. Amen.

God creates and renews all creation, including us, through the Spirit. In Jesus Christ, God reveals the divine purpose and acts decisively to make possible a redeemed creation and the healing of humankind. What God did ultimately in Jesus Christ, God seeks to continue in and through us.

Jesus said, "The one who believes in me will also do... greater works than these, because I am going to the Father. I will do whatever you ask in my name, so that the Father may be glorified in the Son. If in my name you ask me for anything, I will do it."

Is it possible that we can do greater works than Jesus? Modern medicine has eliminated or can cure many illnesses that plagued people of Jesus' day. Technology and science have made available resources for unparalleled healing and have even given humans the ability to create and alter life forms. But these same resources increase our capacity to destroy God's creation and add to human suffering.

The key condition of Jesus' promise is this: "Whatever you ask in my name." To ask in Jesus' name is to ask for that which Jesus desires, and he desires the healing and renewal of God's creation. All healing and renewal that is compatible with the example and teachings of Jesus is the work of God's spirit.

PRAYER: Creating and renewing God, in Jesus Christ you have entered decisively into human existence to heal and renew your creation. You have invited us to share in Christ's ministry. Through your Spirit, continue to shape us into the likeness of Jesus Christ and to use us as instruments of your new creation. Amen.

THURSDAY, MAY 27 • Read John 14:15-17, 25-27

The Spirit enables us to share in God's creative and renewing action in the world. That action is characterized by love. But we cannot love within our own power. Here is the good news: The One who commands us to renew the creation with love gives us the power to fulfill the command. God sends the Advocate, the Spirit of truth, to guide and empower us to participate in God's new creation.

The world is so distorted and damaged that it resists the Spirit. But we who know God's revelation in Jesus Christ recognize the Spirit at work healing and transforming the world into God's new creation. The Spirit abides with us and within us as we obey the commandment to love one another as Christ loves us.

The Holy Spirit reminds us of all that Jesus said and did so that we stay focused on our identity as beloved children of God who share in God's work of transforming the world through Christ's love. The Holy Spirit comforts us in our sorrow, guides us in our confusion, and forgives us when we contribute to the world's sin and destruction.

The Spirit brings peace but not the world's kind of peace that depends upon the pleasantness of circumstances. The peace of the Spirit comes from knowing that we are loved and that we are not alone. Even when the world around us crumbles, the Spirit assures us that the One who is working on our behalf, healing and renewing, has himself been broken but has triumphed. Therefore, the Spirit assures us that shalom, God's peace, will prevail.

PRAYER: Send your Spirit, O God, to guide, comfort, and forgive us. Grant us the peace that passes all understanding, and make us instruments of your peace in our violent, diseased, and sinful world; through Jesus Christ who is our peace. Amen.

God speaks and the world is created. "Then God said, 'Let there be light'; and there was light" (Gen. 1:3). God creates and renews the world with a Word. John's Gospel declares that Jesus Christ is God's eternal Word, and through that Word the world is created and redeemed.

Since the call of Abraham and Sarah, God has been creating a community that embodies the eternal Word through which God continues to create and renew the world. Jesus, the Word made flesh, called a motley group of obscure, frail, and sinful human beings and shaped them into a community that would continue Christ's ministry of healing, reconciliation, and transformation. His death leaves them confused and uncertain as to their future and their mission. They have fallen silent and inactive as agents of God's new creation.

Pentecost is the occasion on which the disciples find their voice once more, and the church is born. The Spirit that moved over the dark and silent chaos and spoke creation into existence now descends upon the chaotic and silent disciples and enables them to speak the triumphant word of resurrection.

Before Pentecost, humankind's language had become confused and chaotic from pride (Gen. 11:1-9), but now the discordant voices unite in mutual understanding: "All of them were filled with the Holy Spirit and began to speak in other languages, as the Spirit gave them ability." The Holy Spirit at Pentecost gives the disciples their voice and transcends the divisions and barriers that thwart God's creative and renewing work in the world.

Our sinful and divided world awaits the Spirit's healing and uniting word. God continues to call the church to embody the Word that creates and renews.

PRAYER: Creating and renewing God, who has spoken to us through your Incarnate Word, Jesus Christ, send your Holy Spirit once more upon your church and help us speak your word of resurrection and new life in our chaotic and confused world. Amen.

The Holy Spirit's gift at Pentecost to the divided people with different languages is the ability to communicate. Divisions among members of God's family threaten creation with violence, competitiveness, and hatred. In Genesis, people sought to "build a tower with its top in the heavens, and let us make a name for ourselves" (11:4). The result was a confusion of language and the inability to communicate.

Pride results in lost communication, alienation, and sometimes violence and destruction, causing us to exploit, scar, and deplete God's creation rather than share in its preservation, healing, and renewal. Needed is the gift of God's spirit that creates, renews, unites, and heals.

The Spirit creates a community out of the diversity of humankind, a community bound together with a common loyalty to the crucified and risen Christ, God's eternal Word. The church is created by the Spirit just as God's spirit brought creation from the watery chaos. As God's spirit was breathed into the nostrils of a lump of clay and Adam became a living being, so the Holy Spirit breathes into Christ's community, the church, and makes it a sign of the living Christ.

The church is created by the Holy Spirit to be a sign, foretaste, and instrument of God's new creation in Jesus Christ. Yet the church today often reflects the pride, divisions, hatred, brokenness, and sin of the old world. We wait for the gift of the Holy Spirit to renew the church, heal its divisions, and restore its voice of life and hope.

While we wait, we come together as Christ's people, remembering God's mighty acts in history and sharing with one another "about God's deeds of power." The Holy Spirit comes among us, and even we will be "amazed and perplexed."

PRAYER: Come, Holy Spirit, renew your church. Shape us into a community that is a sign, foretaste, and instrument of God's new creation in Jesus Christ. Amen.

PENTECOST SUNDAY

People from across the world gathered for Pentecost, the Jewish festival to celebrate the early harvest. Pentecost originated as a celebration of the Creator's blessing in bringing forth grain by the constant renewal of the earth.

The God who creates and renews by the Spirit now initiates a new harvest. The Holy Spirit descends upon the diverse company at Pentecost like "tongues of fire" (NIV). A new community is born, and the confused and speechless disciples of Jesus are renewed and given a message that will renew the whole creation.

At Pentecost the God who brought creation into being with a word and who initiated the new creation in the Word made flesh sends the Spirit upon a silent and barren band of Jesus' followers. A new community, the church, is born. It is a community entrusted with the message of renewal and transformation through the resurrection of Jesus Christ.

In the power of the Spirit, Peter proclaims that in Jesus Christ salvation is brought near. He reminds the people that God promises a time when "I will pour out my Spirit upon all flesh, and your sons and your daughters shall prophesy, and your young men shall see visions, and your old men shall dream dreams." Those without power or speech, including slaves, will have a voice. Even the heavens will declare the coming of God's new creation.

Pentecost brings into focus God's gift of creation and renewal through the Holy Spirit. The Spirit that created the cosmos, holds creation together, renews the earth, and brings forth harvest has called us to be part of the new heaven and new earth brought near in Jesus Christ. We, the church, have been empowered by the Spirit to proclaim in word and deed the coming harvest of God's salvation.

PRAYER: Come, Holy Spirit; empower us to live now in light of the new creation in Jesus Christ. Amen.

School of the Sacred

May 31–June 6, 2004 • Linda R. Douty[‡]

MONDAY, MAY 31 • Read Proverbs 8:1-4

Remember the childhood anticipation of the first day of school? A year of learning, with its zigs and zags, beckoned with fresh potential. I invite you to view life in the Spirit through that familiar learning lens, seeing life as an arena for growth, where all experiences—both the light and the dark—can teach us valuable lessons. The writer of Proverbs implies that this classroom called Life bases its curriculum more on experience than information.

God's guiding spirit nudges us to seek wisdom at the "crossroads" and "gates" of our lives—the birth of a new baby, the untimely death of a loved one, the loss of a job, a mundane meeting that unexpectedly blossoms into love. All these are crossroads that provoke questions of deeper meaning. A "gate" appears through which we pass to a new way of thinking or being where issues are decided. These times of upheaval, whether violent or gentle, are invitations to ask Why? What can I learn?

Our lives are shaped by the questions we ask. If our resident interrogations are, How can I make more money? How can I attain more luxury? What can ensure my own pleasure? then we will live into those answers as these matters claim our highest allegiance. On the other hand, if our unspoken inquiries are, Who am I in relation to God? Why was I created? How is the Spirit weaving its way through my days? then our lives gently open into avenues of meaning and purpose.

PRAYER: Loving God, you invite us daily to learn from our lives. As we consider deep questions of meaning within the container of your love and mercy, may we become willing students in the school of the sacred. Amen.

[‡]Leader of spiritual formation retreats with private practice in spiritual direction, living in Memphis, Tennessee.

One misty morning as I took an early stroll with my two-year-old grandson Andrew beside a lazy river, I heard him gasp. I turned to see his eyes widened with wonder at the sight of an intricate spiderweb, its precision outlined in sparkling dewdrops. I stooped down to join him in astonished gratitude as we examined the spider's daily offering of Victorian lace. It seemed ironic that the skilled creator of this masterpiece was a creature regarded as ugly and repulsive! That shared encounter taught me a number of lessons. It reminded me that God resides not only in the tiny details of nature but in the tiny moments of intimacy between grandmother and grandchild. The spider's handiwork bore evidence that beauty can emerge from surprising origins.

The writer of Psalm 8 confirms the most significant lesson from that morning walk by declaring that even children react to God's glory with praise and amazement. No wonder Jesus so often acknowledged children as examples when the disciples began overintellectualizing! A child is neither jaded by sophistication nor rushing to the next appointment. A child instinctively throws arms open to embrace life, yet sees the details of a butterfly's wing.

As Andrew and I meandered back to the rustic cabin that morning, I was sobered by the realization that I had walked that same path countless times before, yet never stopped to notice the wonder that surrounded me. I had been moving too fast. That leisurely stroll with a two-year-old, an ordinary moment in an ordinary day, had been replete with extraordinary lessons.

SUGGESTION FOR MEDITATION: **Take a slow stroll with a magnifying glass in hand. Stop as you are led, and examine the intricate life of a single object—a leaf, a rock, an anthill, a flower. Marvel at the exquisite detail of creation and breathe a heartfelt thank-you that you are part of this astounding web of life.**

Remember the exhilaration of being asked to be the teacher's helper? Cleaning chalkboards and taking out trash became coveted privileges as class members jockeyed for this position of special responsibility.

The message of Psalm 8 is clear: God has given us not only special status but the challenging task that accompanies it as stewards of creation. However, in our metaphorical school of the sacred, we seem to have misunderstood our assignment! Somewhere along the way, the call to exercise responsible dominion over the earth has become an excuse for arrogant domination.

We abuse and subjugate the natural environment for short-term yields at the expense of long-term consequences and fail to regard this violation as a spiritual matter. In an effort to avoid our culpability, we cleverly separate the spiritual from the secular, religion from politics, church from environment. But the words of Psalm 8 ring in our ears, reminding us of the sacred stewardship to which we are called.

The teachings of Jesus, rich with images of gardens, fields, and wildlife, use nature as tools for sacred instruction. He speaks of the lilies of the field, lambs, a plentiful harvest, nesting birds. Obviously, he valued the symbolism and inspiration of creation.

As we accept our roles as partners in the care of our cosmic classroom, our ecological attitudes need to be in harmony with our biblical theology. We cannot escape the connection.

SUGGESTION FOR PRAYER: Spend some time in silent reflection considering your own actions regarding stewardship of the earth. Does your family honor its responsibility to conserve, recycle? Ask God to increase your awareness of practices that sensitize you to the earth's needs.

"Holy, holy, holy! Lord God Almighty!...God in three persons, blessed Trinity." I grew up singing those words every Sunday at my Methodist church and found the mystery increasingly puzzling. How could this be? God is one, yet three? As the years went by, I seemed to shrug the shoulders of reason and blindly accept this confusing dogma as the church's lofty theory of who God is.

But the concept continued to haunt me, scattered throughout the liturgy, the hymns, the scriptures. I wanted to develop an understanding of this doctrine so central to the Christian message, yet only in experiencing the Trinity can one begin to understand it. Our relationship with God is manifested in our daily lives as we experience God the Father outside, God the Son beside, and God the Holy Spirit inside us.

Hebrew Scriptures identify the first person of the Trinity, the Almighty God outside us, as "I AM THAT I AM." This is the Source of all that is, the Creator of the universe who sets glory above the heavens and establishes the moon and the stars. Our experience of this God prompts us to bow our knees in adoration and thanksgiving.

Though this Divine Teacher commands respect, God is not one who raps our knuckles and sends us to the corner wearing a dunce cap when we fail or disobey. As portrayed in the parable of the prodigal son, this forgiving Father, whom Jesus called Abba (or "Daddy") welcomes us home with open arms and showers us with blessing. And we ask, "What are human beings that you are mindful of them, mortals that you care for them?" This is the experience of God as loving Parent, as Other, a power outside us, a transcendent presence.

SUGGESTION FOR PRAYER: **Find a place to kneel in gratitude before God as the Source of all that is. Rest in the knowledge that this Almighty God loves you profoundly and cares for you as a deeply loving Parent.**

There was an insistent knock at my door. I opened it to find a distraught young woman who, in the midst of a crushing relational problem, needed to talk. Someone had suggested that she contact me because I had experienced a similar situation. I'll never forget her poignant remark, "I can go on with my life only if I see someone else who has gone on with her life." This young woman was beginning the journey from suffering to hope that Paul describes in today's scripture reading.

Oh, the supportive comfort of shared experience! Jesus, the Son, second person of the Trinity, shared the fullness of our human condition. He knew what it meant to be in pain, to feel abandoned by loved ones, to suffer injustice, to be wrongly accused, and to be in utter despair. His divinity did not insulate him from the full range of human emotions and experience. We participate in this aspect of the Trinity every time we sit with a grieving friend, when we lend a supportive ear of understanding, when we minister to those in need; in other words, when we embody the love of Christ to others.

Jesus' life becomes our human model, for his temptations mirror our own. His consistent response of forgiveness on the one hand and a call for social justice on the other challenges us to distinguish between meaningful suffering and meaningless suffering. Paul reminds us that we do not suffer for its own sake but to discover redemptive characteristics in ourselves as we deal with whatever befalls us. Only as we move from suffering to endurance to character to hope will we experience the fullness and grace of God's love.

SUGGESTION FOR PRAYER: Take a companion walk. Stroll along as though Jesus were beside you. Allow a divine conversation to take place, expressing your honest feelings, fears, hopes, dreams, concerns, as you would with a trusted and wise friend.

Have you ever felt a subtle nudge to pick up the phone and call someone? a twinge of despair just after making an unkind remark? a surge of euphoria at the sound of magnificent music? This passage from John's Gospel tells us emphatically that our experience of God the Holy Spirit within us can not only inspire but guide us.

Most of us seek guidance outside of ourselves—an authoritative voice, a recommended book, a wise friend—and trust these voices of discernment. We do not trust our own inner guide.

The gift of the Holy Spirit is a profound, sometimes dangerous, matter. Unspeakable evils have been perpetrated through the years under the guise of "God told me to." Yet we affirm the that the Spirit will "guide [us] into all the truth." Our spiritual task comes in learning to distinguish the voice of God from the host of inner and outer voices that clamor for our attention and allegiance.

We hone the ability to discern the Holy Spirit's whispers in the container of silence. Through faithful time with God in which we open our hearts wordlessly, the competing inner voices expose their identity: protestations of the ego revealed in defensiveness and protection of ego boundaries—*my* feelings, *my* rights, *my* church, *my* nation. Through dedicated and persistent times of silence, the still small voice of love begins to emerge. In subtle, almost imperceptible ways, the fruit of the Spirit appear in seemingly mundane moments. This sensitivity to the Holy Spirit is not a product of our work for God but rather allowing God to work within us.

SUGGESTION FOR PRAYER: Commit yourself to a time of silence and reflective solitude, first five minutes a day, then ten, and so on. Refrain from evaluating what happens; let that be God's business. Trust God's desire to transform you. Dare to believe that your deepest desires and God's will for you can be the same.

TRINITY SUNDAY

The Bible portrays Wisdom as an elusive concept. She seems to weave her web of meaning throughout eternal time as well as through the tiny moments of everyday life, stirring the right questions, preventing us from settling for half-truths, giving us the confidence to live into the answers.

Wisdom illumines the Trinity for us, reminding us that no one concept of God can contain or define God. We cannot catch the Divine in our net of words. Our best attempts fall short of complete understanding of "I AM THAT I AM."

However, we can experience the power and love of God in more ways than we can imagine. God is much more willing to speak than we are to listen! We can relate to God as Father who creates and transcends our existence, a divine presence outside us. We can befriend Jesus, the incarnation of God, the one who saves, who is called Emmanuel, God with us, beside us. We can be inspired by the Holy Spirit, who resides within our very being, guiding us through the authentic self.

This passage portrays Wisdom as foundational—with God before creation, undergirding and infusing our existence in a way that helps us to "put it all together." Perhaps this gift of God called Wisdom can encourage us to be ongoing students in the school of the sacred, where every day can be a meaningful commencement.

PRAYER: Loving God, our minds cannot totally grasp the mystery that is you. May we experience you in every way possible as we open ourselves to new revelations of your divine self. Amen.

Freed by Grace

June 7–13, 2004 • Tony Nancarrow[‡]

MONDAY, JUNE 7 • Read 1 Kings 21:1-7

Today's reading involves three main characters. King Ahab of Samaria, who "did more to provoke the anger of the LORD, the God of Israel, than had all the kings of Israel who were before him" (1 Kings 16:33); his wife Jezebel, a Phoenician princess, who erected a temple to Baal and founded a college of Baal and Asherah prophets; and Naboth, the owner of a vineyard close to Ahab's winter palace in Jezreel. Ahab wants to acquire the property so that he can plant a vegetable garden. He offers Naboth a good price or an alternative piece of land in exchange; but Naboth, believing the land to be a trust from God, will not sell.

The scripture presents Ahab as a weak and immature king who sulks and will not eat. He wants Naboth's property more than anything else but does not force the issue. Not so his wife, Jezebel. She commandeers his royal authority and fulfills her husband's desire for the property by using that power to have Naboth falsely accused of blasphemy and treason. Naboth and his sons are killed (2 Kings 9:26). With no heirs to claim the property, Ahab can claim it for himself. Elijah abruptly appears to call the king and his wife to account for their actions.

This story reminds us of the capacity for evil in those who are a law unto themselves. Modern-day living confronts us almost daily with possibilities for the abuse of power, not only in the business world but in our personal relationships. May we hear Elijah's call to accountability in all areas of our lives.

PRAYER: Bountiful God, protect the innocent victims of political or financial power. Give them peace, and give their oppressors true repentance. Amen.

[‡]Executive director of Mediacom Associates, a not-for-profit communications agency; minister of the Uniting Church; living in Keswick, Australia.

The Canaanite, Baal-worshiping Jezebel hatches a scheme to give to her husband, King Ahab, the plot of land he covets even though it is not hers to give. She takes over Ahab's authority and writes letters in his name, using his seal falsely to accuse Naboth of blasphemy and treason—crimes punishable by death.

Jezebel tells Ahab to go and inspect his ill-gotten possession. Ahab, in his covetousness, breaks the tenth commandment. Such greed may prompt violence, as in this case. A personal covetousness can lead to a breakdown in social order as others are drawn into the web of deceit and betrayal. Elijah, in response to a word from the Lord, confronts Ahab and tells him that his sin will cost him dearly.

Sin is not a popular word in today's society, but whatever word we choose to describe actions that separate us from the love of God, the result remains the same. A petty desire may escalate into grievous offense. The initial feelings of enticement and pleasure are brief, soon replaced by emotions of self-loathing, regret, disappointment, and a sense of failure.

Ahab's sense of joy over "owning" Naboth's vineyard quickly leaves him when confronted by Elijah's strong words. The pleasure is gone now that he knows that Naboth's blood is on the ground. Ahab does repent of his covetousness and its violent result (21:27); judgment is delayed.

Few actions of sinful pleasure do not carry an enormous cost. Rarely are our sins worth the price we ultimately pay for them, but through it all God does not desert us. When God's word of judgment comes to us, it comes motivated by love, offering us forgiveness, acceptance, and hope.

PRAYER: God, you are always ready to accept us, no matter how grave our sins, when we come to you with a contrite heart. Amen.

In today's scripture the psalmist provides a model for beginning each day in God's presence, confident that God hears our cry and responds to the concerns of our hearts.

I'm a morning person. Once awake I can't stay in bed. I begin most days with a forty-minute walk. Like the psalmist, morning is also my time to commune with God.

I cherish this time alone, walking in the streets that surround our home. I spend the first ten minutes centering my mind on the beauty of God's creation that surrounds me. I enjoy the changes that the seasons bring, reflected in the variety of flowers and shrubs. Some gardens on my walks are tended with loving care; others are unkempt and full of weeds. This contrast highlights for me the value of making time and giving attention to my relationship with God. Spending time on and nurturing my friendship with God provide fertile ground for spiritual growth in my life.

The psalmist opens his daily ritual of prayer in verse 1 with a petition: "Give ear to my words." That verse closes with a petition to God as well: "Consider my sighing." Sandwiched between the petitions are the words "O Lord." The psalmist to some extent surrounds God with requests, just as God's natural world now surrounds me. So as I continue on my walk, I too make petition to God, holding before God those people and concerns that are close to my heart—friends who have special needs, my colleagues with whom I work, the needs of the community and world in which I live. Usually I return from my walk focused on the day ahead and sensitive to the needs of those with whom I will relate that day, aware that God is with me.

PRAYER: O Lord, in the morning I cry out to you, knowing that you will hear my voice and answer me. Amen.

Psalm 5 is a song of lament that pleads for God's assistance. The psalmist knows God's great love, a welcoming love that listens, cares, and encourages us to say all that is in our hearts about those who oppose us, trusting that God will lead and make plain the way God wants us to go.

At the beginning of 2000 I underwent major surgery, the culmination of twenty years of chronic illness, held in check by increasing doses of cortisone. The day of my surgery was a long one. During the wait I read a book recommended by one of my friends at The Upper Room. *When the Heart Waits* by Sue Monk Kidd relates the story of Kidd's discovering a cocoon on a tree close to her home. She breaks off the small twig holding the cocoon and tapes it to a tree in her backyard. Over the coming months she watches and patiently waits until one day a beautiful butterfly emerges.

The symbol of the cocoon became one of my life's epiphanies. In my days in the hospital and the weeks of recuperation that followed, God granted to me a new awareness of the road that lay ahead of me, which included a growing trust that God's will was for my wholeness—a wholeness both of body and spirit. I received a new peace that I should not view the waiting as a passive experience.

The caterpillar, cocoon, and butterfly became symbols enabling me to see that my own journey to health involved not only a pleading for God's assistance but an acknowledgment of God's abundant love that had already been revealed to me in numerous ways. In the prison of ill health and long recuperation, I came to know true freedom in God's grace.

SUGGESTION FOR MEDITATION: Be still and center your heart and mind on the presence of Christ. Imagine Christ sitting in a chair facing you. Share with him the concerns that weigh heavily upon you. In the stillness listen to what God in Christ is saying to you.

Today's reading refers to a conflict in the community of Galatia, a Roman province in Asia Minor that stretched south toward the Mediterranean Sea. Paul responds to opponents who claim one must observe the law of Moses in order to be put right with God and be part of the church.

Jewish Christians are demanding that new Gentile Christians adhere to the requirements of Jewish law, particularly the practice of circumcision, in order to be identified as people of God. Paul endeavors to show that faith in Christ is not an add-on to Judaism but rather a radical new way of understanding God's law. Both Jew and Gentile are justified, or saved, in the same way: by grace through faith in Jesus Christ.

In my early years in rural ministry, families loosely attached to the life of our church often brought their children for baptism. In my discussions with them I emphasized the obligations that infant baptism placed on them as parents.

As I reflected on those early years, I came to a new understanding. My emphasis focused too much on parental and congregational obligations and too little on baptism as a sign of God's grace and acceptance. While the important role that parents play in the spiritual nurture and development of their child should not be underestimated, if that becomes the measuring stick, then few of us will measure up.

God's love and acceptance of us are not initiated by what we do. Fortunately God sees us not through our eyes or the eyes of the law but through the eyes of the Son.

PRAYER: Forgiving God, remind us that it is through faith in you that we are saved, and not through anything that we do. Amen.

Occasionally readers confuse the woman in this story with Mary of Bethany who also anoints the feet of Jesus (John 12:1-8) and with the woman who pours ointment over Jesus' head in the home of Simon the leper (Mark 14:3-9). Luke describes this woman's past in one brief phrase: "a woman in the city, who was a sinner."

As Jesus and Simon recline around the table, the woman begins to wash Jesus' feet with her tears, drying them with her hair, kissing them and pouring perfume on them. Expressing both love and gratitude, she is not embarrassed.

Early in my ministry I made a weekly visit to the senior citizens' ward of a large regionally based hospital, a home to many aged and infirm long-term medical patients. One day an elderly woman called out to me in German. She appeared agitated, so I entered her room and knelt beside the chair where she sat. Displaying all the signs of dementia, she sat in a soiled nightgown. I desperately wanted to leave. She looked at me with haunting eyes and continued to speak to me in German. I said, "I'm sorry, but I can't understand what you are saying. Is there something that I can do for you?" She responded, "I'm lonely; please hold my hand."

The quality of love and acceptance so clearly evident in Jesus' dealing with the sinful woman is so often missing in our own relationships. Genuine love, as we see in the life of Jesus, is completely unselfish and unbound by law. May we with God's grace also love one another in the same wonderful way that God loves us.

PRAYER: Gracious God, I regret that often I am more eager to receive love than to show it. Fill me with your love that I might share it with others. Amen.

Simon is appalled that Jesus would allow this woman, a "sinner," to touch him. Having neglected to offer Jesus the customary courtesies of hospitality—foot washing, a kiss, anointing—Simon is affronted by Jesus' tolerance of this woman.

Jesus then tells a parable about two indebted men whose debts were forgiven by a compassionate moneylender. One had been given a large sum and the other a much smaller amount. Jesus asks Simon which of the men would love the moneylender the most. When Simon identifies the one who has been forgiven the most, Jesus draws parallels between the parable and the woman who has anointed his feet.

A marginalized and judged woman responds to the generous love and grace of God in a way that a male religious leader is unable to do. God's way is unbound by legalism. Rather it is a way of grace, forgiveness, generosity, justice, compassion, and inclusion, a message embodied in Jesus.

Like Simon we all know what it is like to make mistakes and to think ourselves always right. But God's love and forgiveness challenge our self-righteousness. If we truly receive the freedom God's grace gives us, we will be slow to judge and quick to forgive.

PRAYER: Gracious God, teach us to value one another. Remind us of the consequences of our actions. Help us to act with compassion toward others and to look at life through the eyes of grace. Amen.

Journey toward Wholeness

June 14–20, 2004 • *Martin Thielen*[‡]

MONDAY, JUNE 14 • **Read 1 Kings 19:1-4**

A man was leaving for church one Sunday morning. His neighbor, who prided himself on his self-sufficiency and independence, asked him, "Where are you going?"

"To church," the man replied.

The neighbor said, "Church is for people who can't walk on their own two feet."

"Perhaps so," said the man, "but who's not stumbling?"

The characters in this week's readings are all stumbling. Elijah, burned out and depressed, told God he wanted to die. The psalmist, full of despair, wondered why God had abandoned him. The Gerasene demoniac, cut off from his community, lived alone among the tombs. Who's not stumbling?

Everybody stumbles at one time or another. Like Elijah in today's reading, sometimes we find ourselves in the wilderness, frightened and discouraged. Thankfully, despair is not the final word. Elijah, along with the psalmist and the Gerasene demoniac, take concrete steps toward renewal. This week we will walk with them on their journey toward wholeness.

A preschooler had worked hard to make a coffee mug for his father. The day finally came for him to take his gift home. In the excitement of the moment he slipped and fell; the mug broke into pieces. Devastated, he dropped to the floor and cried. After the sobbing eased and tears had been wiped away, his mother suggested, "Let's pick up the pieces and see what we can make with what's left." God is in the business of picking up the pieces of our life and making something with what's left.

Prayer: Lord, I stumble in many ways. Please guide me toward wholeness. Amen.

[‡]Pastor, First United Methodist Church, Lebanon, Tennessee.

Andy and Carol had waited for this moment for over a decade. After years of disappointment and endless medical procedures, Carol finally gave birth to their child. The joy of birth gave way to the trauma of complications. Forced to leave the delivery room, Andy found himself in the hospital chapel, praying for his newborn son. However, as he prayed, something snapped. Andy was mad, and he was mad at God. "How can you do this to us?" screamed Andy. "After all these years of waiting and praying, you finally give us a child. And now, as soon as he arrives, it looks like you're going to take him away!"

Andy and Carol's son survived and eventually thrived. And so did Andy's prayer life. That day in the hospital chapel, Andy learned that it was okay to share his deepest frustrations and anger with God.

Elijah does not hesitate to share his disappointments with God. In verse 4 he says, "It is enough; now, O Lord, take away my life." Later, in verse 10, Elijah complains to God, "I have been very zealous for the Lord…and they are seeking my life, to take it away."

The psalmist, like Elijah, also shares his deepest frustrations with God. "My tears have been my food day and night, while people say to me continually, 'Where is your God?'" He later states, "I say to God, my rock, 'Why have you forgotten me?'"

Our journey toward wholeness begins by honestly admitting our brokenness and pain to God. Do not attempt to sanitize your prayers. Openly share your doubts, fears, anger, and frustrations with the Lord. God can take it!

PRAYER: Lord, sometimes I feel abandoned by you. Thank you for understanding how I feel. Help me become more aware of your love, strength, and presence. Amen.

A member of my congregation felt distant from God. She had trouble praying. She also was not sleeping well and had lost her appetite. She dropped by my office to talk about her spiritual life and to request prayer for healing. I listened to her story, asked some questions, and offered a prayer on her behalf. She seemed grateful for my concern. However, she acted surprised when I gently insisted she see her doctor and have a complete physical exam. She set an appointment before she left my office. A few weeks later she told me her doctor diagnosed her as clinically depressed. After a few months of medication, she once again felt close to God.

Taking care of our physical body is an important spiritual issue. We see that clearly in today's reading. This passage finds Elijah deeply discouraged. He is so depressed that he does not even want to live. Notice what God does *not* do: God does not preach a sermon to Elijah. God does not encourage Elijah to pray or go to church. God does not send Elijah to a counselor.

What does God do? God restores Elijah's physical body. Elijah sleeps, then eats, then sleeps again, then eats again. Finally, God sends Elijah on a long walk. Elijah's journey toward wholeness includes adequate sleep, nourishing food and drink, and invigorating exercise. Only after his physical needs are met does God deal with other, more spiritual issues.

Do you feel burned out? The root problem may not be emotional or spiritual but physical. Any journey toward wholeness includes adequate sleep, balanced diet, and regular exercise. The Bible teaches us that our bodies are the temple of God. How are you treating God's temple?

PRAYER: Help me, Lord, to be a good steward of my physical body, so I can better serve you and others. Amen.

Today's reading finds Elijah in a cave at Mount Horeb, spending time in quiet solitude. During this time of solitude, Elijah encounters the living Lord. Probably to his surprise, Elijah discovers God's presence not in the mighty wind, powerful earthquake, or raging fire on the mountain. Rather, Elijah experiences God in the context of silence, where God speaks to him in a "still small voice" (KJV).

We live in a noisy, frantic, and busy world. Few opportunities exist for silence, reflection, and prayer. However, times of solitude when we can "be still, and know that I am God" (Ps. 46:10) are absolutely essential. We cannot be whole without such times of silence. Even Jesus, the son of God, needed regular times of solitude to think and pray. Today's culture would do well to heed the words of the prophet Habakkuk, "The Lord is in his holy temple; let all the earth keep silence before him" (2:20).

The older I get, the more important silence and solitude become to me. I believe that every person can carve out times of silence in his or her daily schedule. Reading *The Upper Room Disciplines* is one way to accomplish this goal. Other possibilities include walking, woodworking, or gardening. For me, journaling has become an important time of solitude. It provides a daily opportunity to reflect on the events of the day and upon my relationship with God. I record events, thoughts, feelings, insights, and prayers. Whatever method of reflection you use, do not neglect to schedule times of solitude. It is an important step in your journey toward wholeness.

Prayer: Forgive me, Lord, for being too busy to think and pray. Help me make time every day to "be still and know that [you are] God." Amen.

Yesterday's reading reminded us of the importance of solitude. Yet in our journey toward wholeness, we also need other people, especially the community of faith. Even Elijah enlisted the help of others. (See 1 Kings 19:15b-21.)

Today's readings affirm our need for relationships. Even in despair, the psalmist longed to worship God with others. Verse 4 says, "I went with the throng, and led them in procession to the house of God,... a multitude keeping festival." Gathering with fellow believers for praise, prayer, word, and sacrament is crucial to our spiritual well-being.

Today's reading from Galatians reminds us that we are not solitary believers but "children of God...one in Jesus Christ." There is no such thing as a "lone ranger" Christian. We always venture forth on our journey toward wholeness with others.

A man sat on a beach and watched two children play in the sand. They were hard at work by the water's edge, building an elaborate sand castle with gates, towers, and moats. Just as they finished their project, a big wave reduced the sand castle to a heap of wet sand. He expected the children to burst into tears, but they didn't. Instead they held each other's hands, laughed a big belly laugh, and sat down to build another castle.

The man reflected that all the things in our lives—all the complicated structures we spend so much time and energy creating—are built on sand. Only our relationships with other people endure. Sooner or later, a wave will come along and knock down what we have worked so hard to build. When that happens, only the person who has hold of somebody's hand will be able to laugh and rebuild.

Prayer: Thank you, Lord, for the important people in my life. Remind me constantly that relationships—with you and others—matter most. Amen.

Over the past few days we have considered several important strategies for seeking wholeness. However, these alone are not enough. Ultimately, authentic wholeness comes from God. A careful examination of 1 Kings 19 reveals that Elijah's renewal came primarily through his encounter with God. Therefore, any journey toward wholeness must include spiritual dimensions.

Today's passage says, "For in Christ Jesus you are all children of God through faith. As many of you as were baptized into Christ have clothed yourselves with Christ." Through our baptism, God adopts us as God's children. And as God's children, God invites us to participate in a lifelong journey toward wholeness. To be sure, wholeness does not come all at once, nor is it finally completed in this lifetime. However, God gives us love, grace, and strength to continue the journey, even when we can only stumble along, incomplete and broken. When we trip and stumble because of sin, God stands ready to forgive us. This kind of love, acceptance and forgiveness is our birthright as baptized children of God and is the secret of authentic wholeness.

Several years ago I heard an interview with an Olympic diver. The reporter asked how she handled the incredible stress as she stood on the platform and prepared to dive off. She said, "On the platform, right before I dive, I always say to myself, *If I blow this, my mother will still love me.* Even when we stumble on our journey, even when we feel more broken than whole, God still loves us. Thanks be to God!

Prayer: Without you, Lord, I am incomplete. Thank you for claiming me as your child. Help me to live like the child of God that I am. Amen.

SUNDAY, JUNE 20 • Read Luke 8:26-39

Over the past week we have examined several important steps in the journey toward wholeness. These steps include acknowledging our pain, taking care of our body, scheduling times of solitude, relating to other people, and becoming children of God. All of these strategies are important, but our effort to achieve wholeness is not to be an end in itself. Faithful Christians seek wholeness in order to better serve God and neighbor.

That was certainly the case with Elijah. God restored him in order to send him back into service. It is no accident that our text ends with God's saying to Elijah, "Go...." We see the same principle in today's Gospel lesson. The Gerasene demoniac was a deeply disturbed person. However, through the grace and power of Jesus Christ, the demoniac was made whole. After healing him, Jesus commissioned him to "return to your home, and declare how much God has done for you." Jesus made him whole—not only for his own benefit but for the benefit of others. In the Bible, people are always saved to serve.

Although we all need times of healing and restoration, seeking personal wholeness can become an obsession. That kind of self-absorption is sinful. Seeking wholeness for its own sake is never God's plan for us; we seek wholeness in order to better serve the kingdom of God.

We know, of course, that we will never be completely whole in this life. However, we must not let our brokenness keep us from serving God and neighbor. Even the great patriarch Jacob stumbled. But then, who's *not* stumbling?

PRAYER: Dear Lord, in my wholeness and in my brokenness help me faithfully serve you and others, through Jesus Christ my Lord. Amen.

God's Commitment to Our Freedom

June 21–27, 2004 • William P. Nagle[‡]

MONDAY, JUNE 21 • Read Luke 9:51-56

At the time of this incident the Jews and the Samaritans have been doing emotional battle for over seven hundred years. The heart of the conflict appears to be the ethnicity of the Samaritans who claim that they are a part of the original twelve tribes of Israel. The Jews have disowned the Samaritans and view them as foreigners brought in to occupy the land after the king of Assyria conquered Samaria in 722 B.C.E. This ancient feud is the basis for the Samaritans' refusal to receive Jesus on his way to Jerusalem.

The tragedy of this story is that Jesus enters the village seeing its people as the children of his heavenly father, while the villagers see themselves simply as Samaritans. As Samaritans they consider it necessary to carry on the tradition of "one-upmanship" with the Jews. They probably don't know how the feud began, but the consequence of this age-old conflict is that they miss out on the good news that Jesus brings to them. They fall captive to a cultural tradition that keeps them bound to the destructiveness of prejudice and hatred.

As a psychotherapist I frequently find myself working with people who are bound to and enslaved by hurtful and painful events from their past. They both see and describe themselves negatively because others have treated them poorly or disrespected them verbally. This is a universal human problem: We cannot hang onto the good news that we are loved and valued unless we can turn loose of the familiar negative images.

PRAYER: Dear Lord, help me to be open to the daily revelation of yourself and your love. Amen.

[‡]Retired American Baptist clergy and semi-retired marriage and family counselor, living in Fallbrook, California.

When Elisha accepts God's call to be Elijah's replacement, he surely realizes that he has some mighty big shoes to fill. Elijah has been a true prophet for God, consistently proclaiming God's word and standing against earthly authority even when his life was threatened. Elijah was a "free" man who lived under the love and authority of God. He was a superhero, and Elisha concludes that he will need a double portion of Elijah's spirit to follow in his footsteps.

To stand up to a declining culture and its authority figures requires a courage no longer bound by the need for approval and affirmation from prevailing societal mores and morals. A faith in the God who always enters our world to set the captives free is a faith that gives us courage to accept a challenge that we know is much bigger than ourselves. The double portion of spirit that Elisha requests is, in effect, a recognition of his need to be healed of his own self-doubts so that God can use him.

The good news is that God not only calls us, but God also equips us to do the task set before us. The truth that sets us free to be all that God created us to be, that gives us the freedom to be active participants in ushering in the kingdom of God, is that we are God's beloved children. Freedom comes in our claiming that gift.

PRAYER: Father, give me the courage to give up my self doubts and the freedom to be all that you created me to be. Help me to be conscious of this new freedom throughout this day. Amen.

In this psalm of lament, the author faces a life difficulty in which his "soul refuses to be comforted" and his "spirit faints." Nothing in the psalmist's present circumstance communicates the nearness of a loving God; life seems bleak and hopeless. In such a "dark night of the soul" he must look beyond the moment in order to hold onto the reality of a faithful God. Putting aside the present circumstances, the psalmist recalls the Exodus in which God freed the Jews from slavery and prepared them for a life of meaning and fulfillment.

Because the kingdom has not fully come, we often find ourselves in rather ungodly circumstances. In such times we must look beyond the moment for assurance deep within our souls that God is active in the world and that things are not always what they appear to be.

Our hope lies in knowing that the light shines in darkness, and the darkness cannot put that light out: Praise God! From cover to cover, the Bible bears witness to God's faithfulness that stretches out over the eons to free humankind from various enslavements. Salvation that brings about our freedom to be all that God has created us to be produces more than a faith in doctrinal statements about God and Christ. Ours is a faith that we are not alone, a faith that lives with the assurance of God's guiding presence in all of life's events.

PRAYER: Father, I long to be in the kind of relationship with you that will quiet my anxious heart and give me the courage to surrender to your gracious care. Amen.

Freedom is a prerequisite for our ability to make choices. In that God's great desire is that we love God, neighbor, and ourselves, we must live in freedom. God desires the kind of love from us that always requires a choice. An examination of the choices we make over a period of time reflects our life's priority.

Today's scripture reading is about priorities but also about freedom. To the first person expressing a desire to become his follower, Jesus questions his freedom from the need for creaturely comforts. A deeper question might have been, "Are you willing to follow me if it means turning loose of the very things by which your culture measures your success and value?" To the second would-be follower Jesus might have said, "Family values are certainly a good thing, but following me will require you to make difficult choices. Are you free to put me first?" The third would-be follower feels the same ambivalence of the first two. Following Jesus sounds right and good, but the good feelings received from his friends is also important.

Our culture's influence on both our mores and our belief systems is difficult to see. Often the recognition of our culture's negative influence on our religious understandings can be quite painful. Only the grace of God who came and lived among us can give us the freedom to take an honest look at ourselves and the context of our lives.

PRAYER: Gracious God, give me the freedom to look honestly at myself and to hear your words of love. Amen.

"For freedom Christ has set us free." This powerful, life-changing insight is easily skipped over by a people who pride ourselves on our independence and our willingness to fight and die for our freedom. Cultures that know from experience what it means to be enslaved might find this insight from Galatians particularly poignant.

Freedom is an absolute, first necessity if we are to turn our lives over to God. We cannot give away something that is not ours. Jesus said at the beginning of his public ministry, "He has sent me to proclaim release to the captives…" (Luke 4:18), a quote from the prophet Isaiah whom God had called to make the Jews aware of their own captivity. Captive to both their own religious dogma and the mores of their culture, they were not free to be God's people, those called to usher in God's kingdom.

Good news! Jesus has set us free from the captivity that keeps us from being all that God created us to be, cocreators with God, taking "dominion" over creation and bringing it under God's loving care. We have been set free to love one another, to prosper in our marriages, and to enable the well-being of our children and neighbors. In short we have been set free to experience the joy of God's creation.

PRAYER: Father, give me the courage to live in the freedom with which you have gifted me. Amen.

SATURDAY, JUNE 26 • Read Galatians 5:13-25

From the beginning of time humanity has faced the choice between the care of God's creation and its own indulgent desire to do what feels good or appears reasonable. Paul informs us that our life choices have consequences. Choosing to live by the Spirit brings peace and other benefits, while living life disconnected from or unconscious of the Spirit brings chaos and enmity.

Paul does not write to the Galatians because they desire to live a life of enmity and carousing but because they want to comply with the law, to be "good" Christians. Paul writes this letter to encourage the Galatians to let the Spirit guide their life. He knows from his own experience that obedience to the law can disconnect us from the Spirit. In that the Spirit resides within us, living by the law may disconnect us from our own soul. Our source of guidance is lost, and we become vulnerable to the temptation of unloving behavior.

Christ came to set our spirit free to resonate with his Spirit, thus enabling us to see new possibilities for ushering in his kingdom. The Spirit also affirms the value of our being as both God's children and God's ambassadors. Paul insists that grace sets us free, affirming our very being (soul) in spite of the reality that our behavior is often less than perfect.

PRAYER: Lord, give me the courage to accept the freedom that you have given me by living in your grace. Allow me to own my brokenness and, at the same time, love the person you created me to be. Amen.

The "good news" that I will celebrate in worship today is that I am free to claim my rightful place in the kingdom of God, that my negative perceptions of myself are no longer in charge of my being. My negative ways of describing myself have been crucified with Christ and have lost their power to control my behavior. I am free to love. That the negative has lost its power, however, does not mean it has lost its voice. Therefore, negative messages will continue to assault me, but I am now free to see that the condemnations of those negative voices are a lie. They have no power over me. I am free to live by the Spirit!

"If we live by the Spirit, let us also walk by the Spirit" (RSV). We cannot separate living and walking from each other. If we don't first "live by the Spirit," we cannot "walk by the Spirit." If we refuse to be led by the Spirit, we cannot "live by the Spirit." We must become conscious of who directs our walk. Are we children of God—loved, valued, and needed for the ushering in of the kingdom? Or is our walk directed by those negative voices that push us into competition with brother and sister in order to bolster our faltering ego?

"The fruit of the Spirit is love, joy, peace, patience, kindness, generosity, faithfulness, gentleness, and self-control. There is no law against such things. Those who belong to Christ Jesus have crucified the flesh with its passions and desires. If we live by the Spirit, let us also be guided by the Spirit."

PRAYER: Lord, help me to know your grace in new ways that will enable me to look honestly at who is directing my walk. Amen.

Restoring the Fallen

June 28–July 4, 2004 • *Gregory V. Palmer*‡

MONDAY, JUNE 28 • **Read 2 Kings 5:1-5a**

In most respects Naaman, commander of the Aramean army, has it all: position, power, prestige, and recognition. But he is nagged with leprosy. The text does not tell us how long he has had the disease. A young Israelite woman who serves Naaman's wife expresses confidence that "the prophet in Samaria" can cure him. Naaman prepares to go to Samaria in search of the prophet Elisha and a cure for his leprosy. The word of an unnamed "servant girl" opens a new future for Naaman.

Howard Thurman in his autobiography *With Head and Heart* shares a marvelous incident from his early teens when he found himself with his back against the wall. He sat crying on the steps of the train station. He was trying to get to Jacksonville to enroll in school but lacked the funds to ship his trunk. A stranger approached him, inquired about his tears, and ultimately provided the funds needed to ship the trunk. Thurman observes, "Then, without a word, he turned and disappeared down the railroad track. I never saw him again."

So much in our culture makes us leery of strangers, of the unfamiliar, the unknown. We often expect that strangers will do us harm. While this wise strategy may help us prepare our children to leave the safe cloister of home, we must also practice and teach the ways that the unnamed, faceless people we encounter may be channels of blessing. More often than not I have been the recipient of kindness rather than hurtful behavior from even those whose names I may not know.

PRAYER: Dear God, thank you for the nameless people who have opened new futures for me. Amen.

---

‡Bishop, The United Methodist Church, The Iowa Area, Des Moines, Iowa.

Naaman proceeds to Samaria with a letter of introduction from the king of Aram, lots of money, and extra clothes—obviously prepared to impress with his position, rank, and prestige. He comes with official credentials and lots of money to spread around if needed. He's prepared to do anything for a cure.

Naaman finally reaches Elisha's house. Through a third-party messenger, Elisha directs Naaman to "go and wash in the Jordan seven times." Elisha promises that such a washing will result in a cure. Naaman is angry, livid.

Naaman's outrage comes on two counts. One, Elisha does not address Naaman personally. No doubt he is offended, having come a great distance. Given Naaman's prestige he surely expects to be treated with more deference. Two, he finds the nonsensical simplicity of the "prescription" insulting.

How often in our lives have we missed a great blessing because it came disguised? We stand ready to entertain the big and the complex as a means to our healing and salvation, and God confounds us with babies and baptism. Naaman indeed is willing to do anything to be cured except take a simple bath in the Jordan River.

Perhaps this story's message to us is not to box God in, not predetermine how God will act. When we box God in through our preconceived notions of how God will act, then God's actions seem ridiculous. We want to bolt in the opposite direction. God welcomes our acknowledgment of our need and rejoices that we seek God's help. God does not need our expertise in determining how God will help us. When help comes, receive it as a gift. The only appropriate response to a gift and its giver is "thank you."

PRAYER: Gracious God, make me open to receive what you offer so I don't miss your blessings. Amen.

A tone of urgency saturates this text. Jesus is expanding the team and multiplying the ministry. He cannot be everywhere at once. The twelve also have their limitations. Now Jesus broadens the base and appoints seventy (or seventy-two) to serve as a sort of "advance team" for him. I have wondered if he sent these followers out figuring that he might never physically get to all the places he wanted to go. After all, Jerusalem is beckoning.

The tone of urgency is conveyed not only by the need for more help but by the specific instructions Jesus gives the seventy. Jesus urges them to stay focused and sends them to announce the inbreaking of God's reign and to be gracious guests. He also instructs the seventy not to tarry where they receive no welcome.

I am persuaded that people in our time, no less than the time of the historical Jesus, hunger for meaning and salvation. The people I encounter yearn for a living relationship with God. They don't always express their hunger and yearning in the vocabulary of Christian faith. But if we engage and probe and live in dialogue with those around us, we often discover that they yearn for the God made known in Jesus the Christ. That yearning may be the sign of a budding harvest.

"The harvest is plentiful, but the laborers are few; therefore, ask the Lord of the harvest to send out laborers into his harvest." With the help of the Holy Spirit, we bring in God's harvest when we help people name their hunger, pointing them to the feast of God, helping them make the vital life-giving connection.

The church must discover anew the capacity to discern the hungers of the heart that surround us. We must be engaged with the cultures where we live, so we can listen deeply to all of God's children. We must be unapologetic in pointing people to the one who is life and who gives life—Jesus Christ our Lord.

PRAYER: God, give me faith and courage to share the gift I have received in Jesus Christ. Amen.

The text says, "The seventy returned with joy, saying, 'Lord, . . . even the demons submit to us!'" They sound rather impressed with themselves, don't they? Who wouldn't be amazed and astonished that they had cast out and subdued unclean spirits. It's heady, inspiring stuff. We church folk can be like that. In fact, I believe we are going through a period of such powerful spirit work in the Christian church that we sometimes think and act like it's our own doing and not the Spirit's.

We often see this attitude in churches that really take off— either starting from nothing and blowing up to thousands of members in just a few years or a long-standing but stagnant congregation finds itself in the midst of phenomenal growth. I visited such a church recently to discern the key to their phenomenal growth. I left the worship service sorely disappointed; I had heard the pastor and people exalted but not the Savior. The message seemed to celebrate success rather than affirm faithfulness.

What is it about success that makes us want to take center stage? Why is it so hard to remember in plenty or little "that this extraordinary power belongs to God and does not come from us"? (2 Cor. 4:7)

So while the seventy are overjoyed at their apparent success, Jesus helps them refocus by saying, "Nevertheless, do not rejoice at this, that the spirits submit to you, but rejoice that your names are written in heaven." Paul offers a helpful reminder to us also. In 2 Corinthians 4:5 he says, "For we do not proclaim ourselves; we proclaim Jesus Christ as Lord and ourselves as your slaves for Jesus' sake."

PRAYER: Deliver me, O God, from allowing my success to seduce me. Help me keep my eyes on Jesus in whose name I pray. Amen.

In spite of our conviction and preaching of the church as a community of love, redemption, and forgiveness, churches really do not restore the fallen very well. I'm not sure what we fear in reaching out to and working with the fallen. But we often seem comfortable with the philosophy of "out of sight, out of mind."

I believe we fear our own vulnerability and weakness. Addressing others' failings in a straightforward way reminds us that we too have "come short of the glory of God." It also serves to remind us of the ways in which we fear that we might fail.

Paul's counsel to the Galatians was this: "If anyone is detected in a transgression, you who have received the Spirit should restore such a one in a spirit of gentleness." If we accept Paul's counsel as helpful and instructive for the church today, we will have to change the way we support and hold one another accountable.

The church as a community of restoration must practice and encourage the sharing of the journey. Sometimes we fail and fall because we have chosen to or been left to walk alone. I find that I cannot be an effective Christian alone, much less live a life of holiness. Ours is a shared journey. We need one another both for support and accountability.

In such a relational context I can both hear and speak the truth in love. When fellow pilgrims, who I know without a doubt love and value me, speak truth to me (even the truth of my shortcomings), I hear it differently than when it is spoken outside the context of covenant and community.

Perhaps truth can only be spoken and heard in the context of binding relationships. The only reason for speaking painful truth is to seek deeper relationship with God and reconciliation with neighbor, a truth speaking that seeks only to heal and restore that which is lost and broken.

PRAYER: Deliver us, O God, from cheap grace. Rescue us from no grace at all. Amen.

Context is everything; knowing the context in which someone said something delivers his or her words from becoming gossipy tools of destruction. Knowing the context of many a beloved, oft-quoted saying may enrich its meaning even more.

Like many persons, I grew up hearing snippets of Bible all the time. Some phrases or sayings from the Bible I heard outside the walls of organized religion. Some were harmless; some even proved helpful in their witness.

If you think context is important, I assure you that tone carries equal weight. I remember as a child hearing Paul's words to the Galatians, "Do not be deceived; God is not mocked, for you reap whatever you sow." I often heard these words as chiding and chastising, or I received them as a negative warning.

Granted Paul is discouraging the saints from "sowing to the flesh"; but he presents a balanced picture, reminding them that in sowing to the Spirit "you will reap eternal life from the Spirit." Paul builds his words, moving to what I think is a great crescendo of hope and encouragement: "So let us not grow weary in doing what is right, for we will reap at harvest-time, if we do not give up." These are not the words of someone shaking a finger in another's face as if expecting him or her to do the wrong thing. These are words of encouragement cheering the saints on as they persist in doing the right thing. Context is everything.

Prayer: Dear God, help me know your word and proclaim it. By the power of your word give me life. Amen.

I am a wimp. I don't like pain. I avoid pain, whether physical, emotional, or spiritual. But none of us gets through this life without it. No matter how great life has been to us, we have all faced pain. If you haven't yet, it's just a matter of time.

That is why I find the psalms so inspiring: They talk about life as it is. The psalmists do not view life through rose-colored glasses. They don't gloss over the painful and unpleasant. Life, according to the psalmists, is filled with great joy, high inspiration, and many reasons to praise God. Life is also touched by disappointment, loss, grief, and many things that drive us to despair.

But these seasons of life are not to be avoided. They are to be acknowledged and even embraced. We embrace them not because they are good in and of themselves, but because even in seasons of "distress and grief" we discover the never-failing presence of God.

When I run from my pain, I also deny myself the assurance that God remains steadfast and faithful even in tough times. When I avoid my pain, I live in an artificial zone of comfort that cannot be sustained, let alone be sustaining.

When I embrace my pain, I experience more fully the God who gives "joy in the morning," who turns "mourning into dancing." God can do that because God journeys with us all the way—not just part of the way. In so doing, God transforms the discouraging seasons of life into new seasons of opportunity.

PRAYER: O God, it seems easier to hide, to cut and run. Reassure me that you are ever with me, in joy and sorrow even "to the close of the age." Amen.

Measured by God

July 5–11, 2004 • *Charlie Morrow[‡]*

MONDAY, JULY 5 • **Read Psalm 82:1-4**

The indigenous people of the land from the great ocean in the east (the Atlantic) to the many lakes in the west (the Great Lakes) know themselves as woodlands people. Pilgrims from Europe called them Indians.

The grandeur and immensity of the forests across this region provided all the timber and wildlife needed for shelter and food. Hunting homes were built by planting long willow limbs in a circle and then bending the supple limbs toward one another. Tying the limbs together formed a dome-shaped frame. Then reed mats or animal skins covered the frame to make a tent the people called a "wikiup." To strengthen the wikiup against wind and rain, the people used a form of plumb line—a string with a rock tied to the end. Holding the string high and letting the rock swing until it stopped in a straight perpendicular to the ground ensured the limbs' straightness. By lining up knots tied in graduating lengths, they tied the limbs at even, parallel heights.

Today engineers might bounce a laser beam off the moon to measure with precision, but the illustration of the plumb line (in the Amos reading for this week) still stands. Careful attention to a high standard ensures a trustworthy result.

Rather than use a rock and string or a laser beam to measure the uprightness of the lesser gods, God uses justice to the weak, protection of the lowly, and rescue of the needy. These means become the laser beams of God's mercy, measuring and penetrating the lives and hearts of those in power who dominate and oppress God's favored ones.

PRAYER: God of mercy, when you measure us, may you find us steady, straight, and trustworthy servants of your Word. Amen.

[‡]United Methodist clergyman; enrolled member of The Chickasaw (American Indian) Tribe; husband, full-time grandparent; Tama, Iowa.

The problem with being a member of a racial or ethnic minority today comes in being invisible. History records horrible epithets hurled at American Indians: "The only good Indian is a dead Indian." "Kill the Indian and save the soul"—all history.

Today people aren't trying to kill Indians. They act as though we're not even here. We wait in line to pay our bills. When our turn comes, the clerk simply reaches around us to serve the dominant-class member behind us. It's as though we're not even in the room.

Indian souls scream, "Hey wait a minute! What am I? Invisible?" The answer shouts from years of domination and oppression saying, "Yeah. You're here, but you don't count. You're poor. You have no clout. You have no political, economic, or social power in our community. You're not one of 'us.'"

In the divine council, God takes the side of the weak and needy. Whatever marginalized category describes a particular people, God calls the gods to judge justly, to rescue those weakened by the wicked, and to deliver them. Race, gender, economics, religion, and politics are among the lesser gods that God judges harshly.

People of color, people impoverished and abused by society, people marginalized and powerless—all sit in the hallways of the divine council. Overhearing this mythological tirade by God, oppressed people cheer and join the psalmist, singing triumphantly, "Rise up, O God, judge the earth; for all the nations belong to you."

PRAYER: God of grace, remind us to hear, see, and serve those who cry out for justice and mercy. Amen.

The wall is straight, level, and square with the land. It was well-built and serves its intended purpose. The people too were well-built, but they had begun to shift, lean, and tilt. And the Lord stands beside the wall with a plumb line in hand—not to test the wall, but to show Amos the necessity of a high standard of measurement. What a vivid illustration!

What a forceful warning! Measured against the plumb line of God's intention (spelled out this week in Psalm 82), the people will fall by the sword, lose their land, and be cast into exile.

Especially when confronted by troubling passages such as this, the men of my Saturday morning prayer group ask themselves regularly, "Where is the good news in this?" Certainly this passage is not good news to those caught leaning on walls that tilt, wobble, and fall, walls failing the test of a plumb line.

The prayer group decided the good news is that the pronouncement of God through Amos begins with a warning, not a condemnation. Warnings provide time, space, and opportunity to turn back. When warnings are heard, mistakes can be acknowledged. When they are heeded, balance can be restored. If the wall that the Lord stood beside had been leaning, repairs could have been made before the fall.

Instead of heeding the warning, Amaziah argues with Amos, accuses him of conspiring against Jeroboam, and sends the prophet away. Only then does the Lord say, "Therefore. . .!"

PRAYER: **Lord, measure us by your loving standard. Show us how we need to realign our lives, so that your will is done on earth as in heaven. Amen.**

Repeated pulpit requests for new lay readers for the worship service had come and many reassurances uttered that through preparation and forethought, "The teacher often learns more than the student." Still no one came forward. Then one day bashfully, hesitantly, a man said he'd give it a try.

The volunteer and I practiced a few times in the weeks before. We began with easy-to-read, familiar passages at first, just to accustom the man to standing at the lectern and familiarize him with the microphone and the reverberating sound of his own amplified voice. I gently suggested that he relax, read loudly and clearly, and slow his reading pace a bit.

When the man's turn to read in worship came around, he faced today's difficult passage. These opening verses of Paul's letter to the Colossians are classics in complexity. Sentences compound upon one another, and many phrases scarcely connect. Read aloud or silently, this passage can twist the mind. Readers and hearers alike yearn for a full-stop break, so minds can grasp this liturgical list of attributes that Paul acknowledges in the Christians of Colossae.

"That's it," my new lay reader exclaimed in an "aha" moment of insight. "These aren't sentences. This is a list of the signs of being Christian." As he noted, the passage lists faith, love, hope, and bearing fruit as Christian qualities in this community of believers. Paul begins his letter to the Colossians by acknowledging their faith in Jesus, their love for others, and the growth of their church. He then prays for them and offers his blessing upon them.

With this new insight the man read this passage aloud in worship without stumbling and with renewed strength and power, giving thanks to God, the Father.

PRAYER: Lord, clear our heads of confusion. Make the rough passages plain. Remove the complexities of our faith that we might see the simple truth of your love. Amen.

The women of the Choctaw (American) Indian Nation are known for their finger dexterity. For more generations than time can count, grandmothers have patiently taught the children how to weave baskets. The women (and some of the men) have developed keen eyes, quick hands, and confident motions. From shreds of bark and twisting reeds emerge works of intricate beauty and abundant capacity.

Modern American industry has discovered the special skills of the Choctaw people, now employing them on production lines twisting cables for electronic auto parts. In another factory on their Mississippi reservation, Choctaw workers cut and paste the most delicate "pop up" features on greeting cards, using their extraordinary eye-hand coordination, gifts from God and from their grandmothers. Ancient basket-weaving crafts trained Choctaw eyes, hands, and attention to detail, preparing the people for contemporary livelihoods.

Paul's greeting to the Christians in Colossae acknowledges and affirms the reeds of Christianity. Like strips of bark and water-softened reeds, love, hope, good works, knowledge, patience, and joy are interwoven to form a basket that holds our faith.

SUGGESTION FOR MEDITATION: **Sit quietly with your hands in your lap, palms up. Imagine each of your fingers as a strip of bark or a reed representing the strands that (when woven together) contain our understanding of Christian community. You might see them as faith, love, hope, witness, and grace on the one hand. The fingers on your other hand might be prayer, wisdom, understanding, good works, and knowledge of God. Now gently intertwine the fingers of your cupped hands and let them become a basket worthy of carrying God's abundant love.**

Jesus answers the lawyer's self-righteous question, "And who is my neighbor?" He goes beyond the mind game and offers a real-life illustration. The story is simple, its meaning obvious. Yet there's more to the story than its words reveal.

Years ago I saw this parable acted out. Volunteers portrayed each of the familiar characters—the hapless merchant, the priest, the Levite, and the good Samaritan. Extras included an innkeeper, and a volunteer agreed to play the role of the pack animal. Without preparation or rehearsal the vignette opened before the audience's very eyes. As the story was read from the scriptural text, each actor pantomimed his or her character's role. Brief pauses interrupted the flow of the story as each gave spontaneous portrayals. Some characterizations were sparse; others were amply embellished.

In the midst of each portrayal, the worship leader would call, "Freeze!" At that signal the actors locked in their positions and stood silently for a brief moment. The effect was that of a snapshot, a moment frozen in time and space.

To the audience's surprise, in every frozen moment the visual focus of the scene was not on the priest, not on the Levite, not even on the good Samaritan. It was always on the victim!

First and foremost, God loves the victim. In doing so, God shows us whom to love with all our heart, soul, strength, and mind. We therefore show our love for God, as (to the same extent), we love those whom God loves.

PRAYER: **Help us, Lord God, to avoid judging others. Inspire us to focus on rushing to the aid of the victims in our society. Amen.**

What if the man who went down from Jerusalem to Jericho had been a Samaritan? The common reading suggests the victim was a Jewish merchant, but that's a traditional bias not necessarily supported by the text. If the stripped and beaten victim left on the roadside was a Samaritan, the parable takes on a decidedly different flavor.

Scripture doesn't say the victim was robbed, only that he fell into the hands of thugs. Maybe he was easy prey for violent bigots, the victim of a hate crime, attacked solely because he was a Samaritan. In that case the good Samaritan would not have crossed a religious boundary. Instead he would have rushed to the aid of his neighbor, whom he might have known: his brother, his cousin, or his neighbor from across the street or down the road from his own Samaritan home.

This different minority view of the story doesn't change the lesson Jesus teaches in the parable. The good Samaritan remains a genuine neighbor to the victim. The two who do not show mercy remain condemned by their refusal to help. But this view floods the story with an emotion that we often miss. The good Samaritan is no longer an extraordinarily righteous do-gooder who crosses cultural lines to rescue a fallen stranger. Now the Samaritan's passion becomes palpable. Tears of anguish are followed by fury at injustice, and his coming to the rescue of his friend makes more sense.

This interpretation of a familiar story offers a new glimpse of God's anger at injustice and determination to do whatever it takes to care for a child who has fallen by the wayside.

PRAYER: **God of passion, may we have pity on and rush to the side of the abused and mistreated. Amen.**

Bitter Mourning to Hope of Glory

July 12–18, 2004 • Leonard G. Goss[‡]

MONDAY, JULY 12 • Read Amos 8:1-8

The basket of summer fruit portrays well the coming of a bitter type of mourning over the end of Israel's northern kingdom. Summer fruit is ripened fruit, and ripened fruit signals the end of the growing season. The Israelites are looking forward to a spiritual renewal in concert with the changing and renewal of the seasons. But with the promise of summer fruit comes the Lord's words, "The end has come upon my people Israel," suggesting no hope for renewal. The Lord declares, "I will never again pass by them." So tragic is this picture that silence is the only appropriate reaction.

Amos directs hard words of indictment and judgment at the greedy merchants who "trample on the needy, and bring the poor of the land to an end" (RSV). Because of their abuse and injustice the needy pay their debts by selling themselves into slavery! These deceitful businesspeople observe the holy days in a technical way but complain about them as interruptions of commerce, and they can hardly wait for them to be over in order to return to cheating their poor brothers and sisters.

But make no mistake. God is indignant at this attitude, and the Lord takes the side of the oppressed. The cheaters think their proceedings are secret, but God swears an oath never to forget these deeds. We are all ripe for a coming judgment, and each of us will be called to account before Yahweh for disdaining the poor and needy among us.

SUGGESTION FOR MEDITATION: **Think of a time in your life when you scorned God's will by scorning someone less fortunate. Ask God's forgiveness for doing that.**

[‡]Editorial director for trade and academic book publishing, Broadman & Holman Publishers, division of LifeWay Christian Resources; coauthor of several books; member of Walker Memorial Baptist Church, Franklin, Tennessee.

The days of final judgment will be dark and bitter. According to Amos, God is the one who will speak and act and sow panic in the land, possibly by causing an eclipse of the sun. "On that day" refers to "the day of the LORD" (Amos 5:18-20), a day of mourning and lamentation. The nation will experience sudden calamity at the height of national prosperity. No longer will joy characterize the Israelite feasts.

Choosing to chase the prophet from their territory, the people of God will face the silence of God; all communication between Yahweh and the people will be broken. The threatened judgment on the day of the Lord is a famine, but not an ordinary famine of bread and water. Rather, it is an absence of the indispensable, life-giving guidance and nourishment of the words of the Lord, which the Israelites have spurned. When the prophetic word is rejected, that word of counsel and hope is withdrawn and heard no more.

Blessings are undervalued until they are withdrawn and missed. When the light of God's revelation is taken away, there will be a great longing for the Word, but this longing will go unsatisfied. The catastrophic and devastating results of God's silence will be seen by the people's wandering from "sea to sea" (i.e., all the world over) and running "to and fro seeking the word of the LORD." But Amos says they will not find it. God's words are to the soul what bread and water are to the body. But when God pronounces judgment on a guilty nation by withdrawing revelation and light, then truly the end has come.

SUGGESTION FOR MEDITATION: **Israel could not live without the word of Yahweh. Consider both the personal and national consequences of rejecting the life-giving qualities of God's revelation.**

David has just experienced a painful parting from Jonathan, his closest friend (1 Sam. 20:41–42). He has also learned that King Saul is still trying find and kill him. He has gone to Nob, where the priest Abimelech offers hospitality to him and his men. The only available bread is that offered to God during worship. Abimelech allows David and the others to eat this bread only when he is convinced that they are spiritually prepared.

One of Saul's men Doeg, a treacherous spy, is also in Nob at this time. Since he now knows David's whereabouts, he seizes this opportunity to hand David over to Saul and thus ingratitate himself to the king. After David and his men leave Nob, morally bankrupt Doeg reports to Saul the assistance David received from Abimelech and the other priests. His action leads to the bloody massacre of eighty priests and all the other men, women, and children of Nob. Not even the animals of the town are spared. All is done at the hands of Doeg. The only survivor is Abiathar, the son of Abimelech. Upon learning of this tragedy, David blames himself. The massacre at Nob is in the background of David's thinking when he writes Psalm 52. David makes no secret that he would like God to deal severely with Doeg.

Having set himself in direct opposition to God, Doeg "love[s] evil more than good." He has a "tongue [that] plots destruction" and is a "worker of deceit." How can anyone expect to prosper when opposing the Almighty? The enemy of God loves "words that devour" and has a tongue that represents evil of the worst kind. Doeg's tongue brought about the murder of hundreds of innocents—all in his claim for glory.

David wants disaster to come upon Doeg: "God will break you down forever;… [God] will uproot you from the land of the living." This prediction of peril is for all who make riches and self-glorification their refuge rather than God.

PRAYER: Lord, do not allow us to rise to the top if if means stepping on the backs of others. May we make you our refuge and not desire glory for ourselves. Amen.

Security is only for those who "trust in the steadfast love of God forever and ever." They are blessed, for they understand that the wisdom, power, and faithfulness of God command our complete trust. The godly, in complete contrast to Doeg, will be "like a green olive tree in the house of God."

The olive tree, an evergreen, was one of the most valuable trees in all of Palestine. The olives could be eaten or crushed to make olive oil, which had many uses. The average tree produced twenty stone of olives or six gallons of oil. The cultivation of olive trees, while a slow and difficult process, was a highly profitable enterprise in the long run. Cultivating faith and godliness is such a process.

Habakkuk speaks of the labors of the olive (3:17). Jeremiah speaks of its goodly fruits (11:16). And Hosea speaks of its beauty (14:6). The olive tree fittingly symbolizes God's people (Rom. 11:17), showing the blessedness of the godly: They are fruitful, beautiful, useful, and prosperous. To trust in the unfailing love of God means we express our thanks and share our faith:

I will praise you forever....
In your name I will hope, for your name is good.
I will praise you in the presence of your saints. (NIV)

The difference between the Doegs of this world and the people of God is that the treacherous arrogantly use their blessings, while the righteous humbly acknowledge God as the source of all good things. Yahweh's "name" is all God is, says, and does. Waiting on God brings us refreshment and restores our souls. Other Doegs will bark at God's people, for the wicked will always plot against the godly, but our Creator will never let us down.

PRAYER: Lord, you are our hope, and we do not look elsewhere. Even if others boast in their riches, we boast in you. Amen.

Paul writes the letter to the Colossians to combat a false teaching at Colossae, but he does not make plain the nature of the heresy. What he does make clear are the main defects of the false teaching, which apparently involves worshiping angelic beings and depending on ceremonies to secure acceptance with God. In order to correct these errors, Paul reveals the divine nature and absolute sufficiency of Christ, "the image of the invisible God, the firstborn of all creation."

The word *image* means a replica or a likeness, but it is also a representation or manifestation—like a head stamped on a coin or a face reflected in a mirror. To show the unique nature and supreme dignity of Christ, Paul says Jesus is the exact representation of God, not just one manifestation of God's power but the *only* manifestation.

Christ, "the firstborn of all creation," was the Creator, distinct from the world, apart from creation. "Firstborn" here is a title of position and power, and it suggests the rank of eminence and dominion. The Lord's rule extends over all cosmic forces in the universe, both the material and the spiritual realms. And in Christ "all things hold together": The cosmic Christ unites the universe together and is its principle of coherence.

Not only is Christ the image of God and the creator of the universe, "he is the head of the body, the church." Whether of the natural creation or the new creation, Christ is supreme. We who have done evil are now reconciled to and part of the family in which Christ is the firstborn. Because "in him all the fullness of God [is] pleased to dwell," Christ's fullness of wisdom keeps us from error; his fullness of grace keeps us from sin; his fullness of mercy helps us in our distress.

SUGGESTION FOR MEDITATION: Reflect on the meaning of reconciliation—the death of Christ and the removal of all estrangements or barriers between God and us. What part do we play in the divine reconciliation?

God achieved reconciliation through Jesus Christ. For Paul this was the gospel, the good news.

Paul's ministry was not free from sufferings and afflictions, far from it; he was beaten, stoned and imprisoned, all for the sake of the church, the body of Christ. If Christ had not suffered, the church would never have come into being. As servants of Christ, we must be willing to share in the Lord's sufferings and to say, with Paul, "I rejoice in my sufferings" (RSV).

Paul's ministry is an apostolic one, a gift to him from God. His task is "to make the word of God fully known, the mystery hidden for ages and generations but now made manifest to his saints" (RSV). The word *saints* describes Christians in general, and the "mystery" now revealed is that God's reconciling purpose includes all people, Gentiles as well as Jews. Gentiles had appeared to be outside God's favor, but now we see their inclusion has been part of God's plan all along.

The gospel is universal, and we are all included in God's plan. But the living Christ, the "hope of glory," is present among us only by indwelling individual believers. In fact, "Christ in you, the hope of glory" is the entire Christian message made simple.

But the Christian message also includes a warning: We must not turn away from Christ but live our lives in him and thus "present everyone mature in Christ." "Present" refers to bringing people into God's presence at the return of Christ (see 1 Thess. 2:19-20; 5:23), and only then will the work of God in each person be complete. Ultimate maturity in faith, hope, love, and understanding is not meant for only a small, inner group of disciples. It is meant for all the saints.

SUGGESTION FOR MEDITATION: **Reflect on the full wealth of God's mercy and goodness that has been revealed in Christ. What is your part in the gospel mission to the whole world?**

We are not all alike, and no right and wrong exists in personality types. So why does Jesus seem to take up for Mary, who wants to avoid helping her sister Martha with more mundane things in the kitchen? After all, Martha is only trying to be kind in service to the Lord by offering him the best meal she can manage. The answer is that Martha shows the wrong kind of kindness.

Jesus is on his way to die in Jerusalem. What he needs most at this moment in the home of Mary and Martha is a time of quiet and reflection. What he does not need is a big spread and a lot of turmoil and rushing around. Dealing with a party of at least thirteen and possibly more, Martha finds her hosting responsibilities so daunting she cannot pay much attention to Jesus—and she even tells him so (v. 40). Yet instead of helping Jesus find calm away from the madding crowd, Martha adds to the tension in his heart. Mary seems to understand, but Martha does not. She has gotten distracted from what really matters.

The real shock of this story is that Mary is welcome to be with Jesus and to listen to his teaching. In that time and place, women were not encouraged to neglect their domestic duties, and they certainly were not taught much about the law and religious matters. Mary represents all those who need the relief from the world's oppression that only Jesus can offer.

Practicing kindness toward others means looking into their hearts to discern their actual needs—being kind to them in their way, not ours. Mary was able to forget her plans and to think of Jesus and his needs. She chose "the good portion" (RSV). But Martha, who tried to be kind in her own way, actually denied Jesus what he needed most—quiet.

PRAYER: Lord, teach us about our priorities as a church and as individuals. Help us remember that hospitality is not just about welcome but also about listening and responding to the needs of others. Amen.

Yearning for Restoration

July 19–25, 2004 • *Geraldine Ives Fowler[‡]*

MONDAY, JULY 19 • Read Psalm 85

Although Judah was mired in economic and spiritual instability over twenty-five hundred years ago, the psalmist's plea for restoration rings in our ears. The lament of Psalm 85 and the conditions it mirrors are timeless. We serve a God who is the same yesterday, today, and tomorrow, so our lack of peace must be the result of a change in us and in our relationship with an unchanging God. In times of financial and moral disarray, we live in fear as we entertain thoughts of threatened danger from those we have labeled enemy. We can cry with the psalmist for the return of order, but we will cry forever if our actions do not change. Isaiah 27:11 reminds us, "When its boughs are dry, they are broken." We, like Judah, too often neglect the Source of life.

Within us is the imprint of a desire for an intimate relationship with God and a return to the Eden of our existence. We long for perfect harmony between the Creator and all of creation. Where do we go to draw water from the bottomless well? Where do we find the finest wheat to feed our hungry souls? When did we rip off our tags with the imprint, "Created in the image of God"?

We hear the melodies of this ancient hymn/psalm casting about for a response, and the crescendo is reached when the attributes of blessedness and tranquillity, righteousness and peace become personified in the redemption of our souls and our community. We trust in a God who forgives, speaking peace and love into world conversations of enmity and righteousness into situations where evil wants to prevail.

PRAYER: O God, help me to be an instrument of your peace. Amen.

[‡]Executive director and retreat leader, Balm in Gilead Ministries, Allentown, New Jersey.

"O Love That Wilt Not Let Me Go," by George Matheson and Albert L. Peace, is one of my favorite hymns. It speaks to me of a love that calls me back to God, even in the midst of my idolatries.

Our God, who makes a way where there is no way, has revealed in these scriptures a redemptive love that waits for us to turn from our idolatrous ways. God's word and ways are revealed to Hosea, the prophet, through personal pain. Hosea's wife, Gomer, will be sexually unfaithful to him, mirroring the unfaithfulness that Israel has exhibited in its relationship with God. Despite the symbolic names of Hosea's three children Jezreel ("Yahweh sows judgment to come"), Lo-ruhamah ("God's pity is exhausted"), and Loammi ("I am not your God") that imply impending disaster, the broken relationship between Hosea and Gomer will eventually be restored to wholeness.

The former relationship between God and Israel had been one of intimate love, but as the Israelites betrayed God and broke the covenant, walked in adulterous ways, and were spiritually unfaithful, they rediscovered a God who loves righteousness and longs to make clean what has been soiled. "Not my people" becomes "the children of the living God." God's divine compassion and unconditional love will not let them go. In the midst of making us aware of our wickedness and hopelessness, God holds out to us an offer of hope and a promise of restoration.

SUGGESTION FOR MEDITATION: **If you were to wake up tomorrow morning and find a sign on your lawn that reveals whatever it is that separates you from God, what would it say? Pray your answer.**

In the first full-time church I served, I foolishly stood on a step that had been placed behind the altar rail for the children to stand on during their anthem. As I finished giving the announcements and turned to move back to the pulpit area, I stepped off into thin air, landing unceremoniously in a heap on the floor. It was one of the most embarrassing moments of my ministry, but one in which I accidentally illustrated how easily we can "fall off our pedestals" when our foundation is not firmly fixed.

Paul felt that the Colossian church was being beguiled by the half-truths of false teachers. He told the people that if they sank their roots into Jesus they would be able to stand fast and would not be persuaded by false doctrine. Whom have we placed upon a pedestal?

False teachers and half-truths abound today as well. Wherever we turn, we are bombarded with the images of our contemporary cultural gods proclaiming a religion of personality or wealth or success or power. Is that enough for you? Are you willing to accept a cultural religion of signs and wonders?

Can we improve upon Jesus Christ? When we place false hope in substitutions for Christ, "I" becomes the center, and the talk of success and self-aggrandizement all "work together for the good of self." It sounds like religious truth, but it is an illusion. Paul exhorts us to establish our faith on the firm foundation of life in Christ—the true gospel message.

PRAYER: O Lord, what of this world masquerades as wisdom and pulls me away from you? Help me to see the truth and to discern your will for me. Amen.

Thursday, July 22 • Read Colossians 2:16-19

Paul's letters are full of approval and affirmation, yet he never fails to exhort and admonish his readers to continue in Christ and not be dissuaded from the truth. "Almost truth" is very beguiling and intriguing. Something or someone proposes an absolutely stimulating hypothesis that seems a viable alternative to the hard way of discipleship, and we are hooked.

We prefer broad roads and glittery paths but, like Alice in Wonderland, we aren't sure which route we should select. The cat tells Alice that if she doesn't know which way she wants to go, then it doesn't really matter which way she chooses. Perhaps Lewis Carroll knew that the magic of new places, characters, and situations can bring a sense of relativity to all choices.

Paul's words fight against the worship of angels, which was prevalent in Colossae. He admonishes the people to remember that in Jesus we find fullness of joy, needing no other accessories to faith. Our hunger for God is fed by the love of Jesus Christ, yet we sometimes fight the exquisite pain of grace. Even when firmly rooted in that love, we become frightened by the passion that arises within us, and we run to find something or someone else to relieve the pressure lest we explode. Paul chastens us not to let imitations take root in our lives.

PRAYER: O God, may the song you desire to write upon my heart spill out in unadulterated freedom. Let me sing, dance, shout, and move with the music of faith when in doubt, the music of victory when in trouble, and the music of praise when in sorrow. You are my prayer, my song, my life. Amen.

This most familiar of all prayers, which the writer of the Gospel of Matthew expands upon (6:9-15), gives us a glimpse of the teaching of Jesus by example. Longing for the right words and for the intimacy that Jesus shares with God, the disciples ask Jesus to teach them what they have seen him practice time after time.

In this five-pronged, intimate, and confident prayer of reverence, petition, and forgiveness, Jesus teaches us to pray words that offer us true harmony with God and one another. We give God permission to act in us and through us in this communal prayer, finding balance and restoration. The theme of grace that has followed us all week looms large and sweet in the Lord's Prayer. Teach us to pray, we say, as we yearn for communion with our heavenly Parent.

My father, a retired United Methodist minister, developed Alzheimer's disease in his eighties. Shortly before he died, this brilliant man couldn't remember the names of his five daughters or recall the practice of Holy Communion, but he never forgot how to pray. In the midst of the isolation of Alzheimer's, he always offered a prayer of love and grace when asked, making sense at a time in his life when sense was stringently rationed. The Lord's Prayer flowed from his lips like sweet honey from the rock. He had learned well. He had practiced. He knew the power of grace.

O Lord, teach us to pray....

**Prayer: Our Abba, holy is your name. Your kingdom come in
_____ (name of situation, place, or group), and give us day by day _____ (name your need). Forgive us our sin of _____ (name your sin), as we forgive _____ (name of group, individual, or institution). And save us from temptation. Amen.**

We had gathered as a family to celebrate a birthday. Everyone was seated around the dining room table with the exception of my two-year-old grandson, who sat in his high chair nearby. As we reached out for one another's hands and closed our eyes, there was a pause as we waited for the prayer to begin. In the silence that fell, my grandson, watching with wide eyes, yelled, "Wake up! Wake up!"

In Luke's scripture concerning prayer, we see that God wants only what is best for us. Our prayer lives might often appear to others a yawning sleepiness rather than prayerful watchfulness. But in this parable, Jesus encourages us to persist in prayer and to ask trustingly for what we need.

Our struggle with prayer is our struggle with surrender. The Latin root word for pray is *precari*. Prayer is a "precarious" place to be, because our human nature wants to wrest power from God. We would much rather go to an all-night store for three loaves of bread than trust God to give us that for which we yearn. The words we use in prayer are often the necessary tools to clear the path of our own uncertainties and selfishness. If we truly believe the words of the Gospel writer Matthew, we will remember that "your Father knows what you need before you ask" (6:8).

PRAYER: O God, we are in a precarious place when we surrender ourselves in prayer. Help us to trust, to rely upon, to appreciate your goodness and grace. May our prayers be not only for ourselves but for our neighbor in need. Amen.

How often have you heard people say that they don't pray for the "little things" or that they never pray for themselves? In these last three readings about prayer, we have reflected upon its place in our lives and come face-to-face with the scriptural premise that we are to pray at all times and about everything. We enter prayer full of requests and leave prayer with a more clearly defined sense of the route we seek. Often the answers we wanted have been rearranged.

In today's passage, Jesus promises that prayer will always be answered. Although petitionary prayer usually explores God's will, Jesus admonishes us to ask, seek, and knock continually, knowing that God wills to give us a better gift than any earthly parent can—the Holy Spirit. We don't have to beg for God's favor, because we already have it. And we are not to see God as a Santa Claus, a fairy godfather, or a genie who will grant us phenomenal wishes. God is our loving Parent who wants us to have the desires of our hearts.

Too often we relegate prayer to on-the-run conversations, laundry lists of petitions for others, or knee-jerk reactions to trauma in our lives. Yet the true blessings of prayer settle upon us when we sit still and allow God's presence to caress us with love. Then our prayers become heart cries in union with the heart cry of God. Regularly submitting ourselves to the embrace of the Lover of our souls, we may believe that our prayers will always be answered.

PRAYER: O holy Lover of my soul, quiet me with your love, and caress me with your presence. Amen.

Let the Redeemed Say So

July 26–August 1, 2004 • A. Safiyah Fosua[‡]

MONDAY, JULY 26 • **Read Hosea 11:1-11**

Every configuration of people that calls itself a family has within its system at least one problem child. In spite of our best efforts to shape and control the environment of those we nurture, some of our children inevitably go astray. The resulting emotions oscillate between self-blame and anger at betrayal.

In today's passage God is the parent of an ungrateful Israel. Ephraim, the second son of Joseph, had, interestingly, been chosen as representative of the entire nation of Israel. Customarily the Israelites had thought of Ephraim as doubly blessed because Jacob intentionally gave Ephraim more honor than his elder brother Manasseh. In case the hearers have forgotten their own blessings, the speaker recalls the intentional love and nurture that doubly-blessed Ephraim received: Ephraim was taught to walk, taken into God's arms and healed, led with love and kindness. We may even picture loving parents lifting infants to their cheeks and bending down to feed them. How can God possibly give up on Ephraim? Clearly God is either unwilling or unable to abandon this investment, despite the people's willful disobedience.

Today's passage offers a word of hope for those who struggle with misguided or confused children and seek to stand with them. Remember your investment and God's as you actively wait for wayward children to find their way home.

SUGGESTION FOR MEDITATION: **Quiet yourself and think about the many ways that God has used others to invest in your well-being. Thank God for them, and then thank God for allowing you to invest your time and energies in the lives of others.**

[‡]Director of Invitational Preaching Ministries, General Board of Discipleship, Nashville, Tennessee.

"Somebody say Amen!" Every time I hear those words, my mind quickly returns to a worn pew in Oklahoma where I attended church as a child. I usually sat sandwiched between two teenagers on the back pew, swallowing giggles until something interesting captured our attention. I was usually attentive during what we called "testimony service," a time when the believers stood to share their faith stories. I don't mean the well-rehearsed ones that had been said so many times that they had lost meaning, but the sobering reports of those who had suffered silently among us. On the other side of a living nightmare, many of them stood to confess the loss of homes, families, or even their faith. But God had somehow turned things around, and they were standing on better ground. During bone-chilling, hair-raising testimonies of deliverance from a bullet or a cancer or another terror that stalked in the back of many minds, instead of giggles, I swallowed tears.

I did not realize at the time the tremendous impact these stories of God's steadfast love would have upon my faith in later years. Remembering those testimonies gave me courage to face many of my own trials, as I learned that life often offers few reasons to giggle. More than thirty years removed from that back pew, I still hear the steadying words of some of those church members, and occasionally I still swallow a few tears.

"Let the redeemed of the Lord say so." The psalmist encourages Israel to tell each generation about Israel's deliverance from Egypt. God's steadfast love is revealed in the lives of the redeemed—those individuals and communities from all over the globe whom God has delivered from trouble. Would that we could hear their testimonies today.

PRAYER: Lord, help me to share what you have done in my life and in my family's life with others who need encouragement. Amen.

Many of us are acquainted with the extremities of hunger or thirst only through news reports or Bible studies. Yet hunger and thirst continue to be a a harsh reality for millions of the world's people. Psalm 107 chronicles a time during the Exodus wanderings when Israel unsuccessfully looked for food and water "in desert wastes."

The trials of Israel's wanderings bear an unnerving resemblance to many personal stories that you and I share with each other. Far too many times we describe ourselves as driven, hungry, unsatisfied, or even insatiable. We wander in desert wastelands; our souls faint within us. Psalm 107 raises an important question: What choices do people have when they find their backs against the wall? What did Israel choose to do when confronted with what we would call dire circumstances? The good news in today's passage is that Israel made a conscious choice to cry to the Lord for help, in spite of their defeated, depleted emotional state. The Lord responded by leading them to an inhabited place, where they could find food and water.

We also have choices to make when we feel overwhelmed by the circumstances of our lives. We can buckle under the weight of our own complaints or look to one another for anemic solutions. Or we can turn to God for help as Israel did. Though the psalmist makes no mention of the time that elapsed between their call for help and God's reply, we are offered a word of assurance in verse 43: "Let those who are wise give heed to these things, and consider the steadfast love of the LORD." In this we take comfort.

PRAYER: Lord, enable me to trust you while I wait patiently for an answer to prayer. Amen.

Where can I find God's presence? Human beings have probably wrestled with that question since the time we first became aware of the otherworldliness of God. The people in Colossae have fallen prey to several religious ideologies that cloud their understanding of Christianity's basic goals. From their local culture some have adopted a form of astrology and other doctrines of "higher knowledge." From Judaism some have imposed the ritual observances of feast days and fast days and piety. Although the lists that scholars reconstruct from the chapters of Paul's letter allude to additional theological variations, none of these satisfied the need for the fullness of God.

Perhaps the Colossians were attempting to address an issue common to us all—disorientation. We have only to look back to the initial days of Iraqi liberation to remember how disorienting it is for any people to absorb the impact of sudden and radical political change. The events that followed September 11, 2001, in the United States vividly illustrate the impact of sudden social and economic change both on a national and individual scale. Political and economic changes are traumatic. What about spiritual change?

Paul directs many of his letters to people whose moral compasses have seemingly changed overnight. Disoriented, they need a positive direction. Paul answers them clearly: Their attention does not belong on the prevailing philosophies of the day or on the less harmful tenets of the religion they once observed. Since they have been raised to life with Christ, they are to seek the things above and pursue things over which Christ presides.

Paul does not advocate the religious escapism of the heavenly minded; he advocates an entirely new orientation to daily life with Christ as the defining compass point.

PRAYER: Begin today, O Lord, to show me how to live as a child of God. Amen.

For Paul, embracing Christianity is more than a matter of understanding who Jesus is and what he has done for humanity. It is more than intellectual reasoning and understanding the scriptures. For Paul, new life in Christ implies a new lifestyle, that drastically differs from the old.

Lest there be any confusion about the new life to which the Colossians are called, Paul lists sins that should be retired along with the old lifestyle. Paul frequently listed both vices and virtues in his letters to the churches. Today's passage contains two such lists of vices spanning from sexual sins to abusive language.

Paul's language is far from genteel. The letter to the Colossians is filled with imperatives that often make us squirm: "put to death," "get rid of," and "do not lie." Yet Paul does not advocate a new kind of legalism; he instead fervently advocates letting go of attachment to vices that imprison us so that we may more fully embrace new life in Christ. Death to the old way of life is a prerequisite for Christian liberty.

If Paul were to have this kind of conversation with today's Christians, would his words bear any similarity to those spoken to the Colossians? The points of division between Christianity and other religions are not as distinct today as they were in Colossae then. To complicate matters further, many who join churches today have a difficult time identifying what, if anything, in their old lifestyle should be put to death. This raises a serious question for believers in the twenty-first century: Could there, should there, be a standard code of ethics to which all Christians give assent? If so, what would it look like?

PRAYER: Lord, it is difficult to discern the difference between legalism and loving response to the gospel. Show me how to live in this complicated world. Amen.

Asking rabbis to give opinions in disputes was a practice dating back to Moses. Perhaps the petitioner in today's scripture felt the new winds of equality blowing in Jesus' teachings. Jesus' answer in favor of dividing the inheritance would provide an opportunity to challenge existing Jewish laws that entitled the oldest male to receive a double portion of the family inheritance. More likely, the petitioner was having difficulty receiving even the one portion due him. Elder brothers were known to take more than their share—sometimes the entire inheritance! The key to Jesus' refusal to get involved in this family dispute is found in his caution to be on guard against all kinds of greed (v. 15).

Did greed motivate the man to seek what he felt was due him or did denial of his due open the door to greed? Poverty and want have a peculiar way of creating a climate for greed. Once we have been conditioned to feel deprived of anything, it is difficult for us to discern when we have enough. What begins as genuine deprivation is thus slowly transformed into an insatiable quest for an elusive objective. Even when we have a great deal, we still want more. Advertising influences us not just to have possessions but to have the *right* possessions.

Jesus' reply to the question indicates that the man's real motive is greed and not his rights. The questioner's greatest problem is not legal but spiritual. What had this situation done to his soul? When money and possessions gain access to the front seat of our attentions, God's priorities will inevitably have to take the backseat.

PRAYER: **Lord, open my eyes to things that have captured my attention so that I may redirect my gaze to the things that interest you. Amen.**

The life of a farmer is filled with toil and risk. Who can blame him for rejoicing over an abundant harvest? The harsh condemnation at the end of today's parable would be a surprise if we had not been given so many clues to its interpretation along the way.

As we look at the parable more closely, we see that the man is not a poor farmer who suddenly strikes it rich, but a rich farmer who stands to grow richer. He is already an island of wealth in a sea of poverty. The parable provides no evidence that he considers giving some of his assets to the poor or of making contributions to the charity of his choice. We only hear him contemplating early retirement, with enough laid up to avoid having to work for years. This perhaps reveals the crux of the problem. When confronted with more than he can use, the farmer focuses on himself, taking no thought for those around him.

Most of those considered poor in one country would easily be considered wealthy in several others. Yet few of us are not actively contemplating bigger barns in which to store all of our wealth. Clearly in this parable attempting to hold on to everything, taking no thought for others, does not court God's favor. The parable challenges us to discern how much is enough to draw the line between necessity and comfort and to discover how and with whom we may share our wealth. Like the rich man in the parable, we are warned to set limits for ourselves in a land of plenty and to store up God's treasure in our hearts, for this very night our life may be demanded of us.

PRAYER: Lord, help me understand where my true wealth is stored. Amen.

Paying Attention

August 2–8, 2004 • *Pete Velander*[‡]

MONDAY, AUGUST 2 • **Read Psalm 50:1-8, 22-23**

It's Monday again! Will I remember God? Or will I find myself torn apart with no one to deliver me? For many of us Monday, not Sunday, marks the beginning of things. With Monday comes the return of responsibilities and the peak of the heart-attack cycle for the week. Lifeless employment, pressure-filled school, mundane household chores, anxious financial strain, overbooked schedules, and difficult relationships seem to sit there waiting for another Monday to arrive.

Because Monday feels like the beginning of the week, I tend to organize my life and behavior based on Monday's assault, an assault that requires a specific set of coping skills. I prepare to be self-protecting, well-guarded, and impervious to pain. I will have to seize every opportunity and avoid being distracted by the needs of others if I am to survive another week.

As a person of faith, I need to reinvent my response to Monday. Rather than head into another week trying to survive it, I need deliberately to bring God with me or, more accurately, to travel with God through the week, remembering that God will set a new frame of reference for what comes my way in the days that follow. A difficult relationship offers an opportunity to be a light shining in the darkness. Financial challenges become the classroom for learning biblical stewardship, the call to life as a faith-filled servant in the world. If we remember God, God promises to deliver.

SUGGESTION FOR MEDITATION: With another day ahead, what circumstances call me to remember God with thanksgiving and to seek deliverance?

[‡]Leadership Team Leader, Logos Productions, Inc., Cannon Falls, Minnesota; member, First English Lutheran Church (ELCA).

Rules for gift-giving have always generated lively discussion in our family. Some argue that providing lists helps ensure that the gifts received will be appreciated. Others argue that a gift is more meaningful if the giver takes the time to observe and know the recipient well enough to come close to hitting the mark. Then there is the "make it or buy it" debate, again the main assumption being that the more of myself that I put into this gift, the more meaningful it will be to the receiver. Recipients of poorly made sweaters, atrocious pieces of artwork, and wobbly furniture items might argue that effort isn't everything. What we all agree on is that thoughtless gifts aren't worth much, no matter what their monetary value.

Sodom and Gomorrah suffered for their immorality in Genesis. Here in Isaiah, religious superficiality has provoked God's ire. "Your sacrifices [gifts] are meaningless because they are thoughtless and do not represent anything real going on inside you," God seems to say. The people's offerings are like the obligatory, hastily purchased greeting card or like flowers sent automatically by a gift service. Their incense and worship are like the five-minute visit to an infirm relative or like the lip service given to the importance of meaningful communication between parents and children.

God is clear about the meaning of sacrifice, creatively combining the certainty of a list with the ambiguity of leaving us to figure out the details for ourselves. Here's what God wants: "Do good, seek justice, rescue the oppressed, defend the orphan, plead for the widow" (Isa. 1:17). These are not the kinds of gifts I can send someone else to buy. I have to be involved.

SUGGESTION FOR MEDITATION: Ask God to reveal specific circumstances where you can do good, seek justice, rescue the oppressed, defend the orphan, or plead for the widow.

When I was in junior high school, I thought it would be great to be a baby-sitter, mostly because I could stay up really late and watch whatever I wanted to on TV—two things that I couldn't do if I were at home. What I discovered was that staying up late is not easy, and there's not much on TV at one in the morning to hold a seventh grader's attention (at least not back in the sixties). I can remember fighting off sleep, knowing that it was my responsibility to stay awake and be on guard while the parents of my charges were away. What a battle, to stay alert when everything around you is fading into oblivion! I was so happy when one couple said it was okay for me to fall asleep on the couch. After all, if they had been home they would be sleeping too!

Jesus' words in verses 35-38 are not about being awake or asleep literally, nor does he ask us to deprive ourselves of adequate rest. But perhaps Jesus' metaphor would have more meaning for us if he had said, "Don't go through life with 'highway hypnosis.' Be alert to what's going on around you. Be aware of opportunities to serve. Act."

A kind of numb tunnel vision sets in on our lives when we become so focused on a routine that we cannot respond in a meaningful way. Opportunities to "be" the grace of God present themselves in many ways throughout the day—helping someone who has dropped something, assisting a stranded motorist, opening a door, offering a simple word of encouragement. Zombie-like living in the TV test-pattern world of a half-sleeping baby-sitter robs life of its vitality and meaning. When fully engaged and alert, we are prepared to receive the holy in the most unexpected people and events.

PRAYER: Gracious God, help me to be truly awake to the world around me so that I might respond faithfully as your servant. Amen.

THURSDAY, AUGUST 5 • Read Luke 12:39-40

Lawrence Kohlberg's theory of moral development promotes the idea that we progress through three basic stages as we make decisions about what is right or wrong. In an oversimplified summary, the first stage has to do with punishment and pleasure. An action is deemed moral if it brings us pleasure and we are not likely to be caught. The second stage is about approval within a social order. The right action has to do with the approval of others. This stage provides the "every one else is doing it" argument. Finally, the third stage is about working out agreements with others within a framework of an internal moral compass. Morality at this stage is beyond conventional rules, oblivious either to praise or punishment. What's right is right.

The first two stages of moral development require some predictability in order to work. When will Mom and Dad get home? Are any police on this highway? What will my colleagues think? Will my spouse approve? All these questions reflect concern about when or how others will respond to our action.

In today's scripture Jesus tells us that if we knew when a thief was coming, we'd be ready to prevent the crime. By the same token, if we knew when Jesus was coming again, we could be on our best behavior at precisely the appropriate moment. But we don't know when the thief is coming or when Christ will come again. If we are to be ready, we cannot live hoping that our timing will be right or that we will be able to predict the unpredictable. Instead, we are called to live faithfully, led by an internal moral compass that means we are always ready—not perfect, but ready for the "unexpected hour."

SUGGESTION FOR MEDITATION: How do I make decisions about what is right and what is wrong? What standards do I use in different circumstances, such as relating to family members, coworkers, the government, my church? What steps could I take to mature in my moral development, helping me to be more "ready"?

"Now faith is the assurance of things hoped for, the conviction of things not seen." This passage is often read at funerals, pointing to the promised gift of eternal life we have in Jesus. However, in the list of examples the writer of Hebrews lifts up in subsequent verses to illustrate faith, none of them refers to the gift of eternal life as the immediate outcome of faith. Rather, whether Abraham journeys to a new home or fatherhood, Moses leads Israel to freedom, or Rahab risks her life to protect Israel's spies—all of them are directed by faith in their everyday choices, not just in their dying-day hopes.

The death-defying promises we have in Christ are central to the our faith. Yet living with "the assurance of things hoped for, the conviction of things not seen" can have a much broader application for us. It can mean an openness to God's leading and and a willingness to be surprised by the outcome.

We feel much more comfortable living our days in the assurance of things planned for and seen than we are in things hoped for and unseen. We prefer the predictable; and if we can't have predictable, we hedge our bets. We prefer insurance over assurance. Many of us turn to faith only when confronted with circumstances beyond our control, like death itself. When it seems that we have no choice, we lean on God's promises. We are called as Christians to turn to God as a first response, not as a last resort.

PRAYER: God of all faithfulness, open me to a faith that is as relevant to my living as it is to my dying. Amen.

The prophet addresses a nation about sin, forgiveness, obedience, rebellion, promise, and punishment, making it clear that these are God's own words. Today we hear quite a bit about forgiveness and promise in our churches, most of which are less enthusiastic in their treatment of sin, obedience, rebellion, and punishment. Perhaps such words are irrelevant for contemporary Christians, too crude for our sophisticated ears. Yet if we appropriate these words spoken to a nation and apply them to our personal lives, we may begin to see their relevance—even if we would choose to soften or alter the images.

Who among us does not feel plagued by some personal failure, a poor decision, an untrue action? Everyone can name a memory from which he or she would like to be set free. The "swords" of our time may be guilt, addiction, stress-related illness, and lost meaning, each one deadly in its own way.

The active life of faith is about renewal, the constant process of recognizing our sin, receiving forgiveness and the promise of another chance, and choosing willing obedience over reckless rebellion. Our involvement in this process engages us in living. When we check out, living in denial at best or active careless living at worst, we have chosen death.

I find few activities more satisfying than putting on a new pair of socks. With God, every day can be a new pair of socks.

PRAYER: O God, today I choose to be aware of my shortcomings so that your forgiveness might provide the beginning point of renewal in my life. Lead me into obedient, fruitful living for your name's sake. Amen.

This week we have considered ways in which we might be more attentive to God's presence and guidance: remembering God, hearing God's call for justice, remaining alert, making right choices at the prompting of God's spirit within, looking for God's direction in life as well as God's promises when we face death, and the promise of forgiveness.

As we alter the path of our living, each day becomes more holy and grace-filled. Life circumstances may not change dramatically, but our responses hold new power, possibility, and integrity. We have begun to realize, like Abraham, that while we may not know where we're going, we know that God is taking us there.

Our faith is more complete when we let our "stuff," routines, security nets slowly slip into the background like instrumental accompaniment—there but not intruding, present but not pervasive. Now we can listen as God alerts us to things hoped for and things not seen. God's desires become the dominant melody in life. And God can play music unlike any we have ever composed on our own.

For Abraham, faith meant the journey to a new homeland, parenthood at a most unlikely age, leadership born out of faithful submission, and risks that yielded unexpected results. Hebrews 11 names many other common folk who experienced uncommon lives simply by recognizing that God knows best. This is the "home" to which Abraham was led and to which we are called. We can join the cloud of witnesses who live by faith. Who knows what God has in store for us!

PRAYER: Faithful God, thank you for inviting me home into your presence and your hope for my life. In sabbath rest, may I ponder the gifts of your faithfulness. I want to be part of that cloud of witnesses who live by faith. Lead me on. Amen.

Strength from God

August 9–15, 2004 • Eleanor L. Scarlett[‡]

MONDAY, AUGUST 9 • Read Psalm 80:1-2, 18-19

This week's readings call us to discern our relationship with God. In today's reading God's people urgently cry for restoration to good grace. We, like the children of Israel, stubbornly refuse to nurture a relationship with God and then become angry at the pain and suffering we create. We no longer relate to God, yet we want and demand that the strong arms of God uphold us. Because we no longer know or wish to know our neighbors, we look over our shoulders in fear. Children die in violent ways. We long for the day when we can once again feel a peace that expresses our renewed relationship with God, and we are angry that it does not happen as soon as we cry, "Where are you, God, when we need you? Why have you turned your face from us?"

We then bargain with God, saying, "Give us life, and we will call on your name. Give us life so we may live." God, our Shepherd offers love, forgiveness, and hope and promises life, not death. If we could but focus on the image of God as shepherd, we could break down the barriers that block God's light from shining on us. "You brought a vine out of Egypt; you drove out the nations and planted it. You cleared the ground for it; it took deep root and filled the land." God's love and goodness planted in the hearts of the children of Israel remain within us today.

We sometimes refuse to admit our desire for a deepening of spiritual awakening in our lives, our need to feel the assurance of God's presence made visible in our lives and in our world. Let us ask God to walk with us and to help us live faithfully in knowledge of and with confidence in one another.

Prayer: Ever-present God, help us to walk in confidence with you, knowing that you are the source of our lives. Amen.

[‡]Ordained minister, The United Church of Canada, currently serving Saint Paul's United Church, Etobicoke, Ontario.

The household of Judah has experienced the loving warmth of God, a caring and tender gardener who plants, cares for, and protects the vines. Yet, despite God's investment, the vines produce wild grapes of pride, deception, malice, and contempt for God.

The prophet Isaiah reminds the children of Israel of God's love for them and foretells the consequences of failing to produce the good fruit their covenant relationship with God requires. Although this text was a challenge to the household of Judah, it remains relevant to us and to our world today.

The gardener not only plants the vineyard in love but even goes so far as to send God's love in human form to nurture and sustain us. But instead of embracing Christ, we cry, "Crucify him! Crucify him!" We too produce wild grapes rather than grapes of prayer and praise to God.

Consider the cries we hear in our communities. This past week a child walking home just before dusk was snatched away, brutally assaulted, and killed. We hear the outraged cry of the people for protection. We hear the cry of the working poor for a living wage and affordable housing. We hear the cry of the homeless, the hungry, the displaced. We hear cries against injustice and unrighteousness. Are the conditions that foster these cries not the result of today's wild grapes—our failure to honor our covenant relationship with God?

God, the gardener of the vineyard, encourages us to produce good grapes for the harvest. God's justice, grace, and righteousness enable us to receive Christ in our midst. Our relationship with God comes with the responsibility to bear fruit to God's glory. Let us focus on God's purpose for us and seek ways to produce the good fruit our relationship with God demands of us. Let us respond to love with love.

PRAYER: Most holy and loving God, you alone created the universe. You are gardener of our souls, in you we place our trust. Guide our path; use and protect us. In the name of your Son we pray. Amen.

The Niagara region of Ontario is one of the largest wine-growing areas of Canada; the land is fertile, the grapes sweet. They produce an especially rich-flavored ice wine. Farmers take great pride in their vineyards and work for a great harvest.

As I reflect upon this text I am drawn to the image of the vine: strong, flexible, lush. The farmers take great care to provide suitable conditions for the vine to produce grapes in abundance. They organize and arrange the vines into arbors, a place of support and nurture so that the vines produce good grapes. Just as the farmer is to the vine, so is our God to us.

God is our source and strength, organizing and supporting us into becoming persons who produce good grapes. The text challenges us and our generation when it speaks of planting choice vines in fertile soil, taking good care of them, only to receive a disappointing harvest of wild grapes.

To produce quality ice wine requires optimum conditions: favorable environment, hot summer, and an early winter freeze. God, like the farmer, plants the seeds of love in the hearts of the beloved and nurtures them in a favorable environment so that love and hope can grow. God expects the best of us from this planting and tending, yet at times we do not use our "fertile soil" to its best advantage, and we become wild grapes. As a result we live in brokenness. Weeds of despair and hopelessness choke our souls. Our spirits are parched by the absence of God's grace in our lives. When we turn from our relationship with God, we do not produce fruit that sustains and nurtures.

PRAYER: Generous God, help me to see your promise in the world you have created. May I sense your special care of me and avail myself of your nurture and care so that I may produce good grapes. Amen.

Today's writer encourages the Christian Hebrews by reminding them of heroic men and women in the past who had endured similar persecution by firm belief in a loving God. Indeed, the Christian community has Jesus himself, the leader and perfecter of their faith, to inspire their perseverance. Stories of faith enable us to find courage when we undergo trials and suffering. Remembering and retelling our stories give us strength to endure and grow in our faith.

In August 1991, my sisters, cousin, two young nephews, and I went to visit a relative in Miami. Unfortunately Hurricane Andrew also made a visit to Miami. As the house collapsed around us, we ran from room to room seeking refuge and protection from the storm. When there was no place left to run, we huddled together in the one room that offered some semblance of shelter. There we prayed and cried out to God. We felt God's guiding hand supporting and upholding us. A sense of peace surrounded us. When the storm had passed, we thanked God for sparing our lives. "By faith the people passed through the Red Sea as if it were by dry land."

Eleven years after the hurricane, the memories still haunt me; storms still frighten my nephews. We will never forget that night's events when, in our deepest and darkest hour of fear, God lifted us out of darkness into the incredible light of Christ. Paul reminded the people that God had brought their ancestors through the Red Sea as if they were walking on dry land into safety. We need to share our stories of faith with our children and grandchildren, so they can know that God will bring us safely through all of life's hurricanes.

MEDITATION: Sit quietly with your eyes closed, take deep breaths, clear your mind, and then ask yourself what you most fear at this time in your life. When you have the answer, pray, asking God to remove your fear and grant you peace. Relax, sit for a while longer, and feel God's warm embrace. When you are ready, give thanks to God for the healing grace, open your eyes, and face the world.

The race had been the constant dream of her life. She had worked hard, enduring long hours of training because she looked forward to the joy of competing. She had become the pride of her family and church community and the Olympic hope of her country. Then a car accident leaves her seriously injured, and her race for Olympic gold becomes a race for life.

The unexpected can often destroy our expectations. Have you ever felt that your entire world had just fallen apart—everything you had hoped, dreamed, and worked for is snatched away in an instant? This young Olympic hopeful heard the news, "You may never walk again."

While lying in the hospital the athlete chose not to be sorry for herself but to confront her fears with hope. She deepened her relationship with God through a daily regimen of prayer, scripture reading, and journaling. Physical therapy became her constant companion and learning to walk again her greatest challenge.

After years of therapy this former Olympic hopeful's dream has become a reality. Running in the Special Olympics, she won gold in every race. She credited her success not to her own merits but, as Paul states, "by looking to Jesus the pioneer and perfecter of our faith, who for the sake of the joy that was set before him endured the cross." Like this young woman, whenever life's struggles confront us and our dreams for gold are shattered, we can win our race if we run with courage and hope in Jesus.

PRAYER: O God, we would run every race of our lives with you, knowing that when we do, we will win. Amen.

Monday, March 26, 2001, was the darkest day of my life. That day "fire came to earth" and consumed my world. My sister, Marcia, and my six-year-old niece, Danielle, were murdered as they slept in their beds.

Jesus warns his followers that the path of discipleship will not be easy—but this? How do we go on when tragedies such as this occur? My family and I walked around as if in a daze. One day as my mother wiped tears from her face, she said, "Now I understand what it was like for Jesus as he faced his own suffering and ultimate death."

As I reflected on today's text I realized that although followers of Christ are not immune to the struggles and difficulties of this world, we are gifted with the grace of Christ to endure to the end. In the early days of intense pain, my family and I took comfort in the love of Christ expressed through neighbors, friends, and strangers—a visible sign of God's kingdom among us.

I still believe that fire had come to earth and kindled me and my family. I also believe that my baptism into the community of faith has sustained, strengthened, and given me hope during these difficult times.

December 6, the designated day to end violence against women and children, I began the incredible journey of speaking out against violence. I pray we use this text to help us rise above our difficulties and to exercise our responsibility to Christ as we embrace transformation.

PRAYER: Compassionate God, be with those who struggle with difficult family situations. Help those who walk in darkness to see your light and feel your presence. May we remember that in your hands fire can refine as well as destroy. In the name of Christ we pray. Amen.

I recently visited with a family and observed that a difference of opinion about a world situation existed. I sat and listened as both parties stated their points of view: Each was deeply consumed by the issues. I sat in awe and listened as they argued and shared their understanding of God for their lives and the world. As this couple struggled with issues of justice and peace from a faith perspective, I sensed discord and division between them. Yet their faith allowed them to remain in the same room in discussion.

Sometimes a disagreement within a family or community can become a healthy environment for those involved, allowing them to engage in lively, meaningful discussions that provide fertile ground for spiritual growth. But in today's text, Jesus has a different sort of division in mind.

The discord to which Jesus refers strikes at the foundation of the status quo. People must decide between the old order and the new, between God's rule and human rule. As Jesus' earthly ministry nears its end, the division between doubt and faith reaches a critical point. Jesus chastises those who can read the signs that foretell the weather but completely miss the signs of God's kingdom among them.

A few years ago our church was confronted with a controversial issue that created an atmosphere of healthy discussion. For the first time in many years, members and friends of the United Church of Canada were talking passionately about their faith. They had read the signs of God's reign on earth and were discerning together their place in it. They have emerged from this disagreement with a renewed spiritual hope in Christ Jesus who offers transformation to all.

PRAYER: Christ, you are the sign of God's kingdom on earth and God's kingdom yet to come. When we struggle with divisive issues, help us remember that you are with us. Grant us peace, wisdom, and understanding. May your divine presence comfort us today and always. Amen.

God within Us

August 16–22, 2004 • *Bruce A. Mitchell*[‡]

MONDAY, AUGUST 16 • **Read Jeremiah 1:4-10**

Almost fifty-five years ago my father, frustrated with my lack of a meaningful goal in life, enrolled me in a psychological testing program to determine my aptitudes and potential for the future. After almost three days of testing I received an evaluation form and a book with which to interpret the results. The book and report were quickly relegated to an attic in my parents' home.

Thirty years later, rummaging through my parents' attic, I discovered the dust-covered book and test form. Evaluating the results I found that I was, in fact, doing exactly what they had projected.

Sometimes we forget or don't recognize that God has set goals for our lives. We may not recognize the goals or respond to God's call; but from the moment of our creation, God has put within each of us the potential to be what God wants us to be.

My wife and I have a daughter who, from her earliest years, pronounced that she wanted to be a nurse. At eleven or twelve she was scheduled to have her tonsils removed. The procedure successfully completed, she was returned to her hospital room, where the surgeon asked what she had thought about the operating room. She grinned and replied, "It was just like Dr. Welby on television." (*Marcus Welby, M.D.* was a favorite weekly TV program in the sixties.) Our daughter went on to become a highly skilled nurse and has used this gift of God for many years.

Like Jeremiah, each of us has been "appointed" by God to fulfill his or her life's potential. The choice is ours—to be what God wants us to be or to go through life wondering what we might have been.

PRAYER: Lord God, remind me each day that I have been yours since the beginning of time. Amen.

[‡]Retired United Methodist pastor living in Oscoda, Michigan.

The Bible is filled with reminders of God's empowerment of the unwilling. The prophet Jeremiah is one such person.

God proclaims that Jeremiah has been appointed to be a prophet to all the nations. Jeremiah quickly protests, saying he isn't equipped to do what God has called him to do: "I do not know how to speak; I am only a child" (NIV). The same kind of rebuttal has been voiced by thousands over the years. Weakness is an argument offered even today. Yet God persists, specifying what Jeremiah is to do, a call replete with negatives: "uproot" and "tear down" (NIV), "destroy" and "overthrow."

We often are called to do things we don't like, to undertake unpleasant jobs that may involve working with disagreeable people or that may seem beyond our capability. If the truth were known, probably every one of us at one time or another in life has protested some assignment. I remember protesting having to insulate an attic in August heat. Children may balk at feeding the dog. Young people may resent having to visit relatives. Pastors occasionally feel overwhelmed about a church assignment in an unpleasant part of town or to a church known for its dissension.

We are called to recognize that God empowers us to accomplish tasks we feel incapable of doing. Following the string of negatives that began the call to Jeremiah, God adds the positive words *build* and *plant*. As with Jeremiah, God is capable of working through any person to accomplish anything God wants done.

Prayer: Eternal God, of my own power I am inadequate. With your power all things are possible. Amen.

One of the treasures of American scenery is Yellowstone National Park. For generations it has attracted people from all over the world who want to marvel at God's monumental creation. In its thousands of acres are verdant forests, rushing rivers, boiling mud pits, wildlife, and one of the greatest attractions of all, a geyser called Old Faithful. Though it isn't the largest geyser at Yellowstone, Old Faithful is one of the most predictable, erupting twenty to twenty-three times a day.

God's constancy and predictability are our Old Faithful. The tides rise and fall at regular intervals. The sun rises each morning and sets each afternoon at clearly defined times.

Throughout all time, humanity has come to rely upon God's consistent presence in all that happens. Ships leave or come into port on the tide. Farmers depend upon growing seasons. Some areas of the world depend upon a rainy season to relieve drought. All the world relies upon predictable events, even as it contends with the unpredictable.

The psalmist offers praise for the constancy of God, expressing a unique trust that God is present in every human event. Even without tangible evidence of God's existence, the psalmist expresses a personal confidence in God's presence, ready to fill the soul with an assurance of wisdom, strength, courage, compassion, and love.

PRAYER: Lord God, "you are my rock and my fortress." I place my life in your hands with confidence, relying upon your Spirit to guide all I am, say, or do. Amen.

One of the classic motion pictures of modern times is *On Golden Pond*, which gently and sensitively looks at the life of a couple nearing the end of their lives. I once saw what could have been a scene from that movie: An elderly man sat on a boat dock jutting out into a New Hampshire lake. He was well along in years and had seen tough times as well as enjoyed success. Now he sat on a lawn chair in the autumn dusk of both a day and a lifetime, reflecting on everything that had happened in his life.

Today's Bible passage reveals an individual doing somewhat the same thing as that old man. The writer of Hebrews reflects on the ministry of Moses, comparing it to the new covenant in which Jesus Christ is revealed as mediator. The earlier part of the passage emphasizes the sheer majesty of God, a God who appears so overpowering, so awesome, that one is required to stand away in fear of God. Indeed, God repeatedly warns those who approach the sacred mountain that they will suffer death if they come even closer.

But the writer of Hebrews sees God in a different light. Jesus has initiated a new relationship with God that offers hope, mercy, and grace to all who will approach God in a spirit of faith and love. We have received from God through Christ "a kingdom that cannot be shaken." Mindful of the awesome God of Moses, however, the writer of Hebrews warns us not to refuse God's grace, "for indeed our God is a consuming fire."

Perhaps the elderly man on the New Hampshire boat dock looked back at past failures. But he might also have offered a word of thanks for Jesus' assurance of a God who is approachable, loving, and rewarding.

PRAYER: Fill my heart, O Lord, with an "acceptable worship" and thanksgiving for your unshakable kingdom. Amen.

Imagine a small band of people, 120 or so, waiting on a Plymouth dock on September 6, 1620. They look at a cockleshell boat, the *Mayflower*, wondering if that frail seventy-ton vessel is strong enough to transport them from England to an unpredictable future in a new and unknown land. Two months and twenty-five hundred miles later, these people will land in Massachusetts. Our history books now call them Pilgrims.

Today we look back in amazement at the courage and faith of these Pilgrims who followed their convictions in search of religious freedom in a new land. The privations and misery they endured during their stormy voyage to the New World were the precursors of the suffering they would endure as they took up a new life in what was to become the United States.

However, the Pilgrims' faith was great, and their trust in God's ever-present power was rewarded. Indeed, as people who loved the scriptures, they could find confidence and assurance in the words from Hebrews: "Since we are receiving a kingdom that cannot be shaken, let us be thankful and so worship God acceptably with reverence and awe" (NIV).

Though their lives were touched by illness and death during that first year in Plymouth, though they had to eke out an existence in an unforgiving land, the Pilgrims never faltered in their belief that God had provided this land of freedom and that God blessed them in all they undertook. A simple faith, perhaps, but an unfaltering one as well.

PRAYER: Remind us, O Lord, that "what cannot be shaken may remain," that you are our strength in our every need. Amen.

It was a small church situated atop a Mississippi River bluff, claiming fewer than a hundred actively involved members. Moreover, the church membership represented diverse interests: a small but influential segment focused on social service and mission outreach; a second group placed its priority on traditional, evangelistic ministry. Interestingly enough, the two segments coexisted well, and the church flourished, even past the day when the pastor was caught working on Sunday.

The pastor had been assigned to the church on a part-time basis. During the week he worked in a factory in a nearby city; evenings and weekends he did the best he could to minister to the community. One Monday the word got around that the pastor and his family had been observed weeding the garden on Sunday afternoon. "Unacceptable," cried traditionalists of church polity. "Nothing wrong with that," said others. "Jesus might have done the same thing."

In the synagogue Jesus was accused of the unthinkable— doing something meaningful and helpful on a sacred day. But, in truth, isn't every day a sacred day that can be used constructively to the glory of God?

Humanity still gets bogged down in legalism and tradition. And the zucchini, potatoes, spinach, and carrots shared with others from the pastor's garden have helped fill empty stomachs. Isn't it possible that a family gathered together to appreciate God's wonderful world became stronger for their Sunday fellowship in the garden?

PRAYER: Lord, set us "free from...bondage on the sabbath day" to do what we can to make the world a better place. Amen.

The meeting was in a historic suburban church that for over a hundred years had been a mainstay within the community. Several former pastors who had served the church were major denominational leaders.

The committee coordinating the arrival of a new pastor made a point of sharing the history of this large facility. With justifiable pride, the members of the committee listed accomplishment after accomplishment recorded by the congregation over the past century.

The candidate asked, "But what ministry vision do you have for the future?" The committee's response: "We're basically happy with the way things are. This church isn't eager for a lot of radical changes."

Apprehensively the minister and family moved into the parsonage, and the new ministry began. Almost immediately the pastor reminded the lay leadership of the church that the neighborhood was changing. "We need to look at new forms of ministry, find ways to touch the lives of people in the neighborhood." The leadership group responded, "We may not be happy with declining membership, but we're happy with the way things have been. We don't want a lot of strangers in the church."

Nevertheless, the minister began visiting people in the surrounding area, and the church hosted neighborhood activities. Ethnic worship services were developed, and the church flourished. Some members left, yet the spirit of the church came alive with new energy and excitement. The joy in the old church signified the church's rebirth. The spirit of Christ provided a healing in the heart of the church and its people.

PRAYER: Eternal Father, remind us that ministry is not regulated by rules but through your Holy Spirit. Amen.

Reaching for Paradise

August 23–29, 2004 • Elizabeth M. Bounds[‡]

MONDAY, AUGUST 23 • Read Jeremiah 2:4-7

Summer is ending. Children return to school, their vacation only a memory captured in the perennial essay, "How I Spent My Summer Vacation." *Vacation* is a dream word, conjuring up for each of us a vision of paradise. Scripture portrays the longing for paradise from Eden onward. But scripture also tells us that we humans have, again and again, denied ourselves the paradise God has given us. We only need to drive by the local strip mall or reflect on the disappearing rain forests to know the truth of God's words spoken through Jeremiah: "I brought you into a plentiful land to eat its fruits and its good things. But when you entered you defiled my land, and made my heritage an abomination."

Yet this denial has borne good fruit and bad, discovery and destruction. Robert Browning captured the paradox perfectly: "A [person]'s reach should exceed his [or her] grasp, or what's a heaven for?" Reaching for paradise pulls us forward to attempt the impossible, to work to make our world a better place. But as soon as we think we know just what that paradise looks like, we are ready to destroy and kill to achieve our dreams.

The discipline of prayer and reflection can help us steer a steadier course. We can ask the question Jeremiah tells us we ignore, "Where is the LORD?" We can spend time with a God who can hold us as we pick our way through contradictions and confusions, saying, as Jesus taught us, "Your will be done, on earth as it is in heaven" (Matt. 6: 10).

SUGGESTION FOR MEDITATION: Set a timer for ten or fifteen minutes. In that time, become as still as possible, hearing only your breath moving in and out. When the timer rings, close with this prayer, "God, your will be done."

[‡]Associate Professor of Christian Ethics, Candler School of Theology, Emory University, Atlanta, Georgia; elder in the Presbyterian Church, USA.

There is no life without fresh water. Those of us who hear and read scripture in the comfort of municipal water supplies cannot have the deep, visceral sense of the truth of that statement. But Jeremiah's Hebrew audience, along with settlers past and present in desert or dry lands or in areas where the water supply is consistently contaminated, do understand the urgency of the image.

By latest estimates, some 1.3 billion people on this planet do not have access to uncontaminated water supplies; not surprisingly, polluted water is a leading cause of infectious disease in many countries. This perennial problem has worsened in recent years through increasing contamination of water supplies by industrial and agricultural chemicals. Consequently, some of the poorest nations in the world now face a double burden: As they struggle to provide citizens with microbe-free water, they must also grapple with the threat of toxic chemicals in their drinking water supplies.

And those in developed countries may come to understand the power of this image as fresh water supplies become increasingly unable to support the demands of urban life with washing machines, multiple bathrooms, and endless cars to be washed.

Beyond the immediacy of survival, clear moving water is an image across cultures for cleansing and rebirth. We step into flowing water to wash away all that harms us. Just as Jesus promised the Samaritan woman, ongoing encounter with the living God is a constant source of renewal, "a spring of water willing up to eternal life" (John 4: 14).

SUGGESTION FOR MEDITATION: **Find a place where you are near water—anything from a glass of water to a fountain to a stream. If the water is still, sit for a few minutes holding it in your gaze. If it is flowing, close your eyes and listen to the sound. Let a prayer to the God of living waters emerge.**

In every episode of the popular TV show *Touched by an Angel*, the moment comes when the angels reveal themselves to the stubborn, confused, hurting humans who are the focus of their mission. As the golden light suffuses the background, giving the angels something just short of a halo, they proclaim that "God loves you. He loves you so very, very much."

Much to my embarrassment, I usually find tears running down my cheeks at this point. How is this possible? The show is contrived; I know this scene is bound to occur. Its theology is not really mine. But there I am, sobbing, as angel Monica earnestly says, "God has always been with you." I have come to realize that I am responding to the message that Christians have responded to for a long time: God loves us, absolutely. As the psalm says, "Open your mouth wide and I will fill it....I would feed you with the finest of wheat, and with honey from the rock I would satisfy you."

Why do we find it so hard to hear these words? Most of us walk around burdened with the idea that we are not good enough. Some of us have been told this by the outside world. For example, here in the United States, children in poor neighborhoods only have to look around their dingy schools with torn books and tired teachers to know that they aren't valued. Others of us have been told by the parents we loved, "You are stupid." Burdened with self-loathing, we either turn on ourselves or spew out vengeance on others.

The news of God's unconditional love is almost unbearable. Yet its acceptance is at the heart of continued discipleship.

Prayer: Dearest God, allow me to feel and to live out your constant love. Amen.

If we could live according to these verses, our world would be a more loving and caring place. Mutual love realizes Jesus' basic command: "Love God with all your heart and your neighbor as yourself." The command is simple, but the discipline and practice are tremendously hard. We would feel what our neighbor feels, and not just the neighbor next to us but the one in prison on the other side of the city or being tortured in a distant land. Living Jesus' command would mean not only compassion ("feeling with") but also action, turning our life over to these feelings and these actions.

Since the earliest days of discipleship, most of us have known that we cannot meet the demands of Jesus' command. It takes a lot of courage to follow his example of sacrificial love. We then have some options: Give up on Christianity completely; divide up the mutual command between our personal life and our public life (it's a little easier to love those already intimate with us); leave Jesus' teachings in an ideal realm that acts as a distant check upon our actions.

Christians have tried all of these options at one time or another, but none of them quite satisfies. And perhaps that's the point. We are not supposed to be satisfied and comfortable but always engaging the questions of discipleship. Jesus' teachings and parables are rich mysteries to be explored again and again, always offering new meanings, new practices, new life. If we are fortunate, we have a community who is ready to engage them with us as the Christian way is always a way of communion, starting with the One who says, "I will never leave you or forsake you."

SUGGESTION FOR MEDITATION: Set aside thirty minutes. Spend the first five minutes listing some ways you try to live out mutual love. Then spend ten minutes writing down some ways you wish you could live out this love. Center on these wishes and spend fifteen minutes in meditative prayer, asking God's support for your journey.

FRIDAY, AUGUST 27 • Read Hebrews 13:6, 15-16

Most Tuesday nights I am in prison in a classroom with any-where from a dozen to thirty women. I mark a change of worlds as I move through the six locked gates and doors, buzzed in by two different officers. Our class is called Journeys, and we try to create a space where everyone is welcomed and valued as a child of God. Some call this kind of space church.

These women have nothing to sacrifice on this journey except praise and sharing—no offering envelopes, no extra con-tributions. But praise is given lavishly in the tradition of the widow's mite and of Mary's oil to anoint the feet of Jesus. Every time of prayer is marked by exuberant thanks to a helper Lord who has enabled another day of life, another moment of hope. And I have witnessed sacrificial sharing as women in the group have sat patiently while a member who can barely read flounders through a text or another who is far too shy to speak in a group stammers and falls silent as she tries to lead us in prayer. The fruits of praise abound as those same struggling women come to find voice and to see themselves as full and responsible members of our class.

Every Tuesday night I drive home renewed by my time with these women—strengthened by their strength, challenged by their pain. The women who start a new life while in prison have confronted what has brought them there and keep finding the strength of discipleship required to "say with confidence, 'The Lord is my helper; I will not be afraid. What can anyone do to me?'" As I drive, I ask God to give us all that confidence.

PRAYER: Helper God, walk with me in all the different valleys of shadows as I praise your name. Amen.

The author of this text knew well the murmurings and the moanings of all disciples, from his community to our own. As we listen to this Gospel in the midst of other Christians, we are encouraged to keep on living out what this new life demands. Basically the new life, as Bonhoeffer put it, is life together. While Jesus included times for solitude and rest, he generally could be found in the midst of it all—teaching, healing, and eating.

Eating together, as in today's passage, is a particularly important place for teaching by example and for embodying the table fellowship at the core of Christian practice. In Jesus' time, meals were socially ordered events, expressed through the seating arrangements. But Jesus models a way that radically challenges any law establishing social ranking and barriers: "For all who exalt themselves will be humbled, and those who humble themselves will be exalted."

Put into practice, the reversal of the exalted and the humble brings us smack up against our own social barriers. Try serving the women who have been preparing that church dinner before serving the pastor. Try having the wait staff sit down during the fund-raising banquet while the guests take their hand at table service. We may not be shocked, as were the people of Jesus' time, but we become very uneasy.

Luke's Jesus points not only to social assumptions but also to the boundaries all of us draw around ourselves: "You are not I; indeed, you are less than me because your being less than me means that I am more than you." This dangerous dynamic destroys the community and solidarity at the heart of the life of the Spirit.

SUGGESTION FOR MEDITATION: Envision a familiar social situation. What would it mean to take the lowest place?

Martin Luther King Jr. frequently remarked that 11 A.M. on Sunday was the most segregated hour of the week. Recent church studies show that little has changed. Although King spoke specifically of black and white relations in the United States, his observation points more broadly to our inability to be in community with those who are not like ourselves. In spite of Jesus' clear invitation to all and his repeated insistence on bringing to the table those who are "different," we really do not want to spend our church time with anyone but those in our own circle. We want our communities to be comforting and reassuring, our status affirmed and confirmed by approval of those who are considered "worthy."

Even when we do reach out to others, we often do not want them at our table, eating with us as equals. At the seminary where I teach, all of the first-year Master's of Divinity students are placed at a site where they work with persons who are poor, imprisoned, sick, or elderly—in other words, marginal in some way to our society. During that year, one of the hardest challenges for students is to see this assignment as a two-way relationship where the giving and receiving for both parties encourage transformation of self.

Rather than letting others affect our lives, we tend to focus on the reassuring credits that will be "repaid at the resurrection of the righteous." Jesus warned against any reliance on assumed pieties or assurances, challenging his followers to a way bound not by convention but by love of God and love of neighbor. We are not reconfirmed but changed by discipleship.

PRAYER: God, you showed us a way through the life of Jesus. Help us to long for that way and to place that longing at the center of our selves. Amen.

The Mind of God

August 30–September 5, 2004 • Jeffery W. Blum[‡]

MONDAY, AUGUST 30 • Read Jeremiah 18:1-11

As I write this, war rages in Iraq, and all sides invoke the name of God. As you read this, the lead story on the news will describe an event that challenges you to bring your faith to bear on a local, national, or international issue.

I was humbled at a lecture by Holocaust survivor Elie Wiesel's description of a burning pit of babies at Auschwitz and his words that, "All statements about God need to be made standing by that pit." I find wisdom in the understanding that God is the best thing; our experience of God is the next best thing; and the very distant third best thing is what we say about God. There is a paucity of speech and a weakness of mind that makes speaking for and about God very risky business.

Jeremiah lives in troubled times. Using metaphor and symbol, Jeremiah calls the people of his age to see how the nature of God is revealed through acts of history both great and small. Through these revelations, Jeremiah finds the direction and the courage to act according to his understanding of God's will.

We modern Jeremiahs are drowning in revelation. Jeremiah's world was limited to a few hundred square miles and a handful of cultures. We have access to an entire planet, thousands of cultures, and an expanding universe that defies understanding. Our temptation is to grab hold of a handful of "third-best things," inadequate statements about God that make us feel comfortable, to call it our faith, and to go on living our life unchallenged. Rather than God shaping us, we shape God to suit our needs.

SUGGESTION FOR MEDITATION: Consider the foundations of your faith—scripture, tradition, reason, and revelation—and discern the importance of each in your faith journey.

[‡]Director of the Campus for Human Development, a service center for homeless people, Nashville, Tennessee.

TUESDAY, AUGUST 31 • Read Psalm 139:1-6, 13-18

On a piece of paper draw a circle. Put a dot in the middle of the circle, a horizontal line two-thirds up the circle, and a small box in the top third of the circle formed by the line.

This circle is a variation on Plato's understanding of the soul. The line separates the conscious from the subconscious. The dot symbolizes what ultimately drives your life. The small box, your ego, is what you think controls your life.

Yesterday you meditated on what shapes your faith journey. For most of us, tradition, reason, and a cursory reading of scripture form that safe little box in our conscious self that anchors our social, political, and religious life. Revelation rarely fits in that box. We reject revelation as irrational thought best left to the likes of Jeremiah.

The psalmist realizes that the shortest distance to God is the journey from that little box in the conscious to that dot centered deep in our being. The box is us shaped in the image of our culture. The dot is the center of us shaped in the image of God. Understanding God is simultaneous with understanding self.

The journey of faith is a journey toward authenticity, a journey into both light and dark, strengths and weaknesses. It is understanding that strengths are gifts to share, not reasons for conceit. Weaknesses are not to be shamefully hidden but harnessed to allow compassion for others. The psalmist is painfully aware of the human condition. He also understands that God is compassionately aware of our humanity.

The psalm provides the map to this journey: "How precious to me are thy thoughts, O God" (RSV). By striving to understand and share in the mind of God through prayer, meditation, reflection, community, and action, we see ourselves as God sees us and obtain the grace to live authentically in the world.

SUGGESTION FOR MEDITATION: **Explore what it means to share in the mind of God by allowing your thoughts to be supplanted by the thoughts of God.**

Filmmaker Cecil B. DeMille has done modern religion a disservice by making the revelations of God so spectacular. Unless the seas part into great walls, rivers turn to blood, food drops from the sky, and instructions are spoken in a resonant male voice from on high, we don't recognize God at work in our lives. Though the revelations of Jeremiah would not make for great cinema, they give us an authentic understanding of God's revelation in the world.

In so simple a vessel as a clay pot, Jeremiah perceives the past, present, and future of Israel. In the way the potter works and shapes the clay with ease, Jeremiah realizes that seemingly great nations are nothing relative to the span of time and power that is God. In the way the pot weakens and collapses in the hands of the potter, Jeremiah sees the eroding effects of idolatry, opulence, and indifference that destroy the vessel from within. In the ability of the potter to form a pot of substance and utility from the ruins of the first, he finds hope that Israel can be reformed into a nation consistent with the will of God.

Whatever the challenge to our faith, if we only consider matters under the narrow constraints of our cultural box rife with subjectivity, we will surely fall victim to vested self-interest and ultimately sin. If, however, we follow the example of Jeremiah and the psalmist and assume the mind of God as we reflect on these events, we may find our "potter" who through simple acts will speak God's words of revelation, understanding, challenge, and comfort.

SUGGESTION FOR MEDITATION: **The world is never at peace. Injustice is always at work. The innocent constantly suffer. Pick a particular issue or event of concern to you and reflect on it with the mind of God.**

The single key that opens the door and allows us access into the mind of God is humility. Awash in the news of war as I am, I have heard the phrase "truth is the first casualty of war" several times. I would contend that humility is the first casualty, and lack of humility allows us to murder truth.

The shame of the world's religions is that most wars have been fought over differing opinions on the nature and the will of God. We destroy human beings made in the image of God in the name of an idol made in the image of our culture. Hubris supplants humility, and the certainty of our righteousness allows us to commit unspeakable acts.

The American Civil War was fought over a variety of issues, none more volatile than the issue of slavery. Paul's writings and his tacit approval of the relationship between Philemon and Onesimus have been construed as acceptance of slavery. We find it disconcerting that a patriarch who gave voice to the Holy Spirit was so bound by the culture of his age that he failed to recognize and speak out against an evil that is painfully obvious to later generations.

With our 20/20 hindsight, we can easily become smug about how far we have evolved in our recognition of the evil of slavery, the Holocaust, segregation, witch-hunts, and other historical events. We question how people of faith could have been involved in such cruel practices. Humility needs to replace our smug hubris as we discern the mind of God and understand the evil of our place and time that we out of ignorance or complacency allow to proliferate.

SUGGESTION FOR MEDITATION: **In 2104 your great-grandchild is going through your personal papers, pictures, magazines, and writings. What practice that you supported or failed to oppose is recognized as an obvious evil by your heir?**

Despite efforts to be egalitarian and democratic, any human endeavor eventually takes on some type of hierarchy. Depending on the situation, certain types of people will gravitate to positions of leadership and authority while others will assume positions of service to those setting the agenda. The kings and queens of an endeavor that require physical stamina and strength may become pawns in a highly cerebral activity and vice versa, but hierarchy is always operative.

The grace found in Philemon is the vision of a compassionate world despite hierarchy. Throughout this short epistle, Paul constantly juxtaposes and compares the reality of the world with the alternative reality of the kingdom. By identifying himself as both a prisoner and an ambassador, Paul simultaneously occupies both the highest and lowest rungs of the social ladder. Without apology, Paul celebrates the bond of brotherhood between Philemon, a man of some means and authority, and the slave Onesimus. While recognizing the existence of hierarchy, Paul dismisses it as irrelevant in light of the kingdom.

Culture defines differences and then assigns values to those differences that create hierarchy. At its worst, this hierarchy runs the gamut from dictator to slave. Even at its best, cultures invariably define an underclass deemed unworthy of serious consideration. Paul ignores culture, assumes the mind of God, and sees Philemon and Onesimus as God sees them: Human beings worthy of love and compassion. Though culture may need hierarchy to operate, the mind of God sees beyond the labels, titles, and organizational charts to the worth of the individual apart from cultural influences. As people of faith, we can do no less.

SUGGESTION FOR MEDITATION: **As defined by culture, who is Onesimus to you as Philemon? Who is Philemon to you as Onesimus? What would it take to go beyond the cultural barriers that separate you?**

The last temptation of Christ in Niko Kazantzakis's book by that title was the temptation to be normal: to climb down from the cross, return to Nazareth, set up a carpentry shop, wed Mary Magdalene, have children, and die of old age. The previous three temptations recorded in Matthew 4:1-11, materialism, power, and idolatry we recognize as sin. To be a good husband, father, and citizen is a virtue we aspire to, not a sin we seek to avoid.

In Kazantzakis's novel, Jesus resists temptation and embodies the words of today's scripture. How cruel of Jesus to force his mother to watch his tortured death when he could have done otherwise. How much hate did Jesus have for his own life to acquiesce to the ignominy of crucifixion? Do we really want to live our lives in this model?

The words of Jesus in Luke are harsh to our ears. Discipleship comes at great cost. As the world becomes increasingly more selfish and focused on individual pleasures, the ability to live for a greater good becomes increasingly more alien to our understanding of what it means to be human. Like the builder of the tower, the king going to war, or the rich young man in Matthew 19:16-30, we have much to lose in following Jesus.

In Luke 14:34-35 Jesus likens his followers to salt. Salt, which amounts to less than 1% of the ingredients in a recipe, can make a profound difference in the flavoring and preservation of food. Jesus' followers are called to be the spice that makes the kingdom of God manifest in the midst of the world. When we assume the mind of God, we realize that discipleship is less about salvation in the afterlife and more about ensuring the presence of love and compassion in the here and now.

SUGGESTION FOR MEDITATION: **When measured by time and commitment, where is your faith in the list of priorities in your life?**

One Monday morning while working as a chaplain at a mental hospital, my wife encountered a psychotic woman. The patient complained that her problem was the way that other people's thoughts intruded on hers. She described how my wife's thoughts about driving in the countryside, a cutting tool, and an unusually large pencil were making it difficult for her to form her own thoughts. My wife was stunned. The day before, we shopped at a yard sale while driving to her family's farm. We purchased a set of electric barber clippers and an oversized souvenir pencil of Niagara Falls.

Some may scoff at the idea of the mind working in this way, but the human mind is a compact and powerful instrument of communication yet to be duplicated by modern science. Like the woman in the story, the problem for us is harnessing its extraordinary capabilities.

Too often we use our brain as nothing more than a calculator. We calculate cause and effect, cost and benefit, assets and deficits. We embrace the Darwinian survival of the fittest and calculate what we need to ensure that we will be among the survivors. In seeking to save our lives, we most assuredly lose them.

The abacus eventually became the computer that now enables me to explore the World Wide Web. Our ancestors' simple, survival-dedicated brains have evolved into minds capable of going far beyond an understanding of our present condition to a vision of what can and should be. Being made in God's image does not mean that we share a basic body form; rather, we share in the mind of God that loves, dreams, creates, and sacrifices.

SUGGESTION FOR MEDITATION: In what ways do you use your brain? as a calculator dedicated to your own well-being? as an organ of communication that ties you to the will of God?

God Knows Our Names

September 6–12, 2004 • David Allison Becker[‡]

MONDAY, SEPTEMBER 6 • Read 1 Timothy 1:12-17

"Let's roll!" Those are the words of Todd Beamer, a passenger on Flight 93 on September 11, 2001. Beamer encouraged other passengers to challenge the hijackers as the jet headed toward Washington, D.C. The plane went down in rural Pennsylvania, perhaps averting a crash into the White House. We can more easily see in our mind's eye a modern hero like Todd Beamer than visualize an evangelist like Paul. Yet both men were champions for Christ.

Paul acknowledges his sinfulness, but through God's grace and the power of the Holy Spirit, he is ready *to roll* in service of Jesus Christ. Christ selected Paul, a bad example and a notorious sinner, and then patiently shaped him into a servant.

Paul's faith comes through in his sermons and other written correspondence to churches. We witness Beamer's faith by eavesdropping on his cell phone conversations as he garnered strength through prayer. Beamer sought the strength of his Lord and Savior, Jesus Christ, and he prayed the Lord's Prayer and the Twenty-third Psalm with a telephone operator.

In his doxology, Paul expresses gratitude to a great God. Todd Beamer, a confessing sinner and servant, availed himself of that same God on that awful day in September three years ago. A decal with an eagle and "Let's roll" is now nose art on the planes of the U.S. Air Force demonstration flying team, the Thunderbirds. It reminds us how we too can serve.

PRAYER: God, thank you for the mercy you extend in our lives. You are unconditional in your love for us, even when we are bad examples to ourselves and others. We love you, God, and pledge to go forth, strengthened and appointed in your service. In the name of Jesus Christ. Amen.

[‡]Grief counselor and chaplain; writing coach in a public high school, Pueblo, Colorado.

Luke quotes Jesus' words about repentance more than any other Gospel writer, reminding us that Jesus wants his followers to be contrite about sinning and to seek forgiveness. Jesus tells his followers to repent because being made whole is a gift.

The Pharisees do not recognize Jesus' spirit of atonement, criticizing him for hanging out with the wrong sort of people. Our Lord even breaks bread with notorious sinners in defiance of Jewish dietary laws. To Jesus, no one is undesirable, no sin unforgivable.

Today Jesus would stand in the line at the charity food kitchen talking to those gathered there, extending his hand in hospitality, and asking why they are unemployed or homeless. Jesus would not embarrass folks by asking questions about the needle marks on their arms, evidence perhaps of their having traded blood for spending money. Rather, he would ask their names and spend time listening to their sacred stories. Sacred stories? Yes. God absolves our sins and calls us to bring the gospel message to others by word and deed.

My friend Jim, a busy plumbing contractor, made a lot of money in real estate and was a good steward of his resources. When the local charity food kitchen could not find an affordable place to build, Jim donated a piece of property. It was a controversial gift in the local community because the surrounding businesses did not want "those types of people" around. Like Jesus, Jim realized that no people are undesirable. He wanted "those types of people" to be part of a caring community. Jim also volunteered in the soup kitchen because he wanted to know their names and to hear their sacred stories.

PRAYER: God, you know us by name. We come as sinners, humble in our petitions for forgiveness. Help us to share your joy "over one sinner who repents than over ninety-nine righteous persons who need no repentance." Amen.

When we have trouble interpreting a portion of scripture, we might look at the passages that precede and follow it. The passages on either side (Luke 15:1-7, 11-25) of today's reading are stories of lost sinners returning to the fold. Luke 15:8-10 concentrates not on *what* is lost but on *how* the Pharisees may search with their own hearts. Instead of dealing with the lost sheep or the lost son as he did in the preceding and subsequent passages, Jesus uses a possession more valuable to the Pharisees—money. When they grumble about Jesus' hospitality toward sinners, he asks the Pharisees how hard they would search for a lost coin.

In *The Preaching Life*, Barbara Brown Taylor says that these parables of Jesus are an open invitation to be good shepherds alongside him in the world. "Repentance is not the issue, but rejoicing; the plot is not about amending our evil ways but about seeking, sweeping, finding, rejoicing. The invitation is not about being rescued by Jesus over and over again, but about joining him... in recovering God's treasure." The lost coin, says Taylor, is a story of "discovering the joy of finding."

God knows each of us by name and calls us to be searchers for sinners lost in the kingdom, not self-righteous judges like the Pharisees. Our attitude and persistence in this search brings us "the joy of finding." Jesus rebukes those who judge others and praises those who journey in search of others, holding us to a higher standard as accountable stewards. As Christians we are both shepherds and seekers who know the good news and pass it on to others. Through us Jesus offers unconditional hospitality to the lost.

PRAYER: God, we lift up to you our lost brothers and sisters. Help us share the good news of Jesus Christ. Guide us as we make folks feel your love and joy at their homecoming. No one of us is insignificant to you. Amen.

God scolds the people who have chosen rebellion over obedience. "My people are foolish…they are stupid children….They are skilled in doing evil." Relating divine anger through Jeremiah, God invites the people to see the desolation their evil will bring on them.

Jeremiah's harsh prophecy reminds us of the family who received an unsigned Western Union telegram: "Trouble coming. Details to follow." Unsigned messages of an unknown fate paralyze us.

This week we solemnize the terrorist attacks on the World Trade Center thirty-six months ago. A short period of time after the airplanes hit the Center, folks trapped in the buildings prayed even as they lived their last moments in ambiguity. Families and friends received telephone calls from loved ones caught in the carnage who had the presence of mind to call to convey messages of affection and contrition. Facing an unknown fate, the doomed victims prayed and delivered messages of love and hope. Then the buildings collapsed.

It is never too late to turn toward God to seek sanctuary from the devastation of the world. Even in the stark destruction foretold by Jeremiah, God is still one sincere prayer away from forgiving the people. God will not desert us, for our doom is God's anguish. God knows us by name and prepares the way so that we may focus our energies on doing good. We hear the message of hope more clearly when we turn from evil and pay attention to God.

PRAYER: God, help us to hear your word and to understand your sorrow when we "have no understanding." Amen.

The psalmist rages against godless people, the evil and wicked in the world who know God but refuse to acknowledge God. The evildoers "shall be in great terror, for God is with the company of the righteous."

Morris Dees, founder of the Southern Poverty Law Center (SPLC) in Montgomery, Alabama, is an advocate for poor people living on the margins of society. When members of the Aryan Nation persecuted minorities, Dees collected significant financial damages against them. When Negroes suffered hate crimes at the hands of the Ku Klux Klan in the American South, Dees collected huge financial judgments, and the victims' families acquired the real estate of culpable Klan members.

God provides *refuge* for noble people. "When the Lord restores the fortunes of his people," there will be rejoicing. People of God oppose those who promulgate evil. Dees is a role model for those who emulate Jesus, helping the oppressed in the world.

On September 10, 2001, the eve of the terrorist attacks in Washington, D.C and New York City, Dees lectured at Texas Christian University. He told those gathered that it is easy to hate people we do not know, outlining a preemptive strike against evil by teaching tolerance to schoolchildren.

It is easy to forget history's lessons about hatred. In front of the SPLC offices in Montgomery is a civil rights memorial that lists the names of men and women who died in pursuit of justice. God knows their names, and it is important that Christians do too.

PRAYER: God, I cannot pursue justice as Morris Dees can, but I can be more tolerant. I cannot preach as Billy Graham can, but I can be a role model and love my neighbor. I cannot write as the psalmist did, but I can serve you by sharing the gospel one-on-one with my friends and family. Amen.

God is angry with the people and prepared to render judgment against them. God wants the people to acknowledge their wicked behavior. Jeremiah uses the image of turbulent desert winds as a metaphor for the shattering events needed to grab human attention. Sometimes only the shock of cataclysmic events turns our eyes toward God. The storm is God's last recourse.

Perhaps it takes an event like the terrorism of September 11, 2001, to shake us into prayer. Violent storms invade the lives of both righteous and unrighteous people. No one escapes them. Some storms God creates; others God allows. All can be, as for Jeremiah, hot winds to judge us and to call us to obedience to God—the only rite of purification we have. Yet even in the storms, God stands with us.

In crisis, Christians receive wisdom through scripture and prayer in three ways. First, we transcend the tumult of the worldly crisis as we find refuge in God. Second, we become instruments of peace as agents of a loving God in the world. Third, we fight against evil in the world, modeling the unconditional love that God showed us, even as we sinned.

God calls us to prepare ourselves to fight evil even before we confront it. On the first page of my study Bible is a quote from Rev. Phillips Brooks, a nineteenth-century American pastor: "Some day, in years to come, you will be wrestling with the great temptation, or trembling under the great sorrow of your life. But the real struggle is here, now, in these quiet weeks. Now it is being decided whether, in the day of your supreme sorrow or temptation, you shall miserably fail or gloriously conquer. Character cannot be made except by a steady, long-continued process." Seeking God's guidance prepares Christians for the ferocious winds of life.

PRAYER: God, help us build character by listening for your voice and turning our backs on evil. We rely on you and look to you for guidance in our lives. Amen.

How many times do we read this passage and focus on the sheep? Jesus wants Christians to model their lives after the shepherd. He calls us to leave the security of our daily lives to search for those who are lost.

Jesus asks, "Which one of you…[will not] go after the one that is lost until he finds it?" After the World Trade Center terrorist attacks, most bodies were never recovered. Yet God knew each person by name. Each individual, each soul and spirit, has value to God in the kingdom. God knows who is lost and, like the shepherd, raises us "on his shoulders and rejoices."

Exemplary of the shepherds that day at the World Trade Center was a Franciscan friar, chaplain Mychal Judge, who counseled firefighters, a tough crew tested by danger everyday. He delivered the gospel message, reminding them that their power came from God. Father Mychal was the first casualty in the World Trade Center attack, crushed by a victim who had jumped from one of the burning buildings.

The firefighters who found Father Mychal's body removed his fire helmet and later delivered it to Pope John Paul II at the Vatican. Folded neatly inside the brim of the helmet was a prayer, now known as Mychal's Prayer:

> Lord, take me where You want me to go;
> Let me meet whom You want me to meet;
> Tell me what You want me to say, and
> Keep me out of your way.

PRAYER: God, we are humbled by the service of the shepherds who love you. Thank you for knowing our names and searching for us when we are lost. We can learn from the lives of people like Mychal Judge, who knows the joy of being with you today. Amen.

Now is the time to order your copy of

The Upper Room Disciplines 2005

Published for over 40 years, *Disciplines* continues to grow in its appeal to Christians who, like you, desire a more disciplined spiritual life based on scripture.

Enlarged-print edition available

THE UPPER ROOM DISCIPLINES 2005

Regular edition (product #9869):
$11.00 each; 10 or more copies $9.35 each

Enlarged-print edition (product #9870):
$14.00 each; 10 or more copies $11.90 each

God's Justice and Love

September 13–19, 2004 • Sharon Hels[‡]

MONDAY, SEPTEMBER 13 • Read Jeremiah 8:18–9:1

The prophetic world is rife with pairs of opposites. Either Israel is righteous or she is wicked; either she observes the covenantal obligations or she breaks them; either she repents or she will die. These extremes echo with the living prophets' fervor. Their spoken word is the active presence of God, the linguistic expression of God's power and authority.

Today's passage levels a dreadful divine accusation against Israel: Israel has ignored the covenant and worshiped false gods; punishment will come in an attack from the north. Jeremiah is right; this disaster will take place, and Jerusalem will be destroyed. Yet he takes no satisfaction in knowing God's plan but rather utters a wail of grief for his people. Jeremiah's laments are matched in other prophetic books by God's own cries of remorse and grief over the judgment against Israel. Yet amid the promise of punishment and destruction is God's endless yearning for reconciliation. The prophetic voice, given to absolutes, is always dedicated to justice, change, repentance, and starting over, no matter how small the start.

This ancient tradition refreshes our vision of the gospel today. In calling Jesus prophet, we honor a vocation that communicates God's desire for justice and mercy in human society. Pledging to listen to God's word as a guide to our spiritual health, we acknowledge that prophetic closeness to God is nonetheless no guarantee of comfort or security. And we understand that the awareness of God's purifying love in our daily lives brings about compassion toward our neighbors.

PRAYER: O Lord, may we listen to the prophets among us and effect change as we need to for the sake of freedom and justice in our community. Amen.

[‡]Layperson, freelance writer; teacher of Hebrew Scriptures, on faculty of Stillpoint, Nashville, Tennessee; member, Christ Cathedral.

This psalm considers the loss of the irreplaceable. God's holy Temple has been plundered by enemies and destroyed. The pragmatic might point out that another building can be constructed on top of the ruins (as it eventually was). But Solomon's Temple is a point of contact between heaven and earth, where God's presence is especially concentrated, emanating in concentric circles into the city, the region, and all the people who live there. This Temple can never be restored.

Now enemies have destroyed this house of God. God's faithful people have been slaughtered and left unburied. Onlookers have offered only mockery and insult.

Though the psalmist implores God's mercy in this disaster, a disabling fear must be acknowledged: What does this event mean? Is God angry with us? Did we deserve this punishment? Against this sickening possibility, the psalmist returns to the intimacy of the relationship between God and Israel. God's nature is compassionate, responding to cries of trouble with salvation as has been true from the time the people were slaves in Egypt.

When the towers of the World Trade Center in New York were destroyed on September 11, 2001, many of us had our first taste of the bitterness of war. Though we were consoled by the outpouring of kindness and sympathy from foreign nations who helped us grieve our loss, we also saw media reports of foreign people dancing in celebration at the success of the attacks.

Every disaster challenges the quality of our relationship with God. It is not enough to say that time heals all wounds. Like the psalmist we pray that in God's presence we will learn what the disaster means and find some truth that will bring us closer to the peace we seek.

PRAYER: O God of truth and goodness, hear my cries of pain and sadness and love me in my weakness! Show me compassion, and teach me compassion, until your will is my will. Amen.

The author of Psalm 79 shares a trait with the writer of several other psalms in begging God to punish Israel's enemies. The terms of this vengeance are not spelled out as they are in Psalm 137, where the faithful are incited to kill the children of their conquerors. But there is no denying that the fabric of this psalm contains both the fear that this disaster is the people's fault and a hatred of the enemy.

Anger has few official outlets in the Christian tradition, yet the psalmist accepts righteous anger as the appropriate response to the insult, dishonor, and diminishment of war. Like her neighbors, Israel's was an honor- and shame-based culture. Events either built up power and reputation or detracted from them. To be conquered by enemies was to be mocked, humiliated, and isolated on a grand scale. Those who die in this way also die to memory; it is as if they had never lived.

Because God's honor is deeply rooted in the fortunes of God's people, the psalmist cannot imagine that God is not deeply offended by this affront and will want to retaliate for the humiliation that God and God's people have endured: "Pour out your anger on the nations that do not know you, and on the kingdoms that do not call on your name."

The Christian tradition often represents itself as entirely peace-loving, with a personal ethic of forgiveness and a preference for "meekness." But the Christian tradition also reflects an intense interest in God's work of justice on earth. Perhaps we would do well to express our anger more freely in God's presence, as the psalmist does, and in that confession feel our anger dissipate as God's healing love surrounds us. There is always a chance that praying for God to exercise dreams of vengeance makes them that much likelier to be carried out as God's own errand. From this distortion, may God protect us.

PRAYER: O Lord, let the seeds of anger in me be converted by your love; and if there is any hatred in me, by your mercy root it out! Amen.

Several centuries after Jeremiah prophesied and the psalmist lamented, a traveling religious preacher wrote a letter to a young protégé. In reading this text, we find ourselves in another time and place and in an emerging new religious faith. The time is the first century; the place, Ephesus in the Roman province of Asia. The emerging religion is Christianity. Paul tells Timothy, "I urge that supplications, prayers, intercessions, and thanksgiving be made for everyone." These words of simple instruction for the early Christians and for Christians today offer a fair and inclusive approach to prayer.

Paul's authority to command Timothy in such a weighty matter is rooted in the spiritual nature of their relationship. In the first chapter of the letter, Paul explains, "I am giving you these instructions, Timothy, my child, in accordance with the prophecies made earlier about you" (1:18). How do instructions relate to prophecies? In the ancient tradition, the vocational call included a commission to service; the appearance of God resulted in a sending forth. Paul reminds Timothy of the prophecy, or "call," of Timothy's ordination, when in the presence of God he was commissioned to "fight the good fight, having faith and good conscience" (1:18-19).

Paul has had a similar experience of God's presence and commission to service that has reshaped his very being, giving him a sense of gratitude and willingness to be used as an instrument for God's good purposes. On that basis, Paul uses his authority to instruct Timothy concerning prayer.

Timothy's response to Paul is not recorded, but we may believe that he came to understand with Paul that he had been "appointed a herald" of the "one God." We may pause to consider the reorienting experience of God's grace in our own lives and how it ties us to others in love and service.

PRAYER: God of grace, send us mentors to help us grow in grace! Give them authority based on your love. Make us faithful spiritual guides to others. In Jesus' name we pray. Amen.

Running a household well is a bit of a lost art these days. The thankless, repetitive tasks that go into housekeeping seem to offer little in the way of satisfaction, let alone achievement or fulfilled selfhood. Glossy magazines feature a domestic perfectionism that few of us can imagine. Most of us live in a world of daily rituals, with the modest goal of safety and comfort at the end of the day.

Paul's message to Timothy relates to the ordering of the spiritual life of the household of believers. Because the early church consisted of congregations that met in people's homes, the proper running of a household provided a powerful image for thinking about the faith.

Like all household tasks, the work of supplication, prayer, intercession, and thanksgiving is never complete. But daily prayer routine does add up to something. To love on a daily basis as God loves, inclusively and without barriers, and to love as Christ, who gave his life for the salvation of all people, leads to "a quiet and peaceable life in all godliness and dignity." What better basis for running a household?

As members of God's household, we all belong in the shelter of God's love and protection. If we commit first to emulating God's universal love in the daily devotions of our prayer life, then we have grasped the most important part of the life of faith. Our prayer quietly and without fanfare tends to God's purposes on earth, sanctifying all who practice it.

Prayer: Lord God, make us faithful in small things, so that our lives add up to a witness of your unchanging love for all. In Christ we pray. Amen.

Our text today may strike us as a tough nut to crack. Yet in some ways, the story of the dishonest steward is a striking echo of the story of the prodigal. Both stories feature men who break faith with their households, carefully devise a plan to overcome their desperate situation, and have the disconcerting experience of indulgence from the person they had most gravely wronged. In one story the relationship with the father is restored; in the other, the relationship with the rich man is fully severed.

Throughout the Gospel, Luke stresses the proper use of money, so that the reader clearly understands that the dishonesty of the steward has nothing to commend it. In this parable money is not the end in itself. That the steward has the wit to use money for other purposes is a little closer to the mark. Notice also throughout religious documents that wisdom accompanies the skill and ability to get things done. Shrewdness, like cleverness, may be admired and respected on its own merit, regardless of its moral context.

The rich man, who rightfully dismisses his dishonest manager but does so with a concession to the man's cleverness, is not the same spiritual figure as the father who runs down the road to embrace his repentant son. But might we garner truth from rough stories and unsympathetic characters? This story, given the force of the dilemma and the adaptability of the characters, may say to Christians, in an unmistakable way: *Wake up and deal with your life.* Use the strength God gives you to bring a difficult situation to closure; do not allow the power or resources of another person to become an obstacle in your path. Could Jesus have considered this meaning? Let us think of him as he appears in the Gospel of Luke, telling this story as he makes his way toward Jerusalem to meet his own fate.

PRAYER: O Lord, life in your service is not always pleasant or easy. Add your grace to our efforts to fulfill our responsibilities in this life. Amen.

SUNDAY, SEPTEMBER 19 • **Read Luke 16:8b-13**

The church's attempts to make sense of the parable of the dishonest steward begin immediately, even abruptly, in a series of wise sayings that follow the story. Granting the dishonest steward's ingenuity, the writer observes somewhat defensively in verse 8 that the "children of light" or pious people are often less capable and clever than the "children of this age" or ambitious, sophisticated people. Verse 9 allegorizes the crafty behavior of the dishonest steward: This story really teaches us that Christians should use money wisely to be welcomed into "spiritual" homes.

The proverbs in verses 10-13 are more substantial and grow in depth when applied to personal experience. The first proverb relates to the nature of faithfulness, which is the essence of stewardship in all its forms. All who handle the assets of others must learn the lesson of faithfulness in stewardship; the proverb implies that nothing else really matters.

The second, more complicated saying adds an edge to the reflection about the wise use of money. We begin with the relationship between a master and a slave. The nature of slavery requires complete obedience to a master; there can be only one. Once we accept this understanding, we are prepared for the insight of the analogy that service to God and service to Mammon are incompatible.

This is the most successful application of the parable of the dishonest steward. Whether we approve of his actions or not, the steward who once stole from his master eventually saw that he had to use money as a means, not an end. Serving Mammon, or greed, prevents this. Beginning with a flaw in perception, it can become the lens through which we see the world. Unchecked materialism is a masquerade of human life; service to God is human life in its fullness.

PRAYER: Loving God, our lives are yours, and we only manage them. Make us faithful in small things, and give us grace to resist unfaithfulness in all its forms. Amen.

God's Provision, Our Trust

September 20–26, 2004 • *Kenneth C. Ulmer*[‡]

MONDAY, SEPTEMBER 20 • Read 1 Timothy 6:6

What does it take to satisfy you? If the word of God is timeless and universal (and it is) regardless of your place in life, this question is relevant to you. Are you content with your station in life? Paul says godliness with contentment is great gain, yet we should not misunderstand Paul. Contentment is not a life of "just making do" or of compromise.

The word *contentment* is only used one other time in scripture. In 2 Corinthians 9:8 Paul declares that it is God who gives us something to give, a grace that produces "all sufficiency in all things." The word *sufficiency* is the same word for contentment in today's scripture. Here, then, is the key to contentment: confidence in the love, provision, and grace of God.

Contentment recognizes that the grace of God always leads us to God's best. It is sufficiency in the knowledge that God's grace is with us where we are now and knows where we ought to be. In stable reliance and dependence on the God of grace, we can make it through today knowing God has already prepared for tomorrow. We can still dream big dreams and look forward to the sunshine after any storm.

PRAYER: God, help me to rely on your provision and guidance, to trust you today to handle my tomorrow. Amen.

[‡]Board of trustees, The King's College and Seminary; senior pastor and teacher, Faithful Senior Bible Church, Los Angeles, California.

Paul compares a life of wandering with a life of pursuit. Many would immediately ask, Why is it either or? Why can't I have both? Coupled with the revelation of Christ we learn that it is possible to "have" both but not "serve" both.

Contrary to what you may have heard, money is not the root of all evil. The *love* of money is the soil out of which the idolatry of materialism grows. Godliness is about the practical display of the character of God, who owns the cattle on a thousand hills and the gold and silver in the hills. It is learning to live life in relationship with the God who says it is better to give than to receive. Life more abundant is the overflow of the character and nature of Christ through our lives into the lives of others.

God promises to bless the faithful who walk in righteousness, yet it is clear in scripture that the essence of that blessing is not financial and material reward. God's ultimate interest is always the interior and spiritual rather than the exterior and visible. Material and financial prosperity is not the ultimate gauge of spirituality. Too often we measure our walk with the Lord by the size of our bank accounts, cars, houses, and diamonds, diminishing the honor and character of God and producing an arrogance that is antithetical to the character of Christ.

The psalmist says one of the products of godliness is prosperity (Psalm 1). Those who walk with the Lord are expected to bring forth godly fruit and to prosper. This prosperity includes, but is not limited to, material success. We are to be as prosperous as God intends, living a productive life of labor and trusting God to bless us. Our obligation is to be content with what God ordains and to honor God with the full measure of our blessings.

Prayer: God, help me always to live my life with a focus on the Blesser beyond the blessing. Amen.

My mother always had a couple of responses when asked for her advice or opinion on matters: "Now, I didn't call you; you called me" or "Now, you asked, so I'm going to tell you." Jeremiah, the prophet of God, has been beaten and locked up for speaking the prophetic revelation he received from God. During his imprisonment, described in detail in chapter 37, Jeremiah is summoned by King Zedekiah who asks, "Is there any word from the Lord?" (Jer. 37:17). My mother would have said, "Now, I didn't call you; you called me. If you really want to know...."

The king does not want to hear a sermon or a cute little speech with three points and a poem. He wants a word from the Lord. And in the midst of a world of turmoil and confusion, Jeremiah's word is a hard one. Even though his freedom and apparently even his life are on the line, he does not compromise the word of God or back down from the word that caused him to be imprisoned in the first place. He stands on the word, even though it has endangered his life.

How far will you go to declare the truth of God? What word are you withholding because of your fear of the response it might elicit? What truth have you shied from speaking because of your fear of criticism or retribution? Jeremiah has not forgotten God's call to him: "You must go to everyone I send you to and say whatever I command you. Do not be afraid of them, for I am with you and will rescue you" (Jer. 1:7-8, NIV). God has placed a word in us, a word to confront, challenge, and change the lives of others. Let no circumstances imprison that word. The question still echoes today: "Is there any word from the Lord?"

PRAYER: God, place your word in me, and give me the courage to speak it. Amen.

Sometimes faith means acting on a holy hunch. When we sense God has told us to something, without equivocal evidence or logical substantiation, we do it. It may look silly, and few may understand it, but we put ourselves on the line. When God calls us to do the extraordinary, we walk by faith and not by sight.

We are in good company. Try talking to a burning bush. Try walking over a path a dozen times in silence with nothing happening. Try going to war against a giant with a slingshot. Sometimes the sovereign signals of the Savior seem silly!

God tells Jeremiah to do something that by all accounts is silly—to buy a field. The field is in the hands of the Babylonians; Jeremiah is in prison; the nation is in captivity. Yet God says buy it. To many the field must seem worthless, and perhaps many laugh, criticize, or make fun of Jeremiah. But God says buy it.

What is God calling you to do that seems ridiculous? When you are finished identifying every reason why you should not do it—God still says buy it. Faith can see what others cannot see, can trust God no matter how unreasonable God's instructions may seem. You do it because God told you. You live a holy life because God told you. You trust God to meet all your needs because God told you.

True faith means obeying God when it doesn't make sense and when others can't understand it. Though we open ourselves to criticism and run the risk of being misunderstood, we do God's will simply because God says do it.

What are you willing to risk? What are you willing to release? What are you willing to do—just because God says do it?

PRAYER: God, what are you calling me to do that seems ridiculous? Help me to trust and obey. Amen.

Few would doubt that the appearance of a man who has been dead and buried is a miracle. Seeing or hearing the testimony of a dead man would seem to be convincing evidence of the benefit of salvation and the perpetual hazards of eternal separation from God. In this parable, however, Abraham counters the argument raised by the rich man that the miracle of a resurrection would be enough to convince his brothers not to come to hell.

The church has produced a generation that is miracle hungry. We flock in droves from one meeting to another, from one crusade to another, from one telecast to another to participate vicariously in healings, deliverances, and spectacular manifestations. But this parable of Jesus reveals that at best the miraculous conveys minimal salvific value. Salvation comes by the proclamation of the gospel truth rather than by the frightening or surprising manifestation of a miracle. Miracles neither save us nor deepen our spiritual growth.

We have only to trace the footsteps of Israel to discover that people don't grow through miracles. The history of Israel is an almost tragically comedic back-and-forth between miraculous revelation and carnal retreat. After manifestations of the miraculous power of God, the Israelites seem to desire a return to the bondage of their old life in Egypt. Though the ministry of Jesus did indeed include miraculous acts, we should be careful to put miracles in their proper perspective. Paul, in fact, does not include miracles as a source of building our faith but clearly declares that our faith comes by the word of God (Rom. 10:17).

Do we want miracles or spiritual maturity? May we desire the majestic face of God over the miracle-working hand of God.

PRAYER: God, help me to seek maturity in my faith rather than miracles. Impress me with your power, and improve me through your gospel. Amen.

R*efuge* is a favorite word of the psalmist. Over a dozen times the Psalms refer to God as a refuge. In today's text, the psalmist speaks of a life that "dwells in" and "abides under" the Lord, suggesting an unbroken continuity and ongoing inhabiting. The word for "abide" refers to a lodging place, while dwelling emphasizes the process or activity of getting to the place. This person actively and continually inhabits a place that could by nature be a temporary dwelling place.

In a context that could naturally and so easily result in murmuring, rebellion, or complaining, the psalmist speaks of a life lived with intentionality in the permanent residence of a relationship with the Almighty. With a confident spirit the psalmist declares the Lord is "my refuge and my fortress; my God in whom I trust."

The nation of Israel designated six cities of refuge as places of protection for a person who had accidentally taken someone's life and was in danger of the revenge of the victim's survivors. In these cities of refuge a person could await a time of vindication. Otherwise, the person's life was in peril.

Where do you go when you are in trouble? Where do you run when you have messed up? Where do you find comfort and refuge? Praise the name of Jesus. He's our refuge, our fortress. He's our deliverer and in him shall we trust.

Faith and trust in God, our city of refuge, pulls us through the difficult times of life when we are in trouble, under attack, confused, or in danger. With the psalmist we declare our faith in the deliverance and protection of God, and the victory that is only in God.

Prayer: God, when I am in trouble help me to trust in you—my refuge, my fortress, my deliverer. Amen.

An interesting dialogue takes place in Psalm 91. The psalmist says he will address the Lord and declare, "God is my 'refuge and my fortress; my God, in whom I trust.'" Later in the song, God responds, "He will call on me and I will answer him; I will be with him in trouble." God is our refuge, the place and person to whom we go when we find ourselves in trouble. Adam and Eve missed that truth. When they got into trouble they tried to get away from God. But the psalmist says when we are in trouble, we should run to God!

Being in trouble from a biblical perspective is an interesting concept. The Hebrew word for "trouble" refers to anything that is narrow or confining, a situation that makes us feel things are closing in on us. Trouble is when we can't figure out how to get out of the tight place, when we don't have room to function according to God's will for our life. Trouble has us hemmed in.

In times like these the psalmist runs to the God of refuge. In Psalm 34 David says he called out to God and God heard him and "saved him out of all his troubles." The word for "save" used here is *yâsha*, meaning to be open, wide, and free or to have space. In other words, to be saved out of trouble means to be given room or space to move. When we are in trouble and go to God as our refuge, we are given room to glorify God while we are still in the tight, troubled place. When God delivers us out of that tight place, we become an example of God's delivering, saving power.

PRAYER: God, deliver me from the tight, troubled places of my life, and help me run to your refuge. Amen.

Living the Lord's Song

September 27–October 3, 2004 • Leontine T. C. Kelly[‡]

MONDAY, SEPTEMBER 27 • Read Lamentations 1:1-6

When the Israelites are taken captive to Babylon, they remember the majesty of the great city Jerusalem. The city now stands alone, "for no one comes to the festivals." Even the priests of the former great Temple groan. Lament in Babylon is the order of the day. God's "chosen ones" understand that the Lord has made Zion suffer for the multitude of her transgressions. Though God had been faithful and Zion had become a great nation, the people failed to understand the sovereignty of a just God who would call them to accountability for their own apostasy and injustices.

Early in the Exodus experience, from slavery in Egypt to freedom, the people had melted down their gold jewelry to mold an idol. They had cut God down to *their* expectations, *their* agendas, and *their* size, wanting a God whom they could shape, handle, control.

Too often in our own lives we behave much like the Israelites, raising in the midst of sorrow our own lament: "Dear God! How could you let this happen?" When individual lament becomes community lament against the action of a just God, we are called to confession. Pardon and forgiveness come through Jesus Christ. Praise the Lord!

PRAYER: "Merciful God, we confess that we have not loved you with our whole heart. We have failed to be an obedient church, we have not done your will, we have broken your law, we have rebelled against your love, we have not loved our neighbors, and we have not heard the cry of the needy. Free us for joyful obedience, through Jesus Christ our Lord. Amen." (*The United Methodist Hymnal*, Service of Word and Table II, 12)

[‡]Retired bishop, The United Methodist Church, San Mateo, California.

In a ceremony of mourning over the destruction of Jerusalem, the Hebrew exiles gather on the banks of the irrigation canals that bring the waters of the Euphrates to fields of the city. When asked to sing their songs, they are overwhelmed by frustration and grief. For them the Lord's song belongs to a Temple that is no more. "How could we sing the LORD's song in a strange land?"

I was quite young when I heard my father preach from this text, but I was old enough to understand his application of this community lament of the ancient Hebrews to American slavery. Eight of us growing up in a Methodist parsonage knew who we were: not merely preacher's kids but children of God, as were all people. The discriminatory laws of the city and racist attitudes even within the church did not diminish our understanding of who God, through Jesus Christ, is.

I was too young to understand the theological concept of God's sovereignty, but I understood and sang,

> So high, you can't get over it,
> so low, you can't get under it,
> so wide, you can't go 'round it,
> you gotta come in at the door.

We always knew who "the door" was. The total community nurtured our faith in Jesus Christ. We acknowledged that we could not make it without the church of Jesus Christ, nor could the church make it without us.

God not only wants us to trust God, but God risks trusting us! How do Christians sing the Lord's song in this strange world today?

PRAYER: Dear Lord, help us to live your song in such harmony that the world will believe us! Amen.

I do not recall Papa's entire sermon, but I remember him clapping his hands and saying, "We have to sing the Lord's song in this strange land!" What other song was worth singing? We tried the blues; and while that is still a part of our heritage, there was no hope for us there. We tried ragtime; we could dance to its rhythm, but there was no solace for our souls there. Only when we understood God's love for us in Jesus Christ did the song, the Lord's song, come to us in a profound and positive manner.

How do we sing the Lord's song today? What do we know as the Lord's song? Do we remember the great deeds of God, as Psalm 137 suggests, in our lives and throughout history even when we sit beside the symbolic rivers of Babylon today? Do we remember in joy and peace? Or do we remember and find within us the anger that erupts from verse 9?

The martial tone of our culture today does not fit the expectation of justice and peace in God's reign. The anger we meet each day does not fit with the power of God's grace. We are called to be instruments of God's peace. Even in the long times of waiting, God invites us to remember that we follow God's agenda rather than our own.

We do not know how the captives responded to their Babylonian tormentors. We know the stories of many others who, despite torment, continued to sing the Lord's song. I remember Nelson Mandela, imprisoned nearly thirty years in South Africa. When released, Mandela came not in bitterness but as a seeker of justice. I remember those who worked for equality and civil rights in the days of segregation. They sought justice, and they could sing! How will you sing the Lord's song by the rivers of Babylon?

PRAYER: Creator God, with Jesus Christ we have come to know that no place is strange to you. Empower us by your Spirit to live and to sing your song in all places. Amen.

A lonely, imprisoned Paul writes from Rome to his "child" Timothy. He wants to talk with Timothy about the persecution of the Christian churches under the emperor Nero and to share his concern for Timothy's well-being. He urges him to guard the gospel and if necessary to suffer for it.

Paul knows the sincerity of Timothy's faith, a faith nurtured by grandmother Lois and mother Eunice. Surely these women sang those very first "old" hymns to nurture Timothy just as mothers and grandmothers have sung such hymns to you and me. Paul reminds Timothy of his ordination and calls to his mind an ordination charge: "God does not give us a spirit of cowardice, but rather a spirit of power and of love and of self-discipline."

Power and love and self-discipline gave the apostles a willingness to witness for Christ to hostile people! No cowardice falls on that list. Nero would not have noticed those first- and second-generation Christians because of their cowardice. Rather, they witnessed to the power of Christ to break the chains of injustice. You and I know of such power and courage. Sojourner Truth could have kept silent, but she spoke out for God's oppressed people. Rosa Parks could have stood quietly at the back of the bus, but with the mighty courage of a disciple, she sat down. Sojourner and Rosa acted with holy conviction.

Perhaps Paul did not ordain us, but God certainly "called each of us with a holy calling." Paul urges Timothy (and the many followers of Christ like Timothy) not to be ashamed of his testimony about Jesus Christ. Live it. Sing it!

Second Timothy invites us to live the Lord's song day by day, no matter what happens or where we find ourselves. The word of God enables us to define who, by God's grace, we are—even and especially in a world that seems estranged from God.

PRAYER: Dear God, help me to identify people who will strengthen my will to do your will. In the name of Jesus. Amen.

Paul writes of the purposes of God "who saved us and called us with a holy calling, not according to our works but according to his own purpose and grace." Before we arrive at this statement of God's purpose, we almost hop over the words "I remind you to rekindle the gift of God that is within you." The words sound gentle and loving, the advice of an older mentor to a younger person needing guidance. Read them again: "I remind you to rekindle the gift of God that is within you." The word *rekindle* makes me wonder if the zeal of faith in Timothy has begun to fade. We rekindle fire because it is dying. Perhaps Timothy's youth has caused him to pursue interests other than his holy calling. Perhaps Timothy has neglected other spiritual disciplines. Whatever the neglect, here is a gentle reminder for all of us. Rekindle the gift of God within you! Recall the purpose of God's invitation in your life. Recall your holy and divine calling. Invite God to rekindle your zeal!

Living the Lord's song is more than mouthing words, even to beautiful music. Living the Lord's song is depositing our faith in the gospel of Jesus Christ and proclaiming with our lives that we believe in a Savior who is Christ Jesus. One of my favorite hymns is "Great Is Thy Faithfulness." We sing it heartily, for it speaks of God's faithfulness to us, but the covenant relationship makes it clear that we are also faithful to God. We live in good faith.

Paul and the many disciples whose lives we witness in the New Testament sang the Lord's song with all their being. They lived out their calling with zeal and passion. Paul's rendition of the Lord's song is a bold fanfare to the God he trusts with his whole life. Every adversity that comes his way is simply another verse in his song of praise. May God rekindle our zeal to live the Lord's song!

PRAYER: Gracious God, rekindle your gifts in me. Grant that I may have a spirit of power, love, and self-discipline for the sake of Christ. Amen.

Luke groups together some sayings of Jesus that include a parable of an unworthy slave. Jesus tells his gathered disciples that repentance and forgiveness are bound together with responsibility for one another. The disciples request that Jesus "increase [their] faith." Jesus first responds that faith is not measured by size, since even faith the size of a mustard seed can do the impossible. (I remember being given a necklace containing a mustard seed when I was a child. Just wearing the necklace made me feel I could move mountains, as in Matthew 21:21). Jesus then tells the parable of the unworthy slave, found only in Luke.

A servant or slave of a farmer works all day in the fields and then is required to serve his master in the evening. He is not invited to eat and drink with his master. It is understood that he will dine only after the master has been served. He gets no reward or thanks for his extra services, having done only what was his duty. Thus, the disciple makes no claim on God but simply obeys the Lord's will. What the disciple receives is by the grace of God.

The attitude expected of the servant is precisely the attitude Paul embraced: I have done only what I ought to have done. Sing not my praises but God's. This understanding of grace is important to our faith development. God's gift of grace is free to all. Money cannot buy it; duty cannot earn it. "By the grace of God" adds a dimension to our faith that only God can provide. Being covered by God's grace is the ongoing desire of persons of faith. In prayer and praise we receive God's grace, always mindful of our unworthiness.

PRAYER: Dear Lord, I know that I can never be worthy of your grace. Thank you for the evidence of your love and the gifts of grace through Jesus Christ. Amen.

SUNDAY, OCTOBER 3 • **Read Luke 17:7-8**

As we gather at the Lord's table on this World Communion Sunday, we acknowledge that despite geographical distances, cultural and racial differences, and class stratifications, we come to the table as one people, all part of the family of God. In affirmation of God's purposes in Jesus Christ, we come to the table singing:

"Let us break bread together on our knees."
(*The bread representing the broken body of our Lord Jesus Christ*)

"Let us drink wine together on our knees."
(*The wine representing the blood of our Lord Jesus Christ*)

"Let us praise God together on our knees!
When I fall on my knees with my face to the rising sun,
O Lord, have mercy on me!"
(*The United Methodist Hymnal*, 618)

Whether in a great cathedral or under a tree, the Eucharist, the Holy Communion, the Lord's Supper is celebrated by millions of believers. On World Communion Sunday we let the false barriers down to become the church of Jesus Christ, remembering that we are all servants at God's table, where we tend to the needs of one another. Jesus, our example, washed feet at his last table. Only God's mercy enables us to know that we are acceptable at God's table by faith in God's love. No one is unworthy of God's grace through Jesus Christ our Lord.

Prayer: "In thanksgiving, Creator God, with your people on earth and all the company of heaven we praise your name and join their unending hymn: Holy, holy, holy Lord, God of power and might, heaven and earth are full of your glory. Hosanna in the highest. Blessed is he who comes in the name of the Lord. Hosanna in the highest." Amen. (*The United Methodist Hymnal*, Service of Word and Table II, 13)

Lessons on Adversity and Faith

October 4–10, 2004 • Adam Hamilton[‡]

MONDAY, OCTOBER 4 • Read Psalm 66

Each of this week's scripture readings touches on the themes of adversity and faith. We'll learn of Israel's bondage in the Exile, of ten lepers who encounter Jesus, and of Paul's final days in a Roman dungeon. But we will begin and end the week with a study of Psalm 66, a psalm of deliverance and praise.

The Psalms contain the response of people of faith to the various seasons and events of life. Some were written during times of extreme adversity, others during times of peace and prosperity. Some psalms were written shortly after God's people were delivered from some threat, hardship, or illness and are characterized by unrestrained joy. Psalm 66 is such a psalm.

The psalmist has done as we often do in times of trouble. He has made promises or vows to God: "If you will deliver me then I will…." Most of us offer prayers like these when we face adversity; but after the deliverance comes, we frequently forget our vows, failing even to see the connection between our prayers and our deliverance. In today's scripture the psalmist does not forget. He fulfills his vows, praises God, offers a sacrifice to God, and tells others of God's goodness.

This psalm calls us to consider the work of God in our lives, to offer genuine praise for these blessings, and to tell others of God's magnificent works. John Wesley is reported to have told his preachers, "Preach faith until you have it!" In sharing our faith and expressing our praise to God, we find true joy.

SUGGESTION FOR MEDITATION: Create a simple outline of your life, noting where God was at work and the ways in which God has delivered you or answered your prayers. Then write your own psalm of praise.

[‡]Senior pastor, The United Methodist Church of the Resurrection, Leawood, Kansas; author; national speaker.

In the spring of 597 C.E. Nebuchadnezzar, king of Babylon, attacked Jerusalem. King Jehoiachin (also known as Jeconiah), most of the royal family, and ten thousand artisans, leading citizens, and the strongest of the "fighting men" were led into exile. Following this victory Nebuchadnezzar appointed Jehoiachin's son Zedekiah as king, ruling as Nebuchadnezzar's vassal.

The letter in today's passage is written to these exiles, but Jeremiah's words are not what the exiles want to hear. They want God to deliver them from the Babylonians, and soon. But Jeremiah has already prophesied that the exile will last not weeks or months, but seventy years! In light of this prediction, the exiles are to settle in for the long haul.

Jeremiah delivers a powerful message: God's timing is very different from our own. This is an important word for our lives today. Accustomed to instant gratification, we don't like to wait for anything and generally don't have to. The Internet, the microwave, the fax, cable and satellite television, the cell phone, easy credit terms all help us have instant access to almost everything. We want God to work in this way as well. We pray and then become disappointed or frustrated when God doesn't answer our prayers within our expected time frame.

Many of the Jews did not live to see God's deliverance, but it did come. God is faithful and God's purposes will be accomplished, though not always as we would like and certainly not in the time frame we would always prefer. Like the exiles, we are encouraged to trust that God is in control, and that the Lord will indeed take care of all things in the end.

SUGGESTION FOR MEDITATION: Invite God to help you have patience and understanding when God's timing differs from yours. Entrust your life to God.

We return today to the last verse of the scripture passage from yesterday's study, in which Jeremiah has written to Jews taken from their homeland to Babylon. Resentment and hatred toward the Babylonian captors is not uncommon. Even the psalmist in Psalm 137 longs for the day when the Babylonian children will be destroyed. Such is the pain and the bitterness of the exiles toward their enemies. In this context, Jeremiah 29:7 is an amazing verse. Jeremiah asks the Jews in captivity in Babylon actually to seek good for their captors and to pray to the Lord on their behalf.

This is a most remarkable idea given the circumstances in which the exiles found themselves. And it is an idea that we find echoed six hundred years later by Jesus in his Sermon on the Mount: "You have heard that it was said, 'You shall love your neighbor and hate your enemy.' But I say to you, Love your enemies and pray for those who persecute you" (Matt. 5:43-44).

Jesus and Jeremiah had very practical reasons for giving these commands: When we pray for those who have wronged us, when we actually seek God's blessings and work in their lives, our bitterness and resentment give way to hope and joy, while our lives reflect the love of God to those who meant us ill. This approach really works. You have perhaps experienced the redemptive power of love in your own life, and if so, this passage may simply be a reminder of a fundamental spiritual truth. But if you have not, you have an opportunity to begin letting go of resentment and bitterness and finding joy as you seek to practice God's word.

SUGGESTION FOR MEDITATION: **Toward whom do you harbor ill feelings? Pray that God would bless those persons and help them to become the people God longs for them to be.**

The setting of Second Timothy is the dungeon of what is now called the Mamertine Prison in Rome. Awaiting his execution in the darkness, stench, and horror of that place, Paul penned today's passage. Yet in the face of these circumstances, Paul's concern is not for himself but for the future of the Christian church in the light of his impending death.

Read verse 14 again. One of Paul's greatest concerns for the churches was that Christians tended to become embroiled in quarreling over "words." Unfortunately Paul's concern was prophetic. Christians have spent nearly two thousand years arguing with one another, splintering the body of Christ, and diminishing the great good that could have been done had they focused on the mission rather than the minutia. Examples are easy to come by: You say "debtors," I say "trespasses"; you say "infallible," I say "inspired"; you like "contemporary," I like "traditional"; and the list goes on and on.

This tendency to argue about inconsequential matters is part of the human condition and is not limited to church life. Husbands and wives, parents and children, Republicans and Democrats all quarrel at times about matters not worth fighting over. Pride and self-centeredness keep us from being willing to accept others' views with grace and love, insisting instead that we are right and they are wrong. Verse 10 captures Paul's perspective: He will "endure everything for the sake of the elect," so that they may obtain salvation. Jesus' second "great commandment" is not, "Be right in every matter, and convince others that this is so." He commands us to "love your neighbor as you love yourself."

SUGGESTION FOR MEDITATION: Invite God to forgive you for times when you have "wrangled over words." Ask for God's help in demonstrating grace toward those who disagree with you and in living a life of love.

Yesterday we focused on verse 14 and Paul's command not to devote ourselves to "wrangling over words." Paul's perspective is captured well by the title of Richard Carlson's popular book, *Don't Sweat the Small Stuff…and It's All Small Stuff*. But Paul also recognizes that not every issue of disagreement among Christians fits into the category of "small stuff."

A key concern in Second Timothy is that the church should not compromise on important theological truths. Thus Paul begins today's passage with a reminder of his gospel, then quotes an early Christian hymn, and ends by challenging Timothy (and us!) to "rightly explain the word of truth." Our task is to study, to understand the gospel, always to be learning but not swayed by the latest theological or cultural fads. We are to present ourselves to God as those who are "approved by him" with no need to be ashamed.

Perhaps the most powerful word in today's scripture concerns Paul's ability to face adversity, finding peace and joy in the midst of it. Sitting in the squalor of his Roman dungeon, awaiting his own execution, Paul could have been angry with God. He might have shouted, "After a lifetime of faithful service to you, is this the reward I receive?" But he does not look at his suffering with bitterness. Rather, he knows that the gospel is not a promise of a life of bliss and views his suffering as an opportunity for the accomplishment of God's purposes. Even in his last hours he proclaims Christ.

SUGGESTION FOR MEDITATION: **Express your desire to "present yourself to God as one approved by him," informed and holding fast to the truths of the faith. Invite God to give you the strength to see every adversity as an opportunity to let God's light shine through you.**

The healing of lepers is an important part of Jesus' ministry, demonstrating his heart of compassion, the power of God working through him, and a sign of the kingdom of God breaking into our world. But today's story focuses on the lepers' response to their miraculous healing. Nine continue on their way. Only one returns to Jesus to express his profound gratitude, "praising God with a loud voice" and falling on his knees before Jesus.

The question this story begs is simple: Will we be among the nine lepers who receive God's blessings but fail to return thanks? Or will we, like the one grateful leper, "praise God with a loud voice" and prostrate ourselves at Jesus' feet, expressing gratitude to him?

About this time of year some years ago, one of my parishioners was dying of a cancer that had left his bones brittle and his body racked with pain. I will never forget visiting him shortly before his death. He sat in his wheelchair in his living room, and when I asked how he was doing he said, "Adam, I am so grateful to God for the blessings in my life. Yesterday my wife took me for a ride in the car so I could see the colors of the fall leaves. It was such a blessing. I am so grateful to God, who made trees with leaves that change in the fall. And I am blessed that God has allowed me to see them one last time." In pausing to express thanks to others and, most importantly, to God, we find joy even in our darkest hour.

Suggestion for meditation: Make a list of the blessings for which you are thankful, and, like the leper, kneel in prayer to express your thanks. Invite God to make you a person who regularly expresses gratitude to others and to the Lord.

We close this week as we opened it, focusing on Psalm 66. I am reminded of two important spiritual truths when I read Psalm 66. The first is that God does not promise us a life without adversity. The psalmist and his people have been tested. They have known prison. They have gone through fire and water and have known the burdens of others laid on their backs. The psalmist himself has known trouble that drove him to his knees in fear and despair. Travails are part of life. We will never know the incredible joy of this psalm without walking through the difficulties of life. And while God does not promise a life without adversity, God does promise that we will be delivered; perhaps not according to our schedule or in the way we may have prayed, but God's deliverance always comes.

The spiritual truth of this psalm is the importance and power of praise. When God has delivered us, our heartfelt and passionate praise ushers us into God's presence. But our praise in the midst of trials is a statement of faith and trust that brings us peace and hope. I am reminded of Paul and Silas, beaten nearly to death, stripped naked, and shackled in a Philippian prison. It is midnight, and they surely don't feel joyous. Yet what are they doing in their cell? They are "praying and singing hymns to God" (Acts 16:25).

In praise we remember the love of God, experience the presence of God, and yield ourselves to the purposes of God.

SUGGESTION FOR MEDITATION: Sing a familiar hymn of praise to God and then invite God to help you give thanks in all circumstances.

Sweeter than Honey

October 11–17, 2004 • Chris Harrison[‡]

MONDAY, OCTOBER 11 • Read Luke 18:1-18

Many of us experience times when we feel far from God. A woman living in Zimbabwe indicated the struggle when she said, "Isn't it funny how we seem to move away from God when we actually need God's strength and love the most?"

This honest reflection is the difference between the two prayers mentioned in today's scripture passage (vv. 9-18). Although both prayers begin by addressing God, the Pharisee's prayer is self-serving. He has the form of religion without its power; his prayer is more about him than about his relationship with God. Because he has fulfilled the letter of the law, the Pharisee believes he is utterly right. When our prayers are about God's serving us, then we have missed out on the wonder of what God has come to do in us.

The tax collector, calling himself a "sinner," offers a prayer knowing that he has not met the requirements of the law. Self-aware and honest in his self-reflection, he is therefore truly connected to God. God sees the inner self and is not fooled by any form of pretense. God's new work starts with an open, honest connection within the relationship. This "new thing" is a life that is being transformed by grace into the likeness of Jesus. Our prayers then have to do with God's changing us.

These parables challenge us to reflect on the nature of our prayers and the faith that sustains them. Like the widow (vv. 1-8) our persistent faith is to encompass our whole being. Further, we must recognize that salvation has nothing to do with merit—it is God's work alone.

PRAYER: Dear God, thank you for the new work you have begun in me. Never stop changing me until you have completed this new work in me. Amen.

[‡]Pastor, West View Methodist Church, Centurion, South Africa.

Jeremiah is both the weeping prophet and the one who offers hope. He is the prophet of judgment and mercy, doom and restoration.

In 2 Corinthians 3:5-14, Paul states that the old covenant about rules and adherence to the letter of the law ultimately brings about death through condemnation of all who fall short of its requirements. Because constant adherence to the law is not possible for sinful people, the glory of living in the law faded with time. This is exactly what happened to Israel and Judah, who experienced being uprooted, torn down, demolished, and overthrown as a consequence of not adhering to God's law.

However, God offers mercy to those who repent (Jer. 18:8) and who, with renewed desire, turn their hearts toward God. As verse 30 in today's scripture says, we are all accountable for our own sins. But the prophet gives the promise that God will "build and plant" (v. 28). Just as an old plant needs to be uprooted to make place for the new plant, so the "heart of stone" must be replaced by a new heart, "a heart of flesh" (Ezek. 36:26).

Jeremiah predicts that the old covenant will be superseded with the coming of the new covenant (v. 33), which is prophesied to fulfill all that the old covenant was meant to achieve. The new covenant will flow from a spiritual renewal both in mind and heart.

When we experience brokenness caused by judgment and condemnation, we can turn our pain into repentance to receive the planting of God's mercy.

PRAYER: Lord, show us our sin. Thank you that you are a God who shows mercy at our point of need. Amen.

Today's passage contains the Old Testament's only reference to the "new covenant." Jeremiah describes God's new-covenant vision in three ways.

First, Jeremiah speaks of the "new." Like the caterpillar's turning into a butterfly, our nature and means of living are being transformed into something completely different (2 Cor. 5:17). Paul writes that the glory of God is revealed in us, and with the renewal of the spirit, we reflect God's glory in ever-increasing measure.

Second, Jeremiah speaks of the unity that God is bringing about. Israel and Judah, divided by arrogance and rivalry, in Jeremiah's prophecy will be brought together again in the new covenant. Christians believe that in time all people divided by sin will be united in Christ. South Africans are still working out what this promise of unity means.

Third, Jeremiah speaks of inclusivity. No longer will a few have exclusive access to God based on their level of spirituality. All, from the least to the greatest, will be able to know God in the new covenant. This knowledge of God goes beyond the intellect. It will be accessible to all, because it will be written "on their hearts."

Entrance into this new covenant offered by God requires only our openness to the transforming grace of the holy. Like the tax collector who knew and confessed himself a sinner, we are asked simply to humble ourselves before God, who is always creating.

PRAYER: Lord, may your vision bring us hope and call us into action to make your new covenant a reality. Amen.

Reflecting the heart that seeks God's heart and God's way, the psalmist refers to God in every one of the one hundred and seventy-six verses of this psalm. This particular set of verses displays more unity than the others. Its theme is the superior wisdom that comes through knowing the law of God.

Although the psalmist desires to walk in the way of righteousness so that every moment is saturated with obedience to the law, he does not live by the letter of the law. The heart is what makes the difference. The psalmist's desire for God is so great that he dwells in God's law at the heart level, seeking the wisdom and insight that come from knowing God's word. Living according to that wisdom gives the psalmist superiority over his enemies, his teachers, and even the elders. His attentiveness to the law has kept him safe from evil and guided his decisions. The psalmist has been so shaped by God's word that he hates evil and injustice.

This kind of expression of faith and love pleases God, who is honored by the psalmist's obedience to God's heart and law. Do we have such a heart? Is there in us such a passion for right living that God's law is our "meditation all day long"? Are we listening to God through scripture? We could reduce our confusion if we knew God's commands and passionately desired to follow them. Worldly wisdom could be shaped by our desire to please God according to God's eternal law.

PRAYER: Lord, may we find your words to be "sweeter than honey" to us and may our hearts seek after you in all we do this day. Amen.

There is a continuity between the Torah and the teaching of Jesus. The new way of living is rooted in the ways of God, revealed through the whole of scripture. The heart that longs for God will be rewarded by knowing God through that word.

The words of scripture weave the message of grace and truth into our lives, enabling us to see who God is and how God works in us and in the world. The words are not meant to entrap us again in law but to enable life. In a soccer game without rules, a referee, and boundary lines, we cause injury and miss the joy of the game. In the same way we need guidelines as to the best way to live and enjoy the new life.

Paul reminds us of the riches of God's word. He exhorts Timothy to go to the scriptures, where he will find all he needs for life and ministry. Timothy's mother and grandmother have taught him the qualities that reveal the life of God in us. Paul wants to encourage that new life with a greater depth of understanding of salvation by faith in Christ. We do not please God by simply obeying the laws. The new heart we receive in the new covenant enables us to live with the same Spirit that inspired the scriptures.

As we meditate on the scriptures in a way that will inform our lives and serve God more effectively, we come to understand that the more we know of scripture, the more it will be in our hearts. Our methods of study and our regular use of scripture allow and ensure that the word will dwell in our hearts richly.

PRAYER: Lord, Holy Spirit, who inspired the scripture, assist us to live in the joy of that truth. Guide our ministries through the knowledge of your word. Amen.

Paul instructs Timothy to minister from a place of grace and not law. The instruction is like a quote from an ordination liturgy: be consistent in your ministry, persevere through hardships, evangelize, and carry out all the work your ministry involves.

The work of Timothy's ministry will involve delivering God's word to as many people as will hear, as well as helping them apply that word to their lives so that individuals and the world may be transformed into the likeness of Christ. Paul warns Timothy that the teachings of scripture in the new light of Christ must not be deterred by myths and concepts that are simply pleasing to the ear of the listener. He is to be faithful to the essentials of the teachings of Christ, which are not always popular and may not always attract crowds.

Whatever our ministries may be, ordained or lay, we are exhorted to remain faithful in our focus on the kingdom of God and the future coming of Christ. If we are to be ministers of Christ, then we constantly seek God's kingdom, knowing that it is for God and with God that we serve God's people.

When we get discouraged and exhausted and even tempted by distractions, we can encourage one another to be faithful to the initial calling. Whom do you know who may need encouragement right now? Maybe a phone call, a visit, or a note quoting this passage will help both of you to "carry out your ministry fully."

PRAYER: Lord, we ask that you would keep our hearts focused on you and your kingdom, that we may be faithful ministers of the gospel. Empower us to be ready at any time to share our faith with others. Amen.

It has been said, "The heart of the problem is the problem of the heart." The widow in this story typically represents people who need to be defended against unjust exploitation. They become targets if not looked after by the wider family. The only way the widow in Jesus' parable can receive justice is through her persistent requests, which wear down the unjust judge until he gives the widow her due.

Like that of the determined widow, the prayer that transforms is the prayer that seeks God's way consistently and persistently. Many churches in South Africa light candles that are encircled by barbed wire to remind us of the injustices that remain around us and the light of the gospel that shines through. When the call for justice is silenced by apathy or other agendas, Jesus urges us to persist in our prayers and actions to bring about a new reality.

When we recognize what it is that makes us passionate as well as what has brought us pain in our lives, we know something of where God is directing us in the causes of justice. God does not waste a pain. When we have felt the pain of some injustice, God may use our pain to call us into action to correct the injustice.

Prayers that evidence passion and consistency in the seeking of God's justice and mercy are prayers that try to solve the problem of the heart at the heart of the problem.

PRAYER: Lord, we seek your justice in our world. Help us to discern the direction of our passion. Amen.

Life in Communion, Life in Abundance

October 18–24, 2004 • Tom Porter[‡]

MONDAY, OCTOBER 18 • Read Joel 2:23-27

What are the consequences of abandoning God? Prior to these verses Joel tells us that the people had deserted God. God was no longer the decisive reality in their lives. The people have experienced a plague of locusts and a drought, resulting in scarcity, hopelessness, and death. No abundance exists outside of communion with God.

How does God respond to this abandonment? Joel recognizes that God, in spite of being abandoned, never abandons God's people. The Holy One calls on them to "return to me with all your heart" (Joel 2:12). Joel tells us that God is "gracious and merciful, slow to anger, and abounding in steadfast love" (2:13). God gives the early rain, a sign of God's righteousness and justice. God fulfills the demands of the covenant relationship and works to restore people to covenant communion. Living in the covenant relationship results in abundance. Abundance seems to pour over the land. The rain comes in abundance. "The threshing floors shall be full of grain, the vats shall overflow with wine and oil." People are "satisfied."

What does Joel tell us about reality? We are created for relationship with God. To abandon our relationship with God is to cut ourselves off from the source of life, from the life abundant. To live in communion with God is to enjoy the early rain and to be satisfied, abundantly satisfied.

PRAYER: Creator and Sustainer of all of life and relationships, may I never forget that life in communion is the life abundant. Amen.

[‡]Executive director, JUSTPEACE Center for Mediation and Conflict Transformation of The United Methodist Church; lawyer, mediator, teacher, and elder in The United Methodist Church; living in Wellesley, Massachusetts.

TUESDAY, OCTOBER 19 • Read Joel 2:28-32

Several years ago I took a sabbatical from my law practice and went to South Africa to study the work of the Truth and Reconciliation Commission. I had spent most of my adult life trying cases as a trial lawyer and managing a law firm. I knew a lot about control—controlling the courtroom, for example. If my life were seen as a sailboat, you would have said that my sail was close hauled for speed and often reefed down for control. I had a tight grip on the tiller. On the long plane ride to South Africa, I experienced these sails being let out to go before the wind. I felt myself loosening my grip on the tiller. In South Africa, I let out the sails even more. I discovered what it was like to be led by the Spirit and to go with the Spirit. What freedom! What joy!

I realized that I needed to give up my desire to control in order to experience the "pouring out" of God's spirit, to feel it wash over me and move me in subtle and careful ways. In South Africa I found people who had lived their lives in openness to the Spirit. People had grand visions, dreamed dreams, and prophesied. In South Africa the visions and dreams of those oppressed by apartheid led a country to truth and reconciliation.

Joel tells us to commune with God: live in the Spirit; live out of the life abundant; and experience prophecy, dreams, and visions. If we release our need to control and allow God to guide us, we will experience this outpouring of God's spirit. We have only barely glimpsed the visions and dreams that will follow.

PRAYER: Gracious and loving God, thank you for pouring out your spirit on me. Amen.

Bishop Tutu of South Africa has said, "There is no future without forgiveness." Without forgiveness we cannot restore relationships. Without forgiveness we cannot avoid the cycle of retribution and violence. Without God's forgiveness we cannot be liberated to live in communion with God, the source of life, with ourselves and with our neighbors.

The psalmist says, "When deeds of iniquity overwhelm us, you forgive our transgressions." For this reason the psalmist can affirm, "You are the hope of all the ends of the earth and of the farthest seas." God's forgiveness provides the key to our deliverance and to life abundant for all creation.

In South Africa, I experienced people and a nation that truly believed in God's forgiveness and the power of forgiveness in human relationships. I listened to horrendous stories of harm, yet heard people say "I forgive you" over and over again. Only in this way could South Africa have avoided tremendous bloodshed and continuing cycles of retribution and violence.

Living out of forgiveness is a way of life that I have witnessed less frequently in my own country. I have seen it in the lives of the members of Murder Victims' Families for Reconciliation. The son of Walter Everett, a United Methodist minister, was killed by another young man. After a long journey, Walter came to the point of forgiving this young man, even officiating at his wedding. You can still see pain in Walter's eyes, but you also see the joy of which the psalmist speaks.

With God's forgiveness and our performing our "vows," we can experience communion with God and all creation. God will fill the furrows with abundant water. Creation will shout and sing with joy. While true for the Israelites, this reality is also for those who live at "the farthest bounds" of the earth.

SUGGESTION FOR MEDITATION: **In what ways have you abandoned God and neighbor? How have you experienced forgiveness?**

"As for me, I am already being poured out as a libation, and the time of my departure has come." This statement is recorded as one of Paul's last testimonies. His death approaches. We have read about the outpouring of God's spirit. Paul, in response, has poured out his life as a sacrifice, a libation, a gift, an act of worship. This reminds us of Jesus, who poured out his life as a living sacrifice, a gift from God reconciling the world.

Looking back on his ministry, Paul can say, "I have fought the good fight, I have finished the race, I have kept the faith." Paul understood the good news of God's grace as the message of forgiveness and reconciliation, of a life restored to communion with God. Paul gladly undertook this ministry of reconciliation and has seen it through to the end. No one told Paul this it would be easy. It was a fight, and at times it seemed like a marathon. But Paul kept the faith—he has accomplished what all Christ's followers are called to do.

For this Paul will be given the "crown of righteousness." Righteousness, or justice, is the fulfillment of the demands of the covenant relationship with God and with the rest of creation. This crown is not just for Paul but for all who yearn for the appearance of the Lord. This text is both an example and a challenge. We also are to pour out our lives as a sacrifice, unwavering in our faith, until we have completed the task God has called us to do.

PRAYER: God, in response to your outpouring, may I pour out my spirit and keep the faith to my dying day. Amen.

"At my first defense no one came to my support, but all deserted me." How poignant to hear these words from Paul, perhaps among his last words. Paul, at the end of his life, having poured out his life for others, finds himself totally alone, deserted by all. How sad! How tragic! How human! How honest!

Paul's words reflect sadness but no ill will. As did Jesus on the cross, Paul asks that the actions of abandonment not be held against those who deserted him. Paul continues to live out the gospel of forgiveness. How can he do this? How can he forgive? Paul replies, "The Lord stood by me and gave me strength." With God beside him, Paul could live through abandonment and face his death with words of praise and thanksgiving.

If this can happen to Jesus and to Paul, could it happen to us? Paul was promised the crown of righteousness, not the adulation and support of the people. Paul remained faithful to his calling "that through me the message might be fully proclaimed and all the Gentiles might hear it." The Gentiles did not come to his defense, but God did. God never abandoned Paul. These words give us hope. God will never abandon us. "To [God] be the glory forever and ever. Amen."

SUGGESTION FOR MEDITATION: Take a few moments to consider times when you felt you had been deserted by everyone or when you felt attacked and no one came to your defense. In what ways were you aware of God's presence with you? When have you felt abandoned by God? How did you respond?

PRAYER: Lord, in the moments when I feel abandoned, may I be attuned to your presence and strength around me and within me. Amen.

This Pharisee is very good. He fasts twice a week, exceeding any requirement. He gives one-tenth of all his income, not just of his foods or animals. He prays, "God, I thank you that I am not like other people: thieves, rogues, adulterers, or even like this tax collector." Yet Jesus says that the tax collector, not the Pharisee, goes home justified because of his humility before God.

Where did the Pharisee go wrong? Why is the tax collector exalted? Striving to be greater than others, whether in regard to money, power, sex, or goodness signifies that we have not heard and appropriated the good news. We were created good. We have our own song to sing. We are accepted as we are. We do not have to prove ourselves better than anyone else.

All were created good; all are sacred and valuable. When we quit striving to prove our worth and to create our own salvation, we begin to live out of God's abundance and grace rather than out of scarcity. Our striving creates anxiety, which causes us to live by comparisons and others' expectations. Anxiety encourages us to think better of ourselves than others, as we build up our identity at the expense of others. This most often leads to abuse of others, domination and exploitation, even in striving for goodness. This striving with the attendant anxiety and harm to others is what creates sin or rupture in relationships, including our relationship with God. Jesus did not condemn fasting or tithing. He simply said, "All who exalt themselves will be humbled...."

SUGGESTION FOR MEDITATION: **How am I like the Pharisee?**

The tax collector was not a popular figure. He had done harm. He had sinned. The difference between the tax collector and the Pharisee was that the tax collector knew that he needed the grace of God. He knew that he was not better than other people and that he was unworthy. He knew that his hope lay in the mercy of God and in his relationship with God. He was humble in his attitude toward God and himself.

As Jesus told the disciples to be like a child (see Matt. 18:1-5; Luke 18:15-17), here again Jesus extols the virtue of humility—only the humble are justified. The tax collector's humility is seen in his understanding of his need for grace and his inability to create the grace he needs for himself.

Jesus tells us to be like a child. The child had the least status of anyone in Roman society. We are called to downward mobility, not upward mobility. We are to identify with those who are the least—the widow, the orphan, the alien. The child never doubts dependence on God and others. The child receives life as a gift, not caught up in striving to be greater than anyone else. The child, naturally less anxious, lives out of abundance and not scarcity, whether in regard to power, money, or goodness. Jesus tells us that we cannot enter the kingdom of heaven without becoming like a child or the tax collector. This is serious business: understanding the reality of God's universe and the importance of living out of grace.

We are abundantly gifted, loved, and exalted. We are invited to live in communion with God and, in so doing, live in abundance.

PRAYER: God of love, we thank you for your faithfulness to us in calling us to be in communion with you. What an awesome gift! Amen.

Our Joy in God's Righteousness

October 25–31, 2004 • *Rosemary D. Gooden*[‡]

MONDAY, OCTOBER 25 • **Read Habakkuk 1:1-4**

In today's passage, the beginning of a dialogue between the prophet Habakkuk and God, Habakkuk complains vehemently to God and questions God, who seems to be silent and inattentive in the face of the tyrannical rule of the Chaldeans: "O LORD, how long shall I cry for help, and you will not listen?"

I have questioned God, even railed against God, not only about my own suffering but also about injustice in the world. Perhaps you have done the same. Like the psalmist who desperately cries for deliverance from personal enemies in the fourfold "How long?" of Psalm 13, we question God and wonder where are God's justice and deliverance in an increasingly scary world.

On March 7, 1965, commonly known as "Bloody Sunday," several hundred people were tear-gassed and beaten with billy clubs as they began a nonviolent march for freedom and justice across the Edmund Pettus Bridge to the Alabama state capitol. The march resumed on March 21 and ended March 25, 1965, before the state capitol, where Martin Luther King Jr. delivered a speech that also included a fourfold "How long?":

> How long? Not long, because no lie can live forever.
> How long? Not long, because you still reap what you sow.
> How long? Not long. Because the arm of the moral
>   universe is long but it bends toward justice.
> How long? Not long....Our God is marching on.

When we experience injustice, unfairness, and intense personal suffering, let us freely cry out to God in our prayers. Let us also live in hope and wait for God.

PRAYER: O Lord, hear my prayer. When I call, answer me. O Lord, hear my prayer. Come and listen to me. Amen.

[‡]Lecturer in Modern Church History and Mission, Seabury-Western Theological Seminary, Evanston, Illinois; Episcopal layperson.

Habakkuk positions himself to hear God's response to the dominant question posed in yesterday's reading, "How long?" In his declaration that he will be at his "watchpost" waiting for God, Habakkuk acts as one who lives by faith, demonstrating hope and expectation despite the despair he voices in the first chapter. God's answer reminds Habakkuk and modern readers that God is sovereign and will deal with injustice, suffering, and evil according to God's timetable and as God deems fit.

As we await God's appointed time, we live by faith. And living faithfully is more than mere survival, getting by, or muddling through. We live fully in the face of suffering, persecution, and violence. We live expectantly, knowing that God will answer personally our cry for help and deliverance: "For there is still a vision for the appointed time...it will surely come."

Martin Luther King Jr. and countless women, men, and children endured suffering, persecution, and violence in the struggle for freedom. Many sacrificed their own lives for the cause of freedom and justice. Along with King's, the names of forty individuals who were killed between 1954 and 1968 are inscribed on a circular black granite table, which is part of the Civil Rights Memorial in Montgomery, Alabama. Designed by Maya Lin, who also designed the Vietnam Memorial in Washington, D.C., it was dedicated in 1989. Another part of the memorial, a curved water wall, includes an excerpt from King's "I Have a Dream Speech," a paraphrase of the prophet Amos (Amos 5:24, KJV): "Let justice roll down like waters, and righteousness like a mighty stream." May we be willing to live by faith in the stream of righteousness.

PRAYER: Gracious and loving God, help me to live by faith. Help me to remember that you are sovereign and will act in your own time and way to bring about justice. Amen.

In this prayer of lament, the longest psalm in the Psalter, *righteous* is a key word and is repeated five times. The psalmist points us not only to God who is righteous but also to God's justice. Like the prophet Habakkuk, the psalmist complains to God but in a different tone. Rather than cry out "why" and "how long?" this lament is contemplative.

The psalmist delights in God's instruction even while facing "trouble and anguish." God responded to Habakkuk's complaint with the words: "The righteous live by their faith" (Hab. 2:4). Similarly, in today's passage the psalmist prays, "Give me understanding that I may live." In *The Message*, Eugene Peterson translates verses 143 and 144 this way:

> Even though troubles came down on me hard,
> your commands always gave me delight.
> The way you tell me to live is always right;
> help me understand it so I can live to the fullest.

Psalm 119 is a hymn of praise for the law. The psalmist's delight is in God's law, the source of understanding. In Psalm 1 the psalmist describes the happiness of the righteous: "Their delight is in the law of the LORD, and on his law they meditate day and night" (v. 2). In the same manner, the psalmist in today's passage speaks of delight in God's law and of the joy in keeping God's law, even during suffering.

To delight in God's commandments when trouble and anguish come over us is a gift from God, not something we conjure up on our own. This disposition goes beyond optimism and mere positive thinking. The word of God and Christ the living Word give us hope and encouragement to be faithful and to live in hope, especially during times of trouble and anguish.

Prayer: Lord, you are my song and my praise: All my hope comes from God. Lord, you are my song and my praise: God is the wellspring of life. Amen.

"Grace to you and peace from God our Father and the Lord Jesus Christ." What a way to begin a letter! Perhaps, like me, you receive voluminous e-mails daily, many unwanted and unsolicited. Yet I also receive personal notes which, despite the intervention of a machine, provide a sense of connection to distant friends and colleagues. Some of these letters close with "Grace and peace."

Today a common practice in many Christian churches is "the exchange of peace," or "passing the peace." In my Episcopal church, we exchange peace with the words: "Peace be with you" or "The peace of the Lord be with you" as we clasp hands, hug, or even plant a "holy kiss" on the cheek of the other person. At the end of the service, a deacon sends us into the world with the words: "Go in peace to love and serve the Lord." In offering peace to others, we also point them to the incarnate Christ, who is our peace.

The church in Thessalonica grows and flourishes, despite problems and hostility from non-Christian Thessalonians. What an inspiring portrait of a Christian church! Paul is moved to offer prayers of thanksgiving to God for this vital community. Like the Thessalonian Christians, we too can flourish through grace freely given to us in God through Jesus Christ. We are enabled to live a life of faith, love, and steadfastness, especially during times of suffering, hostility, and persecution. Grace renews, transforms, and leads us to wholeness.

Just think of what could happen not only in our congregations but in our world if we demonstrated abundant faith in God and love for one another.

SUGGESTION FOR MEDITATION: **In what ways do you extend grace and peace to all, not just members of your church but especially to those who suffer and the strangers you encounter every day? Before attending your next worship service, reflect on the practice of exchanging the peace.**

The first chapter of Paul's second letter to the Thessalonians begins and ends with grace: "grace and peace to you" in a salutation and the "grace of our God" in a closing prayer. Paul often included prayers in his letters to the churches he established. In yesterday's reading Paul indicated that he continues to offer prayers of thanksgiving to God for the exemplary faith, love, and steadfastness of the Thessalonians.

Recently I complimented an elderly woman in my neighborhood on her dark brown shearling coat with matching hat. She responded, "Thanks for the encouragement." Her comment prompted me to think about compliments in a new way. Indeed, sincere compliments are a form of encouragement, as is intercessory prayer.

In today's reading, Paul includes a prayer of encouragement to the Christians in Thessalonica, "asking that our God will make you worthy of his call and will fulfill by his power every good resolve and work of faith." Their steadfastness, love, and faith continue to grow, even in the face of persecution, because of Paul's pastoral ministry, which includes intercessory prayer. We too are called to intercessory prayer.

Like the Thessalonians, we need encouragement and prayer as we seek to live out our call to discipleship, especially in our vocation and daily life ministries. Through God's grace we can reflect the same type of commitment, and thus honor God, even as we suffer and face difficulty.

SUGGESTION FOR PRAYER: **Thank God for family, friends, and others who have encouraged you in your journey of faith. Think about and pray for those who need your prayers of intercession.**

On his way to Jerusalem, Jesus encounters in Jericho a throng eager to see him, a familiar scene in Luke. Jesus also encounters a rich tax collector, also familiar. In the preceding chapter in Luke, Jesus has told two parables: the parable of the Pharisee and the tax collector and the parable of the rich ruler.

Today's reading carries a tone of immediacy, even urgency, in the narrative as well as in the action itself. Aware that Jesus is "passing through" Jericho, the rich tax collector Zacchaeus runs ahead and stakes out a strategic position in a sycamore tree. Its wide, low branches and short trunk make it easy for a short man like Zacchaeus to climb. As Habakkuk positioned himself at his watchpost to receive God's word, so Zacchaeus positions himself above the crowd to see Jesus as he passes by. Miraculously Jesus notices Zacchaeus poised above the crowd. When Jesus reaches him, he looks up and tells him to "hurry and come down; for I must stay at your house today."

Of all the people in the crowd, Jesus fixes his eyes on Zacchaeus. And despite Zacchaeus's occupation, not to mention his reputation and position in the community, Jesus invites himself to his house for a meal.

Jesus' willingness to dine with Zacchaeus is extended to everyone in the crowd, especially outcasts, the marginalized, and those on the fringes of society, including the rich. Jesus looks directly into our eyes, seeks us out of the crowd, and invites himself into our lives. By welcoming Jesus and responding affirmatively to his invitation, we can know the salvation, grace, and wholeness that Christ has generously given to everyone, even those who have caused our suffering.

PRAYER: Gracious and loving God, as you have welcomed me, help me to invite and welcome others, especially the marginalized and dispossessed, to your gospel feast. Amen.

SUNDAY, OCTOBER 31 • **Read Luke 19:6-10**

As Zacchaeus hurries down from his perch in the sycamore tree and welcomes Jesus to his house, everyone witnessing this scene starts murmuring. We can hear them now: "What kind of man would go to the house of a chief tax collector for dinner? Is he out of his mind? Who does Zacchaeus think he is?" Just imagine the scene.

During the time of the Roman Empire, a tax collector, or publican, was an outcast for several reasons. A type of entrepreneur, the chief tax collector contracted to collect taxes and tolls and hired local residents to assist him. He was responsible for paying the government but was also free to collect extra taxes. Such a system invited abuse and resulted not only in the tax collector's making a profit but also in corruption, theft, and fraud's becoming part of the system. Jews rejected tax collectors because, in the course of their work, they came in contact with ritually unclean people.

Despite Zacchaeus's ill-gotten wealth, tainted occupation, and undignified sitting in a tree, Jesus seeks him out of the crowd, showering him with loving attention. Jesus recognizes an outcast, whose entire family probably suffered shame, embarrassment, and rejection because of his occupation. His acknowledgment of Zacchaeus and his family's human worth and dignity fills their need for Jesus' redeeming grace.

Zacchaeus repents, promising to give to the poor and to make restitution to those whom he has cheated. Jesus then tells Zacchaeus, "Today salvation has come to this house." For Zacchaeus and for all of us, the day of salvation brings transformation, deliverance, and new life in Christ.

PRAYER: Holy and life-giving God, thank you for seeing us in the crowd and offering us the gift of salvation through Jesus Christ. Help us humbly to repent and follow you daily. Amen.

Saints Alive!

November 1–7, 2004 • Larry M. Goodpaster[‡]

MONDAY, NOVEMBER 1 • Read Ephesians 1:11-23

ALL SAINTS DAY

The letter to the Ephesians is addressed "to the saints," a common designation for church members in the first century. We are saints not because of some miraculous feat but because of an unwavering, confident faith in Christ! This All Saints Day offers us an opportunity to reflect on our identity as "saints." This passage from Ephesians soars in its lofty descriptions of those who are "in Christ." They have "obtained an inheritance" and have been "marked with the seal" of the Spirit. They set their "hope on Christ" and exhibit "love toward all the saints."

Like many of you, I can name some "saints" who have shaped and influenced my life. For the most part they have been people who were not extraordinary as the world or the church might expect. Instead, they remained faithful in the midst of the ordinary events of life, often in difficult circumstances. For example, I knew a gardener who in spite of severe physical limitations and painful joints raised a plentiful garden, giving most of the produce away "because God has been so good to me."

This week we are invited to think about the characteristics of a "saint" and the manner in which those qualities appear in us. We will not only give thanks for those who have gone before us but also pray that the eyes of our hearts may be enlightened to know what is the hope to which God has called us.

SUGGESTION FOR MEDITATION: Reflect on Luke 6:27-31. Saints do not call attention to themselves but faithfully point the way to God by loving those who would hurt them, praying for those who would abuse them, and going out of their way to help others in the name of Jesus. How will it be so in your life today?

[‡]Resident Bishop, Alabama-West Florida Conference, The United Methodist Church, Montgomery, Alabama.

A saint is courageous.

The people to whom Haggai addresses his prophetic message are struggling. They have only recently returned from their years of exile to find their homeland destroyed, the Temple nonexistent, and their lives in ruins. The reconstruction of the Temple has begun, but the progress is slow and some of the older ones are critical because it will not be anything like the former structure.

What do we do when things do not turn out the way we had hoped? How do we go on when it seems that everywhere we turn, people remind us of the "good old days"? How do we deal with harsh realities when it feels as if there is no tomorrow?

Three times Haggai emphatically encourages the government and religious leaders and the people to "take courage," in essence calling them to continue to work with boldness and not to give up or give in. The God who called them into existence and who was with them in their exile is also with them now.

Some times and circumstances in our lives are beyond explanation; events challenge us and often shake us to the core of our existence. The saints among us know that such times call for courage in the face of uncertainty, a courage based not on our petty efforts or limited resources but on the courage to keep going because God is with us. I can hear one of those saints of my past as she offered me words of encouragement: "You can do this. Do not be afraid. Trust God and be bold!"

SUGGESTION FOR MEDITATION: Read Haggai 2:4 several times. Focus on the words *courage, work,* and *I am with you.* Where do you find the courage to go on? What does the promise of God's presence in your daily life suggest to you?

A saint is hopeful.

The frustrations of restoring the Temple under difficult circumstances are getting to the people. Not only are construction supplies limited and resources scarce, but the discouragers and the naysayers are out in force. Visions of a return to past glory are fading, and a sense of complacency is settling over the people. How do we keep moving forward and building when all that we see is more hardship, more trouble, and more suffering? Surely God has deserted us!

The prophet Haggai sees something different. Certainly he is a realist, and he knows that this new effort will not measure up to the standard of the previous Temple. But he also anticipates a time when God's glory will fill this new construction in a greater way than in the past and with splendor not worth comparing to the way it was.

Saints are those who can see beyond what was, and even beyond what is, to what will be. They can anticipate what God will yet do. Based on promises fulfilled and love revealed, saints anxiously expect God's intervention and participation in life beyond anything imaginable. God's shalom will be unveiled in new, creative, and unexpected ways. Hope involves a dynamic dimension of the spirit that knows God is breaking into our lives and dispersing our uncertainty so that we can face any and all circumstances with confidence.

Nearing the end of his battle with cancer, one of those saints who touched my life recalled a verse of scripture that spoke of his hope in spite of his illness. He whispered to me, "I know in whom I have believed; there is nothing for me to fear even now."

SUGGESTION FOR MEDITATION: Read and reflect on Ephesians 1:20-23 again today. Where is the source of your hope? Where is God breaking into your life today?

A saint is perceptive.

Paul addresses a church where rumors run rampant in a highly charged atmosphere of anxiety and alarm. There is much to fear from outside forces and agencies that are suspicious of this movement known as Christianity and much uncertainty from inside the congregation about the times in which they live. *Are these the last days? How much longer do we have to endure?*

"Let no one deceive you," Paul writes. Deception is the driving force of the anxiety both inside and outside. Paul suggests the need for God's perspective, for recognizing the truth in the midst of meaningless or threatening situations. Paul knows the Thessalonian church is dealing with mean-spirited, destructive forces. And even though the people will have to deal with them continually, Paul also knows that the power of God's love and grace will ultimately triumph. Therefore, he counsels not to be distracted from the core of the gospel.

We too live in days of rumor, uncertainty, anxiety, and fear. We know how quickly false claims and twisted comments take on the appearance of truth. What we need now is discernment—an accurate reading of the signs of God's presence in the world and an accurate assessment of what is of God and what is not. Such discernment requires meditation, study, prayer, and fasting in the settings of both the silence in one's heart and the supportive community of believers. A saint sees through false claims, listens for the voice of God, attends to the movements of God's spirit, and clings to hope in Christ Jesus. Paul cautions us not to get caught up in rumors but to be captured by the grace of God's breaking into the world.

SUGGESTION FOR MEDITATION: Reflect on 2 Thessalonians 2:2 quietly. What things in this day shake you? What things alarm you? Seek God's perspective in those situations.

A saint is anchored.

Sometimes circumstances in life blow over us with hurricane force winds, threatening to uproot us. Moments of suffering, pain, and grief caused by natural forces, disease, or humanity's inhumanity rush into our lives when we least expect them. The church at Thessalonica finds itself surrounded by a culture that brings social pressures and outright opposition to bear on the faith. The Thessalonian Christians must occasionally feel as if they are about to be blown away. Little wonder that they get caught up in idle speculation about the return of Christ—the sooner, the better as far as they are concerned. Perhaps the thought is a source of relief and rest.

Paul has another word for these Christians in the midst of these difficult days. First he offers encouragement by reminding them of what God has done for them: They are "beloved by the Lord"; they have been chosen by God as "the first fruits of salvation"; and they have been called so that they "may obtain the glory of our Lord Jesus Christ." Then Paul offers guidance on dealing with the harsh realities of a hostile situation. "Stand firm," he says. Do not waver from the faith into which you were called and baptized. "Hold fast," he adds. Do not neglect or retreat from that faith tradition that affirms God's never-ending love and constant watchfulness over all God's people.

A well-known hymn includes the poetic imagery of an anchor, holding in the midst of storms and floods. No matter what swirls around us, we know that Christ is our foundation and that it will hold us when all else fails. In that tradition a saint stands firm, anchored in God's love, mercy, and grace.

SUGGESTION FOR MEDITATION: **Reflect on 2 Thessalonians 2:16-17; read it prayerfully several times. Eternal comfort, good hope, strength. How do these blessings anchor you?**

A saint is alive!

The Sadducees were only one of a number of groups proposing its own particular interpretation of scripture. Luke gives us a clue about one of the principles that distinguished them from others ("there is no resurrection"). This is but one of several occasions when members of those groups confront Jesus.

The Sadducees approach Jesus with a hypothetical question involving a rather absurd scenario about resurrection. Jesus sees through the trap they try to spring on him with their riddle and points instead to a God-given reality. The fact is that resurrection is a certainty, but it is not going to be simply a continuation of life as we know it here and now. It will be radically new and different, and therefore earthly language and relationships cannot begin to describe it. This much we know: God is a God of the living, and those who place their faith and confidence in God are indeed the "children of the resurrection."

Those of us who name Christ as Savior and Lord of our lives are Easter people. We are alive to the glory of life with God— starting now! Our living in the glow of Christ's resurrection becomes a response to God's grace restoring us to full, authentic life and renewing the image of God within our souls. We are people who are alive to the wonder of what God has done first in the resurrection of Christ from the dead, and then in raising us to a new, qualitatively different life in Christ. We are alive to the wonder and power of God's grace working in us and for us now and in the world to come.

SUGGESTION FOR MEDITATION: Reflect on Luke 20:38 and Luke 24:5. How do we search for the living among the dead? In what ways are we alive to what God is doing in us and through us?

A saint is joyous!

As a child I learned the simple yet profound table grace, "God is great, God is good...." Taking turns with my sister, we recited it often, perhaps to the point of repetition that robbed it of its powerful message. As I have grown and matured, I have come to experience that childhood prayer as a central affirmation of our faith, grounded in scripture. Psalm 145 affirms the greatness of God; the awesome majesty and creative power that only begins to describe the nature of God; and the goodness of God in mercy and love, in compassion and grace. Above all, this psalm is a call to worship and praise, a reminder of the source of our joy.

In the haste of life in the twenty-first century, it does us good to linger with Psalm 145. To savor the words of this psalmist is to know that joy springs from within and is not contingent upon external circumstances or possessions. To hear that God "fulfills the desire of all who fear him" is to learn that joy is not about what we accumulate but about how we live in relation to God and in response to God's grace.

This week we have visited some of the marks of the believer-saint. Surrounded by turmoil and uncertainty, the believer-saint holds firm to faith in God and courageously faces the future without fear—precisely because God is "just" and "kind" and "near." But above all, the heart of the believer-saint turns toward God in worship and praise. God is the source of life and hope, the foundation for the future. Therefore we rejoice and sing.

SUGGESTION FOR MEDITATION: Reflect on Psalm 145:21. On this day of worship, how will our mouths and hearts offer praise to God? How will the joy of Christ's resurrection permeate our lives and our actions?

Living into the Future

November 8–14, 2004 • Pamela L. Daniel[‡]

MONDAY, NOVEMBER 8 • Read Psalm 118:1-20

This beautiful psalm falls in the exact middle of the English Bible, and it contains the heart of the Bible message as well: The people of God are called in all times and places to celebrate with praise and thanksgiving the all-powerful love of God.

A responsive poem designed for worship, Psalm 118 is a call to worship, a confession of faith, and a prayer of thanksgiving. It is divided into four parts in which Israel, priests, worshipers, and soloist join in a responsive litany.

Psalm 118 is the concluding part of the Hebrew Hallel, a collection of songs of praise used as a part of the Seder Passover celebration of remembrance. Remembering what God has done, the psalmist declares that in all things God's "steadfast love endures forever." Even in the worst of times, when his enemies surrounded him "like bees" and he was "pushed hard" and "falling," the psalmist found refuge in the Lord, "my strength and my might." Because of his utter confidence in God's love and power, the psalmist has no fear: "What can mortals do to me?" The psalm reminds us that the events and circumstances of life that we can't begin to handle reside within God's control.

The Lord is our strength, might, and salvation. We cannot depend on humans or earthly powers or anything else—only God. This psalm is a statement of faith, reminding us all of the central message of our faith: Trust in God, who will not "give [us] over to death." So open "the gates of righteousness" that we may enter and "give thanks to the LORD."

PRAYER: Lord of power and might, we celebrate and give thanks for your mercy. Amen.

[‡]Presbyterian minister and educator, Morganton, North Carolina.

We often hear this psalm read on Palm/Passion Sunday because it is quoted by Jesus and seen as a prophecy of his triumphal entry into Jerusalem: "Blessed is he who comes in the name of the Lord" (NIV). Its focus on the stone that has been rejected becoming the cornerstone makes it an appropriate Easter reading.

Christians understand the image of the rejected stone to refer to Jesus' arrest, trial, and crucifixion by human beings and the cornerstone to his resurrection by God to be the foundation of the coming kingdom. The stone the builders rejected has become the "chief" cornerstone.

We humans reject stones or people or ideas because they do not fit the plans we envision. Builders of societies or even churches reject people and things deemed inappropriate or unsuitable to their overall design. If the "stone" doesn't fit our image of what should be built, we can't see that it has any use. We are all imprisoned by our blueprints—by our limited vision of how buildings, people, societies, churches, even salvation ought to look. Fortunately for us, God holds the master plan.

In God's plan for the world, the one rejected becomes the foundation of creation. We don't understand that concept because we don't understand God's ways of being or doing. But our understanding isn't the important aspect. We only need to know that God has become [our] salvation.

That is good news for all rejects. What humans may think is unimportant, God chooses and uses. We judge and discard; God chooses to save. Thanks be to God. "This is the day that the LORD has made; let us rejoice and be glad."

SUGGESTION FOR MEDITATION: Everyone experiences rejection. How does this scripture help you deal with those experiences?

These words from Isaiah were written during a difficult time in the history of Israel. It had been more than a hundred years since the Hebrews were exiled to a foreign land and Jerusalem was destroyed. Now having returned to their homeland, the people remember God's promise to restore and bless the nation.

It has taken effort and time, but after many generations the Temple and the walls of Jerusalem have been rebuilt. However, nothing else has changed. Israel has no great king. The nation has not been restored to its former glory. So the people ask, "Why have the promises of God not come to pass? Is this all there is?"

Isaiah answers with a resounding no. This passage, the climax of a section of Isaiah that reaffirms all of God's promises, assures the Israelites that something even better is on the way. There will be a new creation. God is not done; God is just beginning. They are not even to think about the former things, neither the amazing exodus from Egypt nor the great reign of King David.

In the new creation, Isaiah says, there will be no weeping or distress. Death no longer will come to the young but only at the end of a wonderful, long life. The people will live in the houses they have built and eat the food they have cultivated, no longer laboring "in vain" for conquering nations. This new creation will not come about because another great king like David ascends the throne but because God will make it happen. The new Jerusalem will be "a joy" and its people "a delight."

Even before they ask, God will hear the prayers of the Israelites. Historical enemies will become their partners, and there will be no killing or destruction or refugees. "The wolf and the lamb shall feed together," and war will not exist. What the world is now is not what it will be. Let us "be glad and rejoice forever in what [God is] creating."

Prayer: God of all creation, we celebrate and give thanks for your mighty acts of the past, your constant presence in our today, and the glorious future you will bring into being. Amen.

The vision depicted in this passage is glorious. But how will God bring this new creation into being? How will the vision of what can be become the reality? We don't know. How God will bring about the new creation is irrelevant, the details unimportant. What is relevant and important is that no matter what, when, or where, we can trust God with the future and the present.

The prophet tells us to let go of the old way of looking at things, to let go of our limited human vision, and to try to see with God's eyes. No matter what good things we want to hold on to, some golden age or the good old days, we must let them go, because they won't compare to the glory of God's vision.

Hanging on to the past or wanting things to return to the way they were is a normal, human state of mind, especially in the church. We take comfort in the familiar. Doing things the way we've always done them and believing in a future that we can control give a sense of security. The glorious future described by Isaiah seems far, far away or even impossible and perhaps a little frightening. Isaiah's words inspire us to hang on to God's vision. No matter what darkness we face, no matter how bad things seem, God's vision is stronger, and we are in God's hands.

But if we cling to our old ways of thinking, we miss out on the unlimited possibilities of joy in the new creation. When we choose to let go of our narrow perspective and our old ideas, the world is not just good; it is great! The lame do not simply walk; they dance. The hungry are not just fed; they come to a feast. We are admonished to open our eyes and ears to the impossible possibility that we are the "offspring blessed by the LORD."

PRAYER: God of possibilities, open my eyes to your vision for my life and the world. Amen.

First-century Judaism centered around the temple in Jerusalem, a mighty, gold-covered edifice erected by King Herod. The people came to this awesome house of worship during the annual festivals. Looking at the huge stones must have inspired them to trust in the strength and faith it symbolized. How could anything be more impressive?

The Temple represented the strength of the Jewish nation and religion. But Jesus tells his followers that they should not trust in or be falsely comforted by appearances. The time will come when the Temple and all its adornments will be "thrown down." No stone will be left.

No matter how permanent they may seem, things made by humans are not perfect, and they do not last forever. When Luke wrote his Gospel, the Romans had already destroyed Herod's Temple. This event had been a major blow to the people. With the symbol of their nationality and religion now obliterated, they must have wondered if the catastrophe was a sign.

Jesus warns us against putting our belief and trust in anything other than God. The Temple may have been awesome, but in comparison to what God has in mind for our world, it was insignificant. That is like saying the cathedrals of Europe were not truly majestic or the Oval Office in the White House is not a great place of power. But in relation to God, that is exactly what Jesus wants us to understand.

Our impulse is to place our trust in what we can see and touch. But when we limit ourselves to this understanding of life and power, we deny ourselves the one thing upon which we truly can depend—the steadfast love and power of God. How could anything be more impressive?

SUGGESTION FOR MEDITATION: Think about in whom or what you place your trust. What difference would it make in your life if you put your trust in God?

"When will the Temple be destroyed? What will be the signs?" Jesus' followers want answers to these questions, and so do we.

Today's scripture is an apocalyptic passage, one of those texts that deal with the end of time as we know it. The end of the world is something people want to know about. "When will there be a time of peace and justice?" we ask. "How will God deal with the evil of the world? What events signal that the end is near?" We want to understand, believing that if we know what to expect, then we wield a kind of control and won't need to be quite as frightened of the unknown. Jesus' response, however, does not provide comfort.

Jesus does not minimize the negative experiences his followers will face. He warns them not to be led astray during the difficult days ahead, which are a prelude to the birth of something new and wonderful. The persecution his followers will endure is not to be dreaded but seen as "an opportunity to testify." Jesus promises to give them in their trials "a wisdom that none of your opponents will be able to withstand or contradict." In spite of betrayals and hate and even death, their endurance will preserve their souls.

Perhaps Jesus' followers asked the wrong questions, for Jesus' response to them may not be about signs at all. We don't actually need signs, and they even get in the way if assurance of the kingdom of God is our ultimate goal. Our Lord assures us that he will be with us, no matter what we encounter. When circumstances challenge our witness, we don't have to worry, for Christ will give us the right words.

If we put our trust not in signs or temples but in the steadfast love of God that endures forever, we will "gain [our] souls."

PRAYER: Lord, we fear what we do not understand. Help us to trust you with the future of our lives and our world. Grant us your peace. Amen.

Living in a community has benefits and responsibilities. In his letter to the community of faith in Thessalonica, the writer reminds them that all should do their part, following the example of Paul and other missionaries, to support themselves while they minister to the community. Idle behavior is unacceptable in a Christian community.

Two thousand years after the life of Christ on earth, we still expect everyone to meet his or her responsibilities. But first-century Christians might have had a different attitude, assuming Jesus' immediate return and an ushering in of the kingdom of God. They must have asked, "If Jesus is coming back in the next few days or weeks, why should we worry about money or work? Would it not be better to spend our time in prayer, devotion, and thanksgiving?" Those who felt that this was the proper response to the imminent coming of Christ found themselves in conflict with those who thought Christians should continue their day-to-day activities.

Our faith affirms life in the present and the hope of the future. We are expected to do our part as individuals and as members of the community of faith to bring God's kingdom into the world. The imminent return of Christ does not make our daily work irrelevant. To the contrary, our belief in the second coming of Christ adds meaning to what we do. We live every day not in idle expectation but serving faithfully and quietly in the vital expectation of our Lord's return. Do not become weary in doing what is right. Stand firm in your faith.

PRAYER: Come, Lord Jesus, into our lives and grant us your mercy. We pray for wisdom as we deal with everyday life. Guide us in every activity. Help us to live with expectation and diligence. Amen.

Christ the King: Yesterday, Today, Tomorrow

November 15–21, 2004 • Beverly Courrege[‡]

MONDAY, NOVEMBER 15 • Read Jeremiah 23:1-4

Jeremiah proclaims God's promise to rescue God's flocks and to establish a good shepherd to care for them. For Christians, Jesus Christ, the Good Shepherd, is the fullness of God's promise.

Christ is our shepherd. Everyone to whom he ministers receives the same attention, whether it is to save a soul, share the food of the Spirit, offer comfort, heal, admonish, encourage, or teach. Above all he shows unconditional love.

All sheep receive attention. But when a sheep wanders or is in danger, hurting or hungry, the shepherd gives special attention to the sheep in need, while continuing to watch the rest of the flock. Our shepherd Jesus is no respecter of persons.

Jeremiah issues a warning of "woe to shepherds who destroy and scatter the sheep of [God's] pasture." He promises that the lost sheep, "the remnant," will be brought "back to their fold" by the Lord, who will "raise up shepherds over them...and they shall not fear any longer."

In today's society Christians play the double roles of sheep and shepherd. As shepherds we treat the flock with love, care, and kindness, reflecting Christ in us. Just as Christ in us has made us part of today's flock, Christ in us has made us one of many shepherds in those flocks. We all receive the same love from God because of Christ. We must also show the same love of God to all persons, because of Christ who reigns today through us.

SUGGESTION FOR MEDITATION: Think of the ways in which you are one of God's flock. Call to mind instances when others have been good shepherds in your life. How are you a good shepherd to others? Ask God today to guide you in your double roles of sheep and shepherd.

[‡]Bible study teacher, conference speaker, author; founder of Women's Ministries at Richland Bible Fellowship Church, Dallas, Texas.

Most of today's young couples want to prepare the perfect nursery for their baby. They have many expectations about who is coming without really knowing what he or she may look like or what personality will burst forth. College funding and estate planning are sometimes part of parents' activities during the nine months of pregnancy. The newborn today often lives a lifetime through parental planning before exiting the womb!

For centuries the Israelites had expected and awaited a messiah. They no doubt had preconceived notions about the exciting life he would lead, expecting a warrior king like other reigning kings of their time. Their king would ride in on dashing stallion, certainly not a lowly donkey! Their warrior king would rid the land of occupational armies, and the people of God would live happily ever after. Yet expectant parents and the Israelites often trip over their own expectations, missing greater things that defy human expectation.

Jeremiah announces God's intention to "raise up" a "righteous Branch" who will save the Israelites. But this savior will not be a warrior king on a white horse, dethroning evil rulers and driving armies from the land. Rather, Jeremiah says, the coming kind of Israel will "deal wisely, and shall execute justice and righteousness in the land."

We know Jesus as the righteous branch that Jeremiah identified and witness Jesus' reign as one of justice and righteousness. We are invited to seek justice and to live in righteousness. "The days are surely coming" and are here.

PRAYER: Dear God, forgive me when I interfere with your divine plan for my life. I know you hold my hand and keep me from falling when I trip over my own expectations. Thank you for loving me in spite of myself. My heart's desire is to see you in all things. May I continually delight in the unexpected works of your hands. Amen.

No doubt about it. Humankind blew it. Not just once but over and over again. God established a covenant relationship with the children of Abraham, faithfully providing for their needs. Their response was less faithful, more often than not blowing it by following their human desires rather than the desires of God. Genesis and Exodus and the other sixty-four books of the Old and New Testaments tell the who, what, when, why, and how of God, Jesus Christ, and the Holy Spirit in their relationship to humanity.

In today's scripture Zechariah praises God who, as promised through the ages in the Old Testament, has sent the Son of the Most High to redeem the world, not only from human oppression but also from moral and spiritual bankruptcy. With spiritual eyes given him through the Holy Spirit, Zechariah recognizes the "mighty savior" who is coming. Unfortunately, the spiritual eyes of the Holy Spirit will not be given to very many before humankind blows it again, crucifying their redeemer.

Humans were created with a lack of knowledge and with a spirit of innocence, and evil was anxious to get our attention. Yet when we blew it, the Lord continued to reign with unconditional love. God has continually "shown the mercy promised to our ancestors, and has remembered [God's] holy covenant." God the Son came as promised to reign as our future and hope, so that we "might serve [God] without fear, in holiness and righteousness…all our days."

PRAYER: Dear God, help me not to blow it yet again. Give me spiritual eyes to see the blessings of your Word. Amen.

I am definitely a people person, which can be a detriment to a person who derives so much pleasure from being a writer. It takes a great amount of discipline to withdraw from friends for a season to work on a writing project. Writers are often misunderstood in that they may zealously pen their passion in order to provoke, inspire, or move, yet remain oblivious to the possibility that some people won't want to read their work!

Today's scripture makes me wonder similarly about John the Baptist. I wonder if John, created and called to be "the prophet of the Most High," ever felt that trying to get the multitudes to understand unfolding events was a thankless task. This "prophet of the Most High" will spend much of his time in the middle of a river, baptizing those whose hearts can understand, while loudly rebuking sin. John the Baptist was called to prepare the way, and he did so with a passion that never waned.

But John is still a baby in today's scripture. He does not know the difficulties that lie ahead for him as he goes before Jesus to prepare his way, nor the ultimate sacrifice that will be asked of them both. Yet we who have read the whole story of his life know that John will experience the "tender mercy of our God," who will "guide [his] feet into the way of peace."

All humans are called to live out life for a purpose, although many never recognize any calling. But Christians, called or not, have a responsibility like John the Baptist to prepare the way for the Most High, who is coming again and who leads the way to eternal life.

SUGGESTION FOR PRAYER: Ask the Lord today for passion like that of John the Baptist so that you can prepare the way of salvation for the lost people with whom you cross paths.

Several years ago my husband and I joined another couple on a boat trip around the Virgin Islands. This was not your everyday cruise—only the four of us as crew on a forty- to fifty-foot sailboat. Our "captain" is our best friend Tom.

By trade Tom is in the medical field. However, on the ocean he reigns over our foursome; we must be ready to follow his instructions without question. We commit ourselves to Tom's authority. He is the only one with the knowledge, understanding, wisdom, endurance, and patience to guide us safely through the glorious experience of this water kingdom. When Tom calls us to help him, we may give him a hard time; but we all know that our pleasure cruise also involves commitment and teamwork if we are to arrive safely at each destination point.

Practical lessons gleaned from our sailing experiences reflect external lessons in Paul's text. We place ourselves under God's authority and trust God to guide us safely to our destination. Like crewing a sailboat, sharing "in the inheritance of the saints in the light" also involves commitment. We may be called to put in extra effort beyond our comfort level as part of the privilege of sharing in God's kingdom. But the reward for being "prepared to endure everything with patience" outweighs any extra effort. Our further knowledge and understanding of God's reign brings us into a more intimate relationship with Christ.

SUGGESTION FOR MEDITATION: When have you felt God requiring a little more, or even great, effort from you to further God's kingdom? In what ways are you committed to doing whatever is asked of you? In what ways are you reluctant?

The reign of Christ is beyond human understanding, for it is unlike any other reign of power in earth's history. Number one, Christ is called "the image of the invisible God." No other king has been regarded as God's image.

Numbers two and three: Christ is "firstborn over all creation" (NIV) and "by him all things were created: things in heaven and on earth, visible and invisible, whether thrones or powers or rulers or authorities; all things were created by him and for him" (NIV). Contrary to what any rulers or kings today or in ages past may think or have thought, they have never had this kind of sovereignty!

Numbers four and five: Christ not only is "the beginning," but he is "the firstborn from among the dead" (NIV). Rulers like the Pharaohs and leaders of other faiths and even those who boast in the technology of cryogenics may think this power is available to them, but they will know with finality when Christ comes again the futility of human arrogance.

Human beings alone will never have the power to make peace with themselves or with others. Rulers and kings throughout history have thought they had the victory of peace, but it was fleeting. Only Christ brings peace. The future and the hope we can have right now comes in knowing that no matter what chaos surrounds us, Christ makes peace available to us amidst the chaos. He guarantees it. No other authority or ruler has this power and can give this assurance.

PRAYER: Dear Lord, thank you for the peace you have given me despite the chaos that surrounds me. Amen.

REIGN OF CHRIST SUNDAY

There Jesus hangs between two criminals. We know nothing of the thieves' backgrounds, nor do we know whether they have heard anything about Jesus before this day.

Mark tells us that in addition to the insults hurled at Jesus by the crowd and the soldiers, "those crucified with him also heaped insults on him" (15:32, NIV). Yet in today's reading from Luke, only one of the thieves mocks Jesus, crying out to him, "Aren't you the Christ? Save yourself and us!"

The second criminal hanging beside Jesus rebukes the other's statement. "Don't you fear God, since you are under the same sentence? We are punished justly, for we are getting what our deeds deserve. But this man has done nothing wrong."

Now when did this second criminal see the light? Suddenly he believes and shows true repentance? Amen, he certainly does! In spite of blinding pain, he can see clearly that Jesus is the Christ, and he makes a movingly humble request. Knowing he deserves only death for his deeds, he asks Jesus to remember him in his kingdom. All the repentant criminal wants is to be remembered. He has no idea he can *join* Christ in his kingdom. I have always pictured Christ taking a final breath, then clasping the hand of the repentant thief and walking into Paradise together.

Two unbelievers are exposed at the same hour, in the same circumstances. How can one see so clearly? The answer the criminal receives is the same one offered to each of us, even in our darkest hours: "Today you will be with me in paradise." We have only to confess Christ as King: yesterday, today, and tomorrow.

SUGGESTION FOR MEDITATION: **Read all of Luke 23.**

Living with Radical Trust in God

November 22–28, 2004 • James Melchiorre‡

MONDAY, NOVEMBER 22 • Read Matthew 24:36-44

Human life is a tangle of biology and chemistry held together by a thread that can be broken in an instant. We New Yorkers, especially, were reminded of that fragile unpredictability on September 11, 2001. Approximately twenty-eight hundred of our neighbors went to work that morning, ate their bagels and drank their coffee, and looked ahead to the tasks of the day. Certainly, almost all of them had plans for that evening, perhaps a date with a sweetheart, a spaghetti dinner at the firehouse, or an important appointment at a child's soccer game. Yet, for them, there was no evening of September 11.

Matthew tells us to be ready, for the hour of Jesus' second coming will arrive unexpectedly, a powerful reminder of the inevitable and largely unpredictable end to our own lives. What do we make of this sobering knowledge? Many an evangelist has employed it to scare listeners into conversion. Although conversion is a good thing, scare tactics are not needed. The simple fact is that we don't know when our end will come, nor do we know when the final end will occur. The scripture tells us not even Jesus knows, only the Father.

So how in the world can we handle such uncertainty? We must live as though this day were our last on earth and, at the same time, work as though Jesus' next coming were centuries, even millennia, away. Our dual purposes ensure that we are in tune with the dual mission of the Messiah—to transform us individually and then to recruit us to transform the world.

PRAYER: Creator of all, make us ever aware of the uncertainty of our earthly life but the absolute certainty of your reign and care. Amen.

---

‡Journalist, member of St. Paul and St. Andrew United Methodist Church, New York, New York.

My work as a journalist once brought me to the home of Phyllis Tickle, a prolific author and committed Episcopal Christian. Tickle has written several books about the Divine Hours, the ancient ritual of specific prayer on specific days at seven or eight specific hours. It's a custom rooted in Judaism ("Seven times a day I praise you…," Ps. 119:164) that became part of Christianity at least fifteen hundred years ago.

In the course of the interview, I asked Tickle why she has practiced this custom for thirty-five years, how it nurtures her spirit, what she gets out of it. She answered that "praying the hours" is not done for our benefit because it's not "about us." It's about praising God. We should do it for that reason alone.

The psalmist understood this simple summons to praise God so much better than those in our utilitarian age. Notice that Psalm 100 never refers to benefits that might flow to those who recite the song; no petition for a blessing, a favor, or an intercession. Not that such petitions are bad.

However, too seldom these days do we simply come before God and offer our praise for no reason other than "the LORD is God. It is he that made us, and we are his; we are his people, and the sheep of his pasture…his steadfast love endures forever, and his faithfulness to all generations."

Indeed, some prayer is not about us.

PRAYER: Great and compassionate God, too often our prayers are one-sided conversations, a shopping list of what we think we need. Open our eyes to the importance of simply entering your court with praise. Amen.

It was a profound moment on a windy night in an old barn in the mountains of northwestern Panama. During a Bible study, a member of our Volunteers in Mission team asked the minister leading the study, "Is any fear other than fear of the Lord considered sin?" The minister answered indirectly but well, saying we are called to have a "radical trust in God." Paul says the same thing in his letter to the Philippians. While we need to spend some of our prayer time simply praising God and often tend to neglect that kind of prayer, speaking to God about our needs is another great way to help center us, to define the relationship between creature and creator, child and parent.

I once heard a man say that his constant prayer leads him to asks God's help in finding a parking space. His audience laughed, but to those of us who drive in New York City, the prayer seemed very practical! Yet praying that the weather will be sunny for the softball game or picnic, while not inappropriate, hardly compares to praying for a child's recovery from cancer.

In prayer about serious needs, the stakes are higher; the trust must be deeper, more radical, especially at those times when we really don't know how we should pray. I remember sitting in a hospital waiting room where my mother was being treated for an overwhelming condition from which she did not recover. I kept thinking of Paul's assurance in Romans that when we don't know exactly how to pray, the Holy Spirit will take over for us.

On any given day our prayers may resemble a child sitting in front of Santa Claus with a list; times when our petitions are literally a matter of life or death; situations where all we can do is throw up our hands and let the Spirit pray for us. What's common to each example are those four words spoken in the barn in Panama: *radical trust in God.*

PRAYER: Good and gracious God, give us the knowledge that we can come to you for all things, large and small, and grant us the radical trust that will remove all anxiety and bring the peace that really does transcend understanding. Amen.

THANKSGIVING DAY, USA

Thanksgiving Day, a widely observed and underappreciated holiday, often merely kicks off the holiday season, the period that also includes Hanukkah, Christmas, and New Year's—five weeks of intense shopping, eating, drinking, visiting, and hurrying.

Too bad. Thanksgiving deserves better than football and parades. Thanksgiving should focus our attention on our common humanity, need, and interdependence, helping those of us in the human family to remember that everything is "gift."

Our food is usually produced through the work of others and only then because of the earth, the sun, and the rain, those magnificent gifts of God. Our homes, our cars, our other "stuff" to which we become so attached come to us largely as a result of circumstances over which we have little control. These benefits are also "gift." Our families, our health, the next breath we take—none of these is perpetually guaranteed. Again, "gift."

Deuteronomy directs the Israelites to take the first fruits and return them to God. Thanksgiving to God is not to stow away three months of food in the basement freezer or sock away twelve months of income in the bank and then show up at the altar to give a token offering. By returning the first fruits to God, we open ourselves to sharing with others and, even more important, to trusting that tomorrow and the next day and the day after that, God will provide for our needs.

Giving God our first fruits is a lesson we need to heed—and practice. By doing so, we might actually reduce the indefensible gap between the marginalized poor and everybody else in this world. We might actually break the punishing power that possessions can exert on us. If we did, we might better appreciate a holiday that reminds us that everything is "gift."

PRAYER: Good and gracious God, help us remember every day that all is "gift" and that you are the giver. May that knowledge profoundly affect the way we live. Amen.

"The night is nearly over, the day is almost here" (NIV). Paul's words seem especially meaningful at this time of year in the Northern Hemisphere. Late autumn is a time of rapidly shortening days when nature's vitality, so visible in spring and summer, ebbs, and the end of this cycle of life nears. Yet in this half of the globe, we anticipate the holiday of Christmas at the very moment when darkness seems in ascendancy. And in the darkness we speak of following the Child of the light, whose birth we remember this season.

The celebration of the coming of Jesus as a babe in Bethlehem is a memorial, an annual observance. Jesus has not been "away." As "Easter people," we know that the power of the Resurrection has caused Jesus and the way of the gospel to be let loose upon the earth, every day of every year. With Paul we know that "salvation is nearer to us now than when we became believers."

Now, there is still a lot we don't know. We don't know the date of the end of the world or the date of Jesus' promised "second coming" in glory. We don't know the date of our own death. We do know that we are, without question, closer today to the end of our earthly existence than we were yesterday. So our knowledge is incomplete—but not inadequate as long as we fill in the blanks with faith and trust in God.

PRAYER: Eternal God, spare us the anxiety of obsessive schedules, and help us understand that everything happens in your own good time. Amen.

Anytime a scripture passage refers to *faith* and *works*, it's likely to get a lot of attention. Many theological debates have focused on the relationship between those two concepts.

Perhaps that's why we find today's scripture so intriguing. When the crowd asks Jesus about the work that God requires, he responds that the work of God is to believe in the One whom God has sent.

Does this mean belief is work? It can be, and it can be hard work at times. The whole idea of Jesus as fully divine and fully human is challenging. How can a human being be God? Jesus' divinity is the point where Christianity splits away from the other two great monotheistic, Abrahamic faiths of Judaism and Islam. The great mystery of the Incarnation has given rise to some fantastic metaphors. I've heard Jesus compared with the surf on the beach that gives us a glimpse of what the incomprehensible ocean that is God must be like.

A colleague once told me that Jesus is like a windowpane. We peek in and get a sense, only a sense, of the God who lives beyond. But we also get a reflection of our own face. In Jesus, we see God and ourselves, divine and human. Not a simple idea, yet everything else in Christianity flows from it.

Believing can be hard work. Even Jesus acknowledges that! So as we strive to overcome our own unbelief, let's be more understanding of our brothers and sisters who also struggle in their faith. Most of all, let's persevere in the hard work of believing, trusting that God will grant us, in due time, faith sufficient to our need.

PRAYER: All-knowing God, you understand the struggles of our human life. May Jesus, fully human and fully divine, always be our model for this challenge, and may his example bring us eternal trust in your care. Amen.

FIRST SUNDAY OF ADVENT

The other day I was glancing through a hymnal and came across a hymn I haven't heard in recent years. I can understand why, because the title is patriarchal. While I understand that concern, I really wish there was some way to rehabilitate the song because its message of sure confidence in God's plan is important.

As we enter this Advent season, we find ourselves surrounded by hunger, poverty, war, terrorism, and the threats of nuclear, chemical, and biological weapons. We read, both in today's newspapers and in our history books, of terrible violence committed by people who profess Christianity, Judaism, or Islam, claiming Abraham as their common father. We still yearn for God's kingdom in its fullness.

Those of us who are Christians know fellow believers who speak and act as though the Resurrection means nothing more than a personal ticket to heaven, who hear no call to do the transforming work of the Messiah to bring more abundant life to the world in which we live.

Maybe that's why we often encounter Christians who sound so pessimistic; yet Christianity should produce optimists! The story line that runs through sixty-six books of the scripture is that of God's reclaiming God's beloved world and children. We don't know the timetable; we do know the intention!

Maltbie Babcock, a Victorian minister, wrote, "This is my Father's world: why should my heart be sad? The Lord is King; let the heavens ring! God reigns; let the earth be glad!" More than two thousand years earlier, the writer of Isaiah said just about the same: We need not worry about the final outcome. Our task is to march in the light of the Lord and invite all nations and peoples to come to the light of God. God reigns—let us *all* be glad.

PRAYER: God of eternity, help us to trust in your ultimate plans and give us the energy and optimism to work as you call us to be about your business here on earth. Amen.

The God of All

November 29–December 5, 2004 • Amy-Jill Levine[‡]

MONDAY, NOVEMBER 29 • Read Isaiah 11:1-10

Advent focuses on the birth of the one Christians call the Savior, and Isaiah's words are traditionally read as predicting his coming. Yet Isaiah's earliest readers would not have made this connection, and all readers today recognize that the peaceable kingdom Isaiah envisioned remains a hope.

For this ancient prophet, the ideal ruler judges with wisdom and understanding and not according to economic gain or political opportunism. Isaiah has no interest in a faith restricted to a personal relationship with one's Savior, and the religion of Israel was never something that could be practiced apart from others. Isaiah speaks of real rulers, real governments, real communities; his vision is not of a revived self but of a refashioned system.

While the wolf has yet to live with the lamb and while hurt and destruction continue to plague God's holy mountain, Isaiah's message continues to offer both hope and encouragement. Advent requires not only celebrating the past but also assessing the present and, especially, approaching the future. Stumps send out more than one shoot; trees produce more than one branch; the spirit of the Lord rests on all God's children. Isaiah's vision thus need not, and should not, be restricted to that Bethlehem stable; it is a vision that can continue to guide us all.

SUGGESTION FOR MEDITATION: **The glorious sights and sounds of Advent sometimes overshadow the ongoing needs of our community, our country, and our world. We might therefore approach this season with two questions. First, what is our vision of the peaceable kingdom, and second, what is our role in helping to make this vision a reality?**

[‡]E. Rhodes and Leona B. Carpenter Professor of New Testament, Vanderbilt Divinity School; member, Sherith Israel Synagogue, Nashville, Tennessee.

First Kings 3 recounts that King Solomon prayed for an "understanding mind" and the ability "to discern between good and evil" (v. 9). Because Solomon did not ask for riches or long life or the death of his enemies, God granted him not only wisdom but also "both riches and honor" (v. 13). Psalm 72 is one of only two psalms (the other is 127) that carries the subtitle "Of Solomon." The attribution is apt, for the psalm celebrates a wise ruler.

But the gifts of riches and honor and wisdom all come with a set of responsibilities. God charges Solomon "to walk in my ways, keeping my statutes and my commandments" (v. 14), and the psalm praises the king who judges with righteousness, defends the poor, and forestalls the oppressor. Solomon, for all his power and glory and wisdom, failed. He used forced labor to build the temple in Jerusalem, his royal palace, and numerous fortifications (1 Kings 9:15ff.); among his wives were seven hundred princesses and three hundred concubines (1 Kings 11:1-8), which indicates not only that his palace had become a seraglio but also that, through marital alliances, Solomon accommodated himself to the values of other kings and courts rather than attending to the needs of his own people.

If wealth, power, and physical enticements can beguile one as great as Solomon, then we all have good reason to pray, "Give the king your justice, O God, and your righteousness to a king's son."

PRAYER: Grant us, O God, the strength we need to judge wisely, act faithfully, and use our gifts responsibly. Bless us with the ability to know the difference between justice and dictatorship, stewardship and selfishness, enjoyment and exploitation. Amen.

Josephus, a near contemporary of John the Baptist, describes him as "a good man" who exhorted his fellow Jews "to lead righteous lives" and "to practice justice towards their fellows and piety towards God." He notes that John's message centered not on ritual but on repentance. Baptism was not designed to gain pardon from sin; rather, it was, as Josephus put it, a "consecration of the body indicating that the soul was already thoroughly cleansed by right behavior."

John recognized how easily even people of goodwill can become complacent and happy with the status quo. To this comfort level, John issued his challenge: "Prepare the way of the Lord." We might think of this as an ancient version of an altar call. But John was no ordinary preacher, as not only his baptismal practice but also his clothing and diet attest. John reminded his fellow Jews of the prophet Elijah, who had ascended into heaven eight centuries earlier and who, Malachi announced, would return "before the great and terrible day of the LORD" (4:5-6). Thus Elijah became known as the forerunner of the messianic age and, for the church, the forerunner of the Messiah. But the work of Elijah and of John is not yet complete. The paths are not yet straight; the way of the Lord is not fully prepared. Advent offers the opportunity to heed John's call again, "Repent, for the kingdom of heaven has come near," even as John, through his association with Elijah, anticipates the age when all sin is abolished.

SUGGESTION FOR MEDITATION: Elijah was persecuted by King Ahab and Queen Jezebel, and John was beheaded by the tetrarch of Galilee, Herod Antipas, with the support of his wife, Herodias. To prepare the way of the Lord means to be willing to risk all. What then do we need to do to make such preparations, and what are we called upon to risk in the process?

John's words seem somehow distinct from the Christian message. He speaks not about a baby but an ax; not gentle water but unquenchable fire; not welcome but condemnation. But to miss his message is to miss that of Jesus as well, for both baby and Baptist proclaim: "Repent, for the kingdom of heaven has come near" (Matt. 3:2; 4:17). Both called their fellow Jews to become a holy nation. Both died at the hands of Rome's lackeys. And both recognized that piety is not something inherited or stored or determined only by belief. Rather, both John and Jesus insisted that all people bear "good fruit" (3:10; 12:33).

It is sometimes claimed that the Pharisees and Sadducees taught "works righteousness," the idea that one earns one's way into heaven by following every jot and tittle of the Law. But this is not what Judaism taught, any more than it was what John and Jesus—two Jews—taught.

Both Jesus and John believed that Israel was already in covenant with God. People did not have to earn divine love; they already had it. Israel's responsibility under the covenant was to "love the Lord your God with all your heart, and with all your soul, and with all your mind…[and to] love your neighbor as yourself" (Matt. 22:36-39). The verses cited by Jesus as the Great Commandment are taken from Deuteronomy 6:5 and Leviticus 19:18.

Both John and Jesus, Judaism and Christianity, teach about law and grace, responsibility and mercy, belief and action. As the epistle of James states it, "Faith by itself, if it has no works, is dead" (2:17).

SUGGESTION FOR PRAYER: When John the Baptist announced, "God is able from these stones to raise up children to Abraham" (Matt. 3:9), he was punning, for the words for "sons" and "stones" in Aramaic sound alike. Dear God, please make us like fruit-bearing trees: firmly rooted in faith, extending our gifts to all, standing tall and proud as your children. Amen.

The first petition of the Lord's Prayer is "hallowed be your name" (Matt. 6:9), and the penultimate verse of Psalm 72 (the final psalm of David) is "Blessed be his glorious name forever." The divine name is to be hallowed and blessed for all eternity. The problem is, however, that the name is ineffable; it cannot be pronounced. More than convenient labels, in the Bible names often indicate a person's role; for example, "Jesus" comes from the Hebrew for "salvation," and "Immanuel" means "God is with us" (Matt. 1:23).

When Moses at the burning bush asks for God's name, the response is usually translated, "I AM WHO I AM" (Exod. 3:14). The name is in fact a Hebrew verb, and an irregular one at that, which may be better rendered, "I will be what I will be." The Hebrew letters that comprise this name are YHWH, and in turn these are sometimes rendered "Jehovah" or "Yahweh." Neither rendition accurately captures the Hebrew; no rendition can, or should.

Why a verb, and why this verb? This is a God not owned by any one people or nation or church. This is the God of Israel, but also the One who fills the whole earth. No simple translation works, and thus no one group or individual can claim possession of God's full identity. This is a God manifest in history, who is and will be a God of freedom.

In this divine freedom God chooses to be with us; and in this same freedom, we can choose to walk with God.

SUGGESTION FOR PRAYER: "Magnified and sanctified be God's great name in the world which He created according to His will. May His great name be praised to all eternity." (The opening lines of the Kaddish, an Aramaic prayer still recited by Jews today)

SATURDAY, DECEMBER 4 • **Read Romans 15:4-7**

Originally the Roman church was almost entirely Jewish, but in 49 the Emperor Claudius expelled all Jews from Rome, and the demographics changed. After Claudius died, Jews returned to find a much different situation. No longer did the church follow the Torah of Moses, the word of God.

Today many Christians find the situation of these Roman Jews appropriate. Why bother with laws about diet and festivals and Sabbath? Isn't Christ the "end of the law" (Rom. 10:4)? But this view is unfaithful both to Paul and Jesus.

The end of the law means not its cessation but its fulfillment. For those under the law, those Jewish Christians who remained loyal to their tradition, following the law was a blessing and joy, not a curse and burden. How horrible it must have been for them to be told that their way of life, a way that had sustained their people for a millennium, was illegitimate.

The church concluded that what became known as the Old Testament was the Word of God, yet too often this text is wrongly regarded at best as preparation for the gospel and at worst as antithetical to it. To the contrary, this text too is divine revelation. Did Gentiles need to follow the commandments given to Israel? No, for these were given to Jews, not Gentiles. Nevertheless, Gentile disparagement of those who kept the commandments was an insult to Christ himself, for Jesus was a faithful Jew. "What was written in former days was written for our instruction, so that by steadfastness and by encouragement we might have hope."

SUGGESTION FOR MEDITATION: "Old" Testament does not mean "outdated" Testament; it was the Bible of Jesus and of the early church. How might the church recover an appreciation for this text as the ongoing word of God, and how might such an appreciation lead to better relationships among all of God's people?

SECOND SUNDAY OF ADVENT

The term *gentiles* (Greek *ethne*, hence the English word *ethnicity*) refers to people who are neither Jewish nor Samaritan; it is a catch-all term that can also be translated "nations." The covenant community of Israel looked forward to the day when the Gentiles would praise the God of Israel. They did not, however, expect all those Gentiles to become Jews. Rather, they envisioned a time when both Jews and Gentiles, Israel and the nations, would worship together in harmony. In effect, they held on to a view of multiculturalism. Thus Paul cites several passages from his own scriptural tradition: "I will confess you among the Gentiles" (Ps. 18:49); "Rejoice, O Gentiles, with his people" (Deut.32:43); "Praise the Lord, all you Gentiles" (Ps.117:1); "in him the Gentiles shall hope" (Isa. 11:10).

Most first-century Jews did not think that Gentiles needed to convert to Judaism in order to be in a right relationship with God. Israel speaks of "righteous gentiles," people who behave with moral fidelity, from Pharaoh's daughter and the midwives who saved the Israelite babies from destruction to their modern-day counterparts who sheltered Jews marked for death by the Nazis.

To praise God does not require that one be a member of a particular nation or church. Christians, Jews, and Muslims all worship the same God and recollect the "promises given to the patriarchs." Just as God's name cannot be contained by any one translation, so God's praise cannot be restricted to any one creed or doctrine.

As Paul recognized long ago, more praising and less condemnation, more hope and less self-satisfaction lead to welcoming, welcoming to joy, and joy to peace.

PRAYER: Holy God, help us to honor the diversity of your world, to celebrate the righteous from among all your peoples, and to hallow the many ways your name is praised. Amen.

God's Signs

December 6–12, 2004 • Luther E. Smith Jr.[‡]

MONDAY, DECEMBER 6 • Read Isaiah 35:1-7

God transforms places and people, and the changes are dramatic. Forbidding places become places of beauty and inspiration. The weak, frightened, and physically disabled are strengthened, assured, and healed. Where life seems forever harsh, new and vital realities burst forth.

God's activity is cause for rejoicing. The transformations are surprising and welcomed. Still, as wonderful as the changes are, their significance is more about the nature of God than about God's ability to transform nature. The transformations are *signs* of God's love and power—signs that tell us God knows and cares about our conditions. These are signs of God's loving intimacy with us, of God's power to create new possibilities for us. God's signs assure us of present help and point us to a future that we do not imagine for ourselves.

With all the splendor of God's transformations, there remains the disquieting message: "He will come with vengeance, with terrible recompense." We are most ready to identify ourselves as the ones God "will come and save." But is it possible that we are a source of oppression for God's people? God's signs of deliverance for the oppressed are also signs of judgment against those who oppress. Are we so living that God's transformations are cause for rejoicing or cause for fear and anguish?

PRAYER: O God, in your transforming work, transform us. Instill in us the desire for your deliverance from oppression and deliverance from our oppressing ways. May our relationships with your people be a sign of your love and power. Help us to live our lives so that we delight in your coming and you delight in us. Amen.

[‡]Professor of Church and Community, Candler School of Theology, Emory University, Atlanta, Georgia; clergy member of the Christian Methodist Episcopal Church.

Highways are reassuring signs that a route has been charted to get us from here to there. Yet we know that travel on a highway is no guarantee of arrival at our destination. Dead ends, detours, and wrong turns can cause us to be lost. Isaiah's description of God's highway eliminates anxiety about such an outcome. God's "Holy Way" is certain to get us where we need to be. Even the foolish among us can make the journey.

Highways can be dangerous. Travelers may experience life-threatening encounters on the road. In Isaiah's description, *absence* is a sign of God's protection—a highway absent persons who attempt to pervert God's transformed order, a highway absent attacking animals that destroy pilgrims on their journey. Absence is also a sign of protection and life in current contexts. Schools post notices that neither illegal drugs nor guns are allowed on their premises. Restaurants prohibit smoking and pets to maintain a healthy environment for customers. Sometimes our security is defined not only by what is present but also by what is absent.

Presence is a sign of God's transformations. Isaiah says that the very name ("Holy Way") of this highway is confirmation, a sign, of its trustworthiness. Another sign is the presence of those once alienated from their homeland returning to the place God has prepared for them. They return with a testimony and joy that can only be expressed through singing. And the presence of "joy and gladness" forces the absence of "sorrow and sighing."

All this coming and going is how God creates newness. The highway itself is a sure sign of God's transforming activity, and so is its traffic.

PRAYER: God, help us to journey faithfully on the way you have prepared for us. May the joy you have given us inspire us to sing the songs of Zion and to be lifted by the singing of all you have called home. Amen.

Do you trust God with your life? Do not answer too quickly. Spiritual formation relies upon your honest assessment of how you live in answer to this question. As people of faith we often profess, sing, and pray about surrendering our lives to God. However, our decisions about careers, social relationships, financial stewardship, and seeking power that controls others suggest that God is often, at best, an afterthought. Or God is our backup commitment when our primary loyalties fail. Or we may use God's name as a convenient device to justify our desires and behavior.

Earlier the psalmist warned against misplaced devotion (vv. 3-4). In this particular psalm the warning is not a comparison between bad princes and a good God. The morality of mortals is not the concern. The contrast is between those who die (and whose abilities die with them) and God who "keeps faith forever." The God who created everything is also the One who cares for the most vulnerable (the oppressed and hungry), including us. Power and compassion. Whom do you trust with your life?

Our motivation for choosing God may reveal how much we truly understand about entrusting our lives to God. The spirit of the psalm does not turn to God out of resignation to God's power. Turning to God is not a lament that other loyalties have died. The psalm sings praises again and again because of the joy of life being given to God. This joy may be a sure sign of whether we trust God with our lives.

PRAYER: We praise you, O God, for all that you are to us. We rejoice and relax in the assurance that when we give our lives to you, we experience the fulfillment for which you created them. May our lives be a sign of our trust in you in times of failure and success, laughter and tears, certainty and doubt. And thank you, O God, for your everlasting love. Amen.

Amazing signs appear throughout the land, and identifying the source of these signs is the intent of the psalmist's praise. The Lord sets free. The Lord opens eyes. The Lord lifts up. The Lord loves. The Lord watches over. The Lord upholds. The recitation of deeds with the repetition of their cause accentuates these transformations as holy activity. Sacred work looks like this.

The recipients of this holy activity are also signs of God's passion. Prisoners, the blind, those bowed down, the righteous, strangers, orphans, and widows may be discounted by rulers and the masses; but God chooses to express power and love through them and their plight. The overlooked and outcast are signs of the pervasiveness of God's love. If you want to be where God is manifest, follow the signs!

The litany of inspiring transformations is another sign of God—the way of the wicked brought to ruin. Who are these wicked? Unlike the listing of those favored by God, the psalmist does not specify a list of wicked deeds and persons. Throughout the Psalms, however, such naming of deeds (see Ps. 37) and persons (see Ps. 135:9-11) does appear. The wicked are those who oppose the holy commands and activity of God. While many of us may not imagine ourselves as among the wicked, we must ask ourselves if we clearly interact with the overlooked and outcast whom God chooses. The indifferent are as culpable in sustaining oppression as those who oppress with zeal. May our commitment lead us to serve God's holy activity of transformation rather than to become a sign of what God has brought to ruin.

PRAYER: God, guide us to the places and people you choose. Save us from the wicked and from wickedness. And may our praise of you honor generations past and inspire generations to come. Amen.

Advent is a season of anticipation. And what a difficult season it can be. We could easily cope with the strain if it only involved that childhood impatience for the day of gift giving to arrive. But we are desperate for a fulfillment that only God can provide. This desperation does not question if time will pass; the life-and-death matter is whether fulfillment will come. Perhaps we begin to understand the meaning of Advent to the extent that we experience this sense of desperation.

James's admonition for patience comes to believers who experience this desperation. The pressure upon the believers is so great that he employs three examples of patience in desperate times to encourage them: first, the farmer whose crop is a life-and-death matter; second, the prophets who suffered yet remained faithful through rejection; and third, Job, who endured unimaginable tragedy. James hopes to encourage believers to anticipate the future by drawing upon the witness of those whom God has sustained in the past. The past thus becomes a resource for the future. Sacred history sustains us for Advent.

In proclaiming God's transforming power, we often refer to insufferable conditions changed into joyful ones by God. However, we also experience circumstances where God does not change the conditions but changes us through the gift of endurance. This endurance is not a second-class gift of God. Too often endurance is what we are left to do when better options have failed. Yet endurance is not the default practice that signals God's absence but the experience of God's sustaining love and joy even when distressing conditions continue. During this Advent season, your endurance may be a sign to other pilgrims that God keeps us through crisis and through the waiting for the fulfillment to come.

PRAYER: God, we confess that often the waiting gets to us. Teach us how to endure so that bitterness is held at bay and your joy is our companion. Amen.

"Are you the one who is to come, or are we to wait for another?" John's question is asked from death row. And like his prison cell situation, the question is unpretentious and critical. A death row inmate needs forthright answers. The direct question seems to beg for a truth that is revealed best in a simple yes or no response. Instead, Jesus answers by referring to the results of his holy activity. These signs bear testimony to his identity.

Jesus' answer matches descriptions from Isaiah regarding the coming of the long-awaited and promised Messiah. If John were not familiar with the signs of the Messiah, then Jesus' response might be received as an evasive riddle. But John's work as herald of God's new reality suggests that he was rooted deeply in his faith traditions. Jesus' answer regarding the signs was a more direct, trustworthy, and revealing response than any yes or no could ever be.

Awareness of the manifestation of God's promises requires knowing the signs. What we so desperately desire may be expressed all around us. But unless we discern the signs, we can easily feel uncertain about hope.

How do you witness to what God is doing in the world? Do you develop relationships among people of different races, ethnic groups, nationalities, economic class, and physical ability? Do your spiritual practices deepen your understanding of sacred scriptures, Christian traditions, and God's activity in others and in you? Consider your availability to the disheartened and oppressed. Jesus answered John's disciples by saying, "Go and tell John what you hear and see...." How do your routines and commitments place you in opportunities to "hear and see" God's presence and compassion?

PRAYER: This Advent season, O God, guide us to anticipate your coming through the practices, people, and causes that are both sources of preparation and inspiration for our discipleship. Amen.

THIRD SUNDAY OF ADVENT

Earlier in this chapter, John inquired about Jesus' identity (v. 3). In today's scripture, Jesus tells the crowds about the identity of John. Identity clarification is prevalent in Matthew 11. Jesus is clear about the meaning of John's prophetic witness, and he praises John as fulfilling a role that advances God's coming realm. With rhetorical skills at full stretch, Jesus could not deliver a greater tribute than, "Truly I tell you, among those born of women no one has arisen greater than John the Baptist."

Then Jesus immediately says, "Yet the least in the kingdom of heaven is greater than [John]." Not meant to diminish John's significance, this statement is about focusing on those for whom God's holy activity is done. As one of God's signs, John points to God's realm; and God's realm comes to make whole those who are the passion of God's heart. What an amazing stratification of status! The "least" are the "greater." They are the purpose for God's radical transformations of persons and systems of authority and power. They (we) can experience a fulfillment that was not available to John and the earlier prophets.

Today personal greatness is often determined by one's ability to gain wealth, prestige, and power. Jesus speaks about the greatness of those who surrender themselves to the fuller manifestation of God's activity. To participate in God's movement throughout the earth is to become a person of privilege—not privilege to which others defer but privilege attendant to an invitation from God. Rather than squander our privilege to witness, we must bear witness to God's realm as never before.

PRAYER: O God, help us to read the signs of your advent, including one another, so that the fulfillment of our greatness is not lost to us nor to you. Amen.

Invited to the Feast

December 13–19, 2004 • Duffy Robbins[‡]

MONDAY, DECEMBER 13 • Read Isaiah 7:10-13

King Ahaz is between a rock and a hard place, his city squarely in the cross-hairs of Syria and Israel. His last remaining hope is the alliance he had forged with Assyria's king, Tiglath-pileser, his forces, and their pagan god, Ashur. But now, with enemies at the gate and the Assyrians not yet at hand, comes the amazingly gracious offer of verses 10-11.

For the evil king Ahaz, welcoming divine help is like the thief who is discovered midheist by a security guard who, unaware the man is stealing, offers to turn on the light so the man can see better. The last thing Ahaz wants to do is expose his idolatrous and unfaithful rule to the light of God. With what appears to be humility, he replies, "I will not ask; I will not put the LORD to the test." But, of course, God sees the charade for what it is: pride disguised as modesty.

It is a remarkably uncomfortable moment for Ahaz. He has refused the help of a God he desperately needs. We are stunned to think that Ahaz can be so foolish. Stunned, that is, until we realize that the story of Ahaz may be our own story as well.

SUGGESTION FOR MEDITATION: How often do we bank on the false hopes of our own resources or the false "Ashur-ances" of gods that are no gods or the false alliances of our own networks rather than humble ourselves under the mighty hand of God? Perhaps guilt keeps us in the dark or maybe we believe that accepting divine help would require us to give in return. Perhaps pride in our own self-sufficiency keeps us from the help we need so desperately. Whatever it was for Ahaz and whatever it is for us, this brief encounter reminds us that we are in deep need. Our only hope is that God will provide a sign or a Savior in whom we might find refuge.

[‡]Chair of the Department of Youth Ministry, Eastern College, St. Davids, Pennsylvania.

King Ahaz's stunning refusal to accept God's offer of help is, no doubt, rooted in a deadly combination of fear and pride. But ultimately it took root in a view of life that is too small and shallow to encompass the wide vistas of God's goodness. "Ask the LORD your God for a sign, whether in the deepest depths or in the highest heights."

The tragedy of those who refuse God's hand is not that we want too much but that we want too little. The blinders of human greed and insecurity keep us from seeing the wide-open places of God's grace, a generosity measured in "deepest depths" and "highest heights." The normal puny standards of human expectation: financial gain, elevated status, increased power, and momentary pleasure are inadequate to measure the vast expanse of grace and abundance that is God's goodness.

Ahaz, like a slave who has for so long been stealing from his master, now suspects the master's offer to join the household. He cannot believe life holds more than the deception, guilt, and impending doom he lives with daily.

From our vantage point centuries later, we look back on Ahaz and wonder why he said no to God. What did he think he could need that might fall outside the boundaries of "highest heights" and "deepest depths"? But that was precisely the problem. Ahaz suffered from a failure of imagination. He could not conceive of boundaries deeper and higher than those he already knew. He swapped his God-sized longings for pathetic, little "king-sized" dreams.

SUGGESTION FOR MEDITATION: In a world where dreams are mapped by Wall Street, desires are shaped by Hollywood, and spiritual longings are defined by dime-store prophets of self-help and self-realization, there is great danger that we might fall into Ahaz's error. We need to heed the grave warning of settling for a life surrounded and sinking when God calls us to an abundance of "highest heights" and "deepest depths."

In the first verse of Psalm 80, its writer, Asaph, revisits an image that we have seen before in other psalms, the image of God as our Shepherd. It is a wonderful image of the God who leads us (80:1; 23:3), feeds us (23:5), carries us (28:9), protects us (23:4) and grants us rest (23:2). It is a vivid picture of sacrificial concern and consistent, watchful care.

But the notion of God as a Shepherd is also noteworthy, because it provides two powerful images of God's love:

(1) Dying to find us. Jesus' own teaching about the Lord our Shepherd tells the story of a God who passionately seeks lost sheep and expresses great joy when they are found (Luke 15:3-7). He pursues the lost sheep, not as a sheriff who hunts for the purpose of prosecution but as a shepherd who seeks for the purpose of protection.

(2) Dying to save us. Even more powerful than the notion of the Lord as our Shepherd is the stunning fact that this Shepherd became one of the sheep. As we celebrate this Advent season, we stand in awe with John the Baptist who said of Jesus, "Here is the Lamb of God, who takes away the sin of the world!" (John 1:29). So full and complete is the love of God that the very same Shepherd who seeks lost sheep becomes one of the sheep so he can be slain for those that are lost (Isa. 53:7).

This is the wonder we celebrate at Christmas: that lying in the manger, surrounded by shepherds from the local countryside, was God incarnate, a Shepherd of the shepherds and a sheep among the sheep.

PRAYER: Lord Jesus, our Shepherd and our sacrificial Lamb, we join those who centuries ago gathered in wonder at your birth, and, alongside the shepherds of old, we kneel in the throne room disguised as a stable. Amen.

They used to be everywhere—the omnipresent little yellow buttons and stickers on which was printed a simple, perpetual smiling face. Beaming from the surfaces of T-shirts, neckties, frisbees, and windshields, the smiley faces began to be annoying after a while, as if a full life were one lived in perpetual stupor, a paste-on smile, emotions unfazed by everyday reality.

The danger comes when we project the perpetual "smiley face" of pop culture onto the face of God—as if the eleventh commandment were "Don't worry; be happy." When we get to that point, we are in danger of creating God in our own image.

We may prefer to think of God as some jolly deity, sort of a Friar Tuck character who remains mildly amused by human affairs. But Psalm 80 reminds us that such a portrait is a caricature of the God who both smiles and frowns, a God who shines with favor and a God who smolders in anger.

Perhaps this portrait of God is difficult to square with the Disney-esque character we often hear described from both pulpits and pundits. But a God who truly loves must be more than the Great Eternal Happy Face. A truly loving Father cannot look on disobedient children, lost opportunities, broken lives, and human misery with an eternal smirk. It is no wonder we are told that "the Lord disciplines whom he loves" (Heb. 12:6).

Indeed, as the raw remorse of Psalm 80 demonstrates, to take this relationship seriously is to move beyond phony stick-on smiles and to plead for the authentic joy that is the reflection of God's favor. The psalmist's growing intensity—moving from "O Shepherd" (v. 1), to "O God" (v. 3) to "O God Almighty" (v. 7), to "O Lord God Almighty" (v. 19)—reminds us that tears of grief are often the seeds for a harvest of restored joy.

PRAYER: O Lord God Almighty, may we seek your face with the reverence of those who understand that your face can be marked by both a smile and a frown. Amen.

As he does in every letter, Paul begins his letter to the Romans with a brief word of greeting and introduction, often referred to by Bible scholars as the prescript of his letter. In fact, the prescript of Paul's letter to the Romans is one of the longest of all of his letters, some six verses before he actually addresses the recipients of the letter in verse 7.

In that opening prescript we read these words: "Paul, a servant of Christ Jesus, called to be an apostle" (Rom. 1:1). It is a phrase quite typical of Paul and one he often uses to describe his calling (Gal. 1:10; Col. 1:25, 27; Titus 1:10), a calling that combines his apostolic mission with a call to servanthood.

In reading those words we can easily hear them as a mandate different from our own. After all, most of the time the New Testament uses the word *apostle* to describe someone who has seen Christ personally and has been commissioned especially by him to serve as a foundation of the church (Eph. 2:20; Acts 1:12-26). Surely that is a title none of us reading these words can claim.

And yet, there is this observation to be made. The only place in the whole of scripture where the word *apostle* is used in a general sense with reference to all the disciples of Jesus is when Jesus said in John 13:16, "I tell you the truth, no servant is greater than his master, nor is a messenger (*apostolos*) greater than the one who sent him." It is a reminder that, at least in this one sense, all believers are messengers or apostles.

Jesus made this statement, of course, in the upper room just after he had taken up a towel to wash the feet of his disciples. This is especially noteworthy because it reminds us of two significant truths: (1) servanthood will always be at the foundation of the church; and (2) while we may not all be apostles of the foundation, we are all called to be apostles of the towel.

PRAYER: Lord, make us conscious today that while our title may be different from Paul's, our task is the same: servanthood as the hands of Jesus Christ. Amen.

Perhaps we've all had the experience of hearing about some party event and hoping that we have been invited. Maybe it's a birthday party, a banquet, a sleepover (remember those when you were a kid?), a dinner party. As others begin to receive invitations, we start to wonder but don't dare hope, *Will mine be coming too?* And then finally the envelope arrives, "The pleasure of your company is requested...."

That is the same sense of joy and wonder we should feel when we read that little phrase in Romans 1:6, "And you also are among those who are called to belong to Jesus Christ." Three little words, "And you also...", that usher in a whole vocabulary of great news: We too are called to belong to Jesus Christ.

"And you also..." We cannot read these words without a profound sense of awe, awe that we are invited to the Great Banquet Feast of the Lamb. Especially since we have done nothing to endear ourselves to the Host. We have disobeyed, acted as if the Host didn't exist, changed our address before the invitations were sent, ignored all follow-up calls, and even occasionally forsaken the party, believing that we can cook up something better.

Through the grace of God, the Lord of Hosts has invited even you to the party. As Paul says elsewhere in this same letter, "God demonstrates his own love for us in this: While we were still sinners, Christ died for us" (Rom. 5:8).

SUGGESTION FOR MEDITATION: **Read prayerfully through the words of this great hymn by Charles Wesley. Sing it quietly to God as your own personal doxology.**

> **And can it be that I should gain an interest in the Savior's blood? Died he for me? who caused his pain! For me? who him to death pursued? Amazing love! How can it be that thou, my God, shouldst die for me?**

Fourth Sunday of Advent

The gospel contains a mystery; and no matter how much we might wish it weren't so, it can't be smoothed over or explained away. It begins in words like those we read here in the first portion of Matthew 1:23: "The virgin will be with child and will give birth to a son..." (NIV). It continues with the unfolding of the truth we read in the latter part of verse 23, "They will call him Immanuel—which means, 'God with us'" (NIV). Such a mystery troubles us, insulting the majesty of our own supposed wisdom and our ability to maintain control and order; we resist the notion that Jesus was actually born of a virgin.

Our attempts to explain away the virgin birth by suggesting that the scripture means only to say that Mary was a "young woman" makes nonsense of Joseph's concerns in the preceding verses (Matt. 1:18-21). But such mysteries may offend us for another reason. What we really want from scripture is a how-to manual. We want life with God reduced to easy, simple steps: five easy steps to a happy life, four easy steps to wonderful children, three easy steps to a pain-free life. Essentially, that was the Pharisees' mistake. They sought the Word become word. Jesus was the Word become flesh.

God calls us to a relationship, a dance of passion and movement, intimacy and adventure. We want God to give us the steps. The mystery of the gospel is that God calls us to seek God's face, read God's word, take the time to develop that growing intimacy. In the mystery of that relationship, we find we are moving in unison with the holy.

Whether we try to sidestep the mystery of God's plan or simply reduce it to steps, neither does justice to the event described that day by the angel of the Lord. That's why God didn't just send us a how-to manual; God sent us Immanuel, "God with us."

Prayer: God of wonder, may I dance in unison with you. Amen.

From Darkness to Light

December 20–26, 2004 • Vigen Guroian[‡]

MONDAY, DECEMBER 20 • Read Hebrews 2:10-18

One night in Armenia after the devastating earthquake of December 1988, I sat with a father who mourned the loss of his ten-year-old son. Together we read the last chapter of the book of Job.

Afterward I said, "Kevork, it says that God instructs Job to pray for his friends who have misrepresented God in their counsel. Why do you suppose God accepts the prayers of Job, who has angrily cursed God?" Kevork answered unhesitatingly, "Vigen, I suppose it is because Job suffered." I responded, "Kevork, I think you are right. This reminds me of Jesus. Maybe Jesus is near to you now and also to all the other husbands and fathers we saw today in the park who wander in dark paths of despair and fear."

Nothing I said that night could bring Kevork's son Armen back. I thought, however, that Paul answered Job's question and Kevork's: "But mortals die, and are laid low; humans expire, and where are they?" (Job 14:10). Paul responds, "But in fact Christ has been raised from the dead,…so also in Christ shall all be made alive" (1 Cor. 15:20, 22, RSV).

On Christmas we celebrate joyfully the birth of the Christ child who brings salvation. The writer of Hebrews reminds us, however, that eternal life is purchased at the price of the suffering and death of Jesus who "is not ashamed to call [us] brothers and sisters." Even now we should not forget that in a sinful world, suffering is mysteriously the highest credential for redeeming prayer, and the full meaning of Christmas is fulfilled by the cross and the empty tomb.

SUGGESTION FOR MEDITATION: How does suffering purify us for prayer?

[‡]Professor of Theology, Loyola College, Baltimore, Maryland; Armenian Orthodox.

Eastern Christian icons of the Nativity depict the Christ child lying in a dark cave, conspicuously wrapped in swaddling clothes that glisten white with a supernal light. Yet, strikingly, the swaddling clothes also strongly resemble the burial wrappings that the three myrrh-bearing women find folded in the empty tomb of the Easter icon.

This juxtaposition of images is a reminder that the Savior comes into a world darkened by sin and death, bringing life and light into that world. In order to rescue and redeem humanity, however, he himself must die and be buried and descend on Holy Saturday into black Hades to lift with his strong arms Adam and Eve and all of their descendants into the luminous heavenly city. In that city, says the seer, there is not even a "need of sun or moon..., for the glory of God is its light, and its lamp is the Lamb" (Rev. 21:23, RSV).

"God's flesh was a light-bearing torch and dissipated the darkness of Hades," an Orthodox Easter hymn proclaims. This is the light that John speaks of when he says, "The light shines in the darkness, and the darkness has not overcome it" (John 1:5, RSV).

Nevertheless, let us never forget that first there is darkness. Our sin has made this world a darkened cave and burial tomb. Were it not for the Lord of Life and Light coming into this world and into our flickering lives, night and death would triumph. This is why Christmas is a source of great joy and hope.

SUGGESTION FOR MEDITATION: **"A star showed plainly to the Magi/The Word that was before the sun, who has come to make transgression cease./They saw Thee wrapped in swaddling clothes, within a poor and lowly cave,/Who shares all our sufferings,/And in joy they gazed upon Thee, who art both man and Lord."** (Orthodox hymn for the Nativity)

Why do we consider Psalm 96 a birthday song for the Christ child? Does not the Incarnation concern humankind alone? We are in the habit of thinking so, but this is a mistake. There is more than a grain of truth in admonitions that an extreme anthropocentrism is not a good thing.

"Let the heavens be glad, and let the earth rejoice; let the sea roar, and all that fills it; /let the field exult, and everything in it." John helps us to understand the meaning, for Jesus Christ is the preexistent Word of God become flesh. He "in the beginning ... was with God...all things were made through him, and without him was not anything made that was made.... [For] the Word became flesh and dwelt among us, full of grace and truth" (John 1:1-3, 14, RSV).

God's redemptive act in Jesus Christ is continuous with God's original creative purpose. Pleased with creation in the beginning, God would have it right in the end. Although everything God made was "very good" (Gen 1:31), since Adam, human sin has covered all creation with a shroud. "The earth lies polluted under its inhabitants;...Therefore a curse devours the earth" (Isa. 24:4-6). Now the divine Word, through whom all things came to be, enters this world as a man. He begins his great redemptive and restorative work, which is to set all of creation "free from its bondage to decay" so that it may obtain "the glorious liberty of the children of God" (Rom. 8:21, RSV).

SUGGESTION FOR MEDITATION: An Eastern Orthodox Christmas hymn explains what is depicted in all traditional Nativity icons: "Every creature... offers Thee thanks. The angels... , a hymn; the heavens, a star; the Magi, gifts; the shepherds, their wonder; the earth, its cave; the wilderness, the manger; and we offer Thee a Virgin Mother."

Herod was intent upon putting an end to the newly born Messiah once he heard the testimony of the Magi (Matt. 2:7-8). Murder was in his heart, and it did not matter how many children must die in order to accomplish that end. When the Magi did not return, Herod realized that they had tricked him. Coveting his own power, he sent his soldiers to kill "all the male children in Bethlehem and in all that region who were two years old or under" (RSV).

Herod's cruelty left a deep impression upon the early church. The murder of the innocents was nearly as strong a memory as the scene at the manger. These children were the first martyrs of the Christian faith. Their memory contributed mightily to the church's objection to infanticide and abortion in an ancient culture that did not much value the lives of little ones. The Feast Day of the Holy Innocents is December 28 in the West and December 29 in the East. Yet among modern Christians, the story and the feast are forgotten or repressed, perhaps because they rub uncomfortably against sentimentalist pieties.

Some modern poets have tried to revive the memory of the Innocents. In W. H. Auden's Christmas oratorio *For the Time Being*, Herod justifies his deed, reminding us of our own excuses for evil:

Why can't people be sensible? I don't want to be horrid....How dare [God] allow me to decide? I've tried to be good. I brush my teeth....I'm a liberal. I want everyone to be happy. I wish I had never been born.

SUGGESTION FOR MEDITATION: "They heeded not a jot/The rending voice of Ramah/And the children that were not." (G. K. Chesterton, "The Neglected Child")

CHRISTMAS EVE

The Orthodox Christian tradition and the Roman Catholic Church venerates Mary for her faith and holiness, for being the first disciple and, in that sense, not only the mother of Jesus, Son of God and Son of Man, but also the mother of the church. Thus, in icons of Jesus' ascension, Mary stands at center among the apostles, with her arms raised upward as she looks toward the glorified Jesus lifted in a cloud.

Luke reminds us that Mary does not cease, after the freshness of Jesus' birth, to store and ponder the wonders that surround him. When she and Joseph find him in the temple in Jerusalem at age twelve teaching the elders and scribes, Luke says, "His mother kept all these things in her heart" (2:51, RSV). Though she does not fully understand her son or his mission, she stores up the treasure of every moment spent with him.

Mary, writes Cardinal John Henry Newman (1801–90), is "our pattern of faith." Dwelling upon and considering what she has seen and heard, she does not believe blindly. Neither does she insist on understanding completely in order to submit and act. She believes because she also loves. Belief and love light her understanding, which grows because she continues to have faith and to listen and observe.

SUGGESTION FOR MEDITATION: Jesus says, "As for that [which fell] in the good soil, they are those who, hearing the word, hold it fast in an honest and good heart, and bring forth fruit with patience" (Luke 8:15, RSV).

CHRISTMAS DAY

Who is this babe lying in a manger over whom not only humanity rejoices but all of the elements and the whole creation (Ps. 148)? The psalmist says he is the Lord: He is God come among us, Immanuel. "O sing to the LORD a new song;/sing to the LORD, all the earth./Sing to the LORD, bless his name; tell of his salvation from day to day./Declare his glory among the nations" (Ps. 96:1-3). And our reading from the letter to the Hebrews declares that he is the Son of God, reflecting all the divine glory and "bears the very stamp of [God's] nature, upholding the universe by his word of power" (RSV).

Jesus' birth is not the comfortable and cozy domestic scene we like to imagine. The invisible God has been made manifest in our flesh, taken from a mother, Mary, and exposed to grave danger for our sakes. Herod (and all his cruel imitators through the whole of history, among whom even I may be counted) would put an end to Jesus if they could. For his power is greater than theirs; his holiness is the purifying blaze of the burning bush, which destroys even death, the last bitter fruit of sin.

Eastern Nativity icons remind us that darkness and danger surround this birth. The cave signifies this sinful world and also is reminiscent of the sepulchre in which Jesus is buried. Even the babe's swaddling clothes resemble burial wrappings. The devil, dressed as a shepherd, tempts a dejected and confused Joseph in a lower left-hand corner. And the Magis' presence signals danger, for we should not forget that Herod has interrogated them and is intent upon destroying the Messiah child (Matt. 2:7-9). Yet despite all of these dangers, our salvation is secure in Jesus, who "reflects the glory of God...upholding the universe by [God's] word of power" (RSV).

PRAYER: Lord Jesus Christ, Son of God, have mercy on me, sinner that I am. Lord Jesus, thank you for the blessings of this day. Amen.

FIRST SUNDAY AFTER CHRISTMAS DAY

On the cross, Jesus says to the penitent thief, "Today you will be with me in Paradise" (Luke 23:43, RSV). Christians take great comfort in this assurance, in part because it is so consistent with the promise of Christmas.

What will heaven be like? Origen of Alexandria (185–254) says that Jesus is the kingdom of heaven in person. Paradise is in the cave of the Nativity. An Orthodox hymn proclaims: "Bethlehem has opened Eden…, let us take possession of the paradise that is within the cave." In Christ, humankind is renewed and restored to wholeness and unity with its surroundings. Eden is revealed and opened once more within a humble manger, the home of dumb creatures.

The ox and the ass stand over the Christ child, so near that he breathes in their breath. They are present in the earliest known Christian depictions of the Nativity. Isaiah's prophecy is fulfilled: "The ox knows its owner, and the ass its master's crib" (Isa. 1:3, RSV).

If Paradise is inside that cave, if Bethlehem opens to Eden, then are we not permitted to believe that heaven is earth renewed? If everything that comes fresh from God's hands, through God's eternal Word, is good, then surely heaven includes Eden's plenitude, only more real and beautiful than anything before, luminous with the Son's glory, enlivened with the breath of the Spirit.

Thus Psalm 148 brings the whole cast of God's creatures, first introduced in Genesis, back to the praise of the Lord: "Mountains and all hills, fruit trees and all cedars!/Beasts and all cattle, creeping things and flying birds!/ Kings of the earth and all peoples" (RSV).

SUGGESTION FOR MEDITATION: "The heavens and the earth are around us that it may be possible…to speak of the unseen by the seen; for the outermost husk of creation has correspondence with the deepest things of the Creator." (George MacDonald, *Unspoken Sermons*)

Living for the Praise of God's Glory

December 27–31, 2004 • Beth Porter[‡]

MONDAY, DECEMBER 27 • Read John 1:1-18

This week we continue to celebrate God's gracious Self-gift by reflecting on what it means to live "for the praise of [God's] glory" (Eph. 1:12). Two experiences have profoundly influenced my spiritual understanding: I live in a L'Arche community with people who have developmental disabilities and with their assistants. L'Arche (French for "the ark," meaning Noah's ark), is inspired by the Beatitudes, the conviction that the poor person is also blessed with gifts for others, and that in our own poverty we discover God. Several Jewish or Muslim members introduced me to the second influence on my spiritual understanding—the encounter with other religions. In this week's reflections, I draw on L'Arche and interfaith experiences.

In his opening verses, John recapitulates christologically the opening of the book of Genesis. As in Genesis, light is at the beginning in John: Jesus represents light overcoming darkness, order overcoming disorder. The image is pregnant with the promise of goodness to come.

An artist friend named Marta is Jewish. She survived a concentration camp but lost most of her family members in the Holocaust, an experience that touches all her art. I had expected her paintings to be dark. But Marta chooses to spread life and beauty through her art, painting in vibrant colors. One work she titled simply *Bereshit*, the Hebrew word for "in the beginning." An abstract piece full of blues, greens, and shades of rose, it evokes light, freedom, and possibility.

SUGGESTION FOR MEDITATION: When we pay attention to the light, darkness doesn't triumph. To what darkness in your life might you say, "I beg to differ"?

[‡]Pastoral team member, L'Arche Daybreak community, Toronto, Canada; writer on spirituality and interfaith matters.

In today's passage the psalmist enumerates some of God's many blessings. And in wonder (not arrogance) the psalmist exclaims that God has not dealt thus with any other nation! Wonder is a path to gratitude.

Sometimes we may wonder at another's goodness. When an assistant leaves one of our L'Arche homes we are sad, but we gather to celebrate his or her time with us. Each person in the household has an opportunity to say something to the assistant. What emerges is usually a litany of the practical ways the assistant has blessed the rest of us, almost like a psalm of praise and thanksgiving: "You took me to see my family. You played the piano for us. You went shopping for new clothes with me. We went to the beach together. You always cleaned up the kitchen. I think Tracy (who doesn't talk) would like to thank you for helping her make candles at the craft studio. I'm glad you stayed home with me when I was sick. You were flexible when I needed to change the schedule." Gratitude has been called "the attitude of beatitude." Indeed, by the end of these times of sharing, our feelings of sadness about saying good-bye have usually lifted, and as we join in a concluding prayer and song we are filled with a sense of having been deeply blessed.

Whether life has been fair to us is often a matter of perception. Psychotherapists talk about helping patients "reframe" their experiences so as to see them differently. Moving against darkness by celebrating whatever small rays of light we may find can open new vistas. If we begin by offering a sacrifice of praise and thanks, we may find that spontaneous praise and happiness follow.

SUGGESTION FOR MEDITATION: **Create a psalm of thanksgiving for someone close to you. Sing it to God. Perhaps also share it with the person.**

As today's psalm passage indicates, the ancient Hebrews knew that God's Law, given them at Sinai, was the most precious of gifts. It formed them into a people and gave them a social order based on justice exercised with mercy, not on appeasing the whims of unpredictable warring deities such as were worshiped by peoples around them.

As a young student I picked up on the common Christian law-grace dichotomy suggested in John's Gospel. I thought of the law as stern and fearsome and of the new dispensation of grace initiated by Jesus Christ as loving and gracious.

Only years later, when I began to take my Jewish friend Ellen to synagogue services, did I perceive a different vision of the Law and realized my former understanding was simplistic and misrepresentative of Judaism. As the Torah, the five books of Moses containing the Law, is carried through the congregation before being read, members reach out to touch or kiss it. Ellen loves to be called up for the Torah reading or to open the ark where the Torah is kept. There is often a lively discussion on the contemporary relevance of the passage read. As the Torah is restored to the Ark, a lovely song expresses the belovedness of God's Law: "She is a tree of life to all those who follow her...."

Of course, grace and judgment are found in both testaments of the Bible. In what, then, do Christians rejoice? Not that Christianity has replaced the Jewish religion but that by God's grace and through the faithfulness of Christ Jesus, we understand ourselves to have been redeemed, forgiven, and adopted (Eph. 1:5-9), so that we also are God's people. While rabbinic Judaism developed its own vibrant character over the past two thousand years and today is as diverse in its expression as is Christianity, we share with Jews the rich heritage of the Hebrew Scriptures.

PRAYER: Thank you, God, for your love made evident in our experiences of law and of grace. Amen.

What does it mean to live "for the praise of [God's] glory"? Possibly it means being in daily relationship with our best spirit—trying to listen, admitting mistakes, communicating truthfully and with love, doing justice. But perhaps these days it means one other thing. An international relations specialist refers to "the interfaith imperative," the necessity of knowing those of other faiths if we are to make it as a global society and not self-destruct in massive fear and suspicion of one another.

Seeking to understand "the other" can be challenging and upsetting. After the 9/11 terrorist attacks, the invasion of Afghanistan several years ago, and the invasion of Iraq more recently, discrimination against Muslims has increased. To reach out to the family of Alia, a woman who has disabilities and is a member of our community, we invited Alia's father to share about their family members who live in Pakistan and his life here in Toronto as a Muslim. We felt shame as Canadians as he told of racist epithets shouted at him. How could someone treat so nastily this kindly gentleman, a Canadian citizen!

He spoke also of the social and economic disruption in northern Pakistan that accompanied present and past wars in Afghanistan—the refugees, leftover weapons, crime, and frustration that allowed extremists a foothold. Hearing the personal account of this friend was quite different from hearing a newscast. It was hard to realize that "our side" contributed to his family's suffering, and harder still to have no solution.

Alia's father concluded by sharing the dying wish of Alia's grandfather, that his descendants be "decent human beings." "This surely," he added, "is more important than any practice of any religion!"

SUGGESTION FOR MEDITATION: Hatred, it is said, is a failure of the imagination, an inability to move from the particular, from one's own world of experience, to the general, to a sense of our common humanity and to empathy for the other. How am I called in light of this statement?

Like most prophets, Jeremiah not only predicts God's judgment when materialism takes over but also makes clear that mercy and restoration follow judgment. Today's scripture, full of promise of a new beginning, may help us prepare for the new year. We might also be inspired by the Jewish practice during the High Holy Days (the Jewish New Year) of self-examination, repentance, and the seeking of forgiveness from others and then from God, so as to begin the new year with a sense of a clean slate.

In lavish poetic images, Jeremiah conveys God's faithful love and generosity toward the remnant who will return to the land of Israel. Why does God especially mention the blind, the lame, the expectant mother—the very people whom the able-bodied majority might see as burdens best left behind? Surely, this mention comes because the restored community will be spiritually healthy to the extent it is able to put those who are most vulnerable at its center. The measure of any civilization (or church) lies in the way it treats its weakest members.

L'Arche people who have disabilities know the suffering of marginalization. And even in L'Arche, it is easy to exclude others. Thankfully people with disabilities are usually masters of forgiveness! Celebration comes naturally in an atmosphere of forgiveness. At an anniversary gala, Ben, a young Dutch assistant, picked up diminutive Alia, who can neither walk, talk, nor see but who loves music and motion. As Ben twirled Alia before the audience, her smile illuminated the theater. In the background a chorus sang, "You can change the world with love, one heart at a time." It was this petite Muslim woman, her gift freed by Ben, who changed our hearts that evening.

SUGGESTION FOR MEDITATION: Can you envision your life as a watered garden? What is blooming? What fruit ripens as you prepare to enter the new year? What needs tending? What needs forgiveness?

The Revised Common Lectionary[‡] for 2004
Year C—Advent / Christmas Year A
(Disciplines Edition)

January 1–4

New Year's Day
Ecclesiastes 3:1-13
Psalm 8
Revelation 21:1-6*a*
Matthew 25:31-46

January 6
EPIPHANY
(These readings may be used Sunday, Jan. 4.)
Isaiah 60:1-6
Psalm 72:1-7, 10-14
Ephesians 3:1-12
Matthew 2:1-12

January 5–11
BAPTISM OF THE LORD
Isaiah 43:1-7
Psalm 29
Acts 8:14-17
Luke 3:15-17, 21-22

January 12–18
Isaiah 62:1-5
Psalm 36:5-10
1 Corinthians 12:1-11
John 2:1-11

January 19–25
Nehemiah 8:1-3, 5-6, 8-10
Psalm 19
1 Corinthians 12:12-31*a*
Luke 4:14-21

January 26–February 1
Jeremiah 1:4-10
Psalm 71:1-6
1 Corinthians 13:1-13
Luke 4:21-30

February 2–8
Isaiah 6:1-13
Psalm 138
1 Corinthians 15:1-11
Luke 5:1-11

February 9–15
Jeremiah 17:5-10
Psalm 1
1 Corinthians 15:12-20
Luke 6:17-26

February 16–22
THE TRANSFIGURATION
Exodus 34:29-35
Psalm 99
2 Corinthians 3:12–4:2
Luke 9:28-43

February 23–29
FIRST SUNDAY IN LENT
Deuteronomy 26:1-11
Psalm 91:1-2, 9-16
Romans 10:8*b*-13
Luke 4:1-13

February 25
ASH WEDNESDAY
Joel 2:1-2, 12-17
   (*or* Isaiah 58:1-12)
Psalm 51:1-17
2 Corinthians 5:20*b*–6:10
Matthew 6:1-6, 16-21

March 1–7
SECOND SUNDAY IN LENT
Genesis 15:1-12, 17-18
Psalm 27
Philippians 3:17–4:1
Luke 13:31-35
   (or Luke 9:28-36)

March 8–14
THIRD SUNDAY IN LENT
Isaiah 55:1-9
Psalm 63:1-8
1 Corinthians 10:1-13
Luke 13:1-9

March 15–21
FOURTH SUNDAY IN LENT
Joshua 5:9-12
Psalm 32
2 Corinthians 5:16-21
Luke 15:1-3, 11b-32

March 22–28
FIFTH SUNDAY IN LENT
Isaiah 43:16-21
Psalm 126
Philippians 3:4b-14
John 12:1-8

March 29–April 4
PALM/PASSION SUNDAY

Liturgy of the Palms
Luke 19:28-40
Psalm 118:1-2, 19-29

Liturgy of the Passion
Isaiah 50:4-9a
Psalm 31:9-16
Philippians 2:5-11
Luke 22:14–23:56
   (or Luke 23:1-49)

April 5–11
HOLY WEEK
   Monday
   Isaiah 42:1-9
   Psalm 36:5-11
   Hebrews 9:11-15
   John 12:1-11

Tuesday
Isaiah 49:1-7
Psalm 71:1-14
1 Corinthians 1:18-31
John 12:20-36

Wednesday
Isaiah 50:4-9a
Psalm 70
Hebrews 12:1-3
John 13:21-32

Maundy Thursday
Exodus 12:1-14
Psalm 116:1-2, 12-19
1 Corinthians 11:23-26
John 13:1-17, 31b-35

Good Friday
Isaiah 52:13–53:12
Psalm 22
Hebrews 10:16-25
John 18:1–19:42

Holy Saturday
Job 14:1–14
Psalm 31:1-4, 15-16
1 Peter 4:1-8
Matthew 27:57-66

April 11
Easter Sunday
Acts 10:34-43
   (or Isaiah 65:17-25)
Psalm 118:1-2, 14-24
1 Corinthians 15:19-26
John 20:1-18
   (or Luke 24:1-12)

April 12–18
Acts 5:27-32
Psalm 150
Revelation 1:4-8
John 20:19-31

April 19–25
Acts 9:1-20
Psalm 30
Revelation 5:11-14
John 21:1-19

April 26–May 2
Acts 9:36-43
Psalm 23
Revelation 7:9-17
John 10:22-30

May 3–9
Acts 11:1-18
Psalm 148
Revelation 21:1-6
John 13:31-35

May 10–16
Acts 16:9-15
Psalm 67
Revelation 21:10, 22–22:5
John 14:23-29
  (*or* John 5:1-9)

May 17–23
Acts 16:16-34
Psalm 97
Revelation 22:12-14, 16-17,
  20-21
John 17:20-26

May 20
ASCENSION DAY
*(These readings may be used Sunday,
May 23.)*
Acts 1:1-11
Psalm 47 (*or* Psalm 110)
Ephesians 1:15-23
Luke 24:44-53

May 24–30
PENTECOST
Acts 2:1-21
Psalm 104:24-34, 35*b*
Romans 8:14-17
John 14:8-17, 25-27

May 31–June 6
TRINITY SUNDAY
Proverbs 8:1-4, 22-31
Psalm 8
Romans 5:1-5
John 16:12-15

June 7–13
1 Kings 21:1-21*a*
Psalm 5:1-8
Galatians 2:15-21
Luke 7:36–8:3

June 14–20
1 Kings 19:1-15*a*
Psalm 42
Galatians 3:23-29
Luke 8:26-39

June 21–27
2 Kings 2:1-2, 6-14
Psalm 77:1-2, 11-20
Galatians 5:1, 13-25
Luke 9:51-62

June 28–July 4
2 Kings 5:1-14
Psalm 30
Galatians 6:1-16
Luke 10:1-11, 16-20

July 5–11
Amos 7:7-17
Psalm 82
Colossians 1:1-14
Luke 10:25-37

July 12–18
Amos 8:1-12
Psalm 52
Colossians 1:15-28
Luke 10:38-42

July 19–25
Hosea 1:2-10
Psalm 85
Colossians 2:6-19
Luke 11:1-13

July 26–August 1
Hosea 11:1-11
Psalm 107:1-9, 43
Colossians 3:1-11
Luke 12:13-21

August 2–8
Isaiah 1:1, 10–20
Psalm 50:1-8, 22-23
Hebrews 11:1-3, 8-16
Luke 12:32-40

August 9–15
Isaiah 5:1-7
Psalm 80:1-2, 8-19
Hebrews 11:29–12:2
Luke 12:49-56

August 16–22
Jeremiah 1:4-10
Psalm 71:1-6
Hebrews 12:18-29
Luke 13:10-17

August 23–29
Jeremiah 2:4-13
Psalm 81:1, 10-16
Hebrews 13:1-8, 15-16
Luke 14:1, 7-14

August 30–September 5
Jeremiah 18:1-11
Psalm 139:1-6, 13-18
Philemon 1-21
Luke 14:25-33

September 6–12
Jeremiah 4:11-12, 22-28
Psalm 14
1 Timothy 1:12-17
Luke 15:1-10

September 13–19
Jeremiah 8:18–9:1
Psalm 79:1-9
1 Timothy 2:1-7
Luke 16:1-13

September 20–26
Jeremiah 32:1-3a, 6-15
Psalm 91:1-6, 14-16
1 Timothy 6:6-19
Luke 16:19-31

September 27–October 3
Lamentations 1:1-6
Psalm 137
2 Timothy 1:1-14
Luke 17:5-10

October 4–10
Jeremiah 29:1, 4-7
Psalm 66:1-12
2 Timothy 2:8-15
Luke 17:11-19

October 11
THANKSGIVING DAY, CANADA
Deuteronomy 26:1-11
Psalm 100
Philippians 4:4-9
John 6:25-35

October 11–17
Jeremiah 31:27-34
Psalm 119:97-104
2 Timothy 3:14–4:5
Luke 18:1-8

October 18–24
Joel 2:23-32
Psalm 65
2 Timothy 4:6-8, 16-18
Luke 18:9-14

October 25–31
Habakkuk 1:1-4; 2:1-4
Psalm 119:137-144
2 Thessalonians 1:1-4, 11-12
Luke 19:1-10

November 1
ALL SAINTS DAY
(May be used Sunday, Nov. 7.)
Daniel 7:1-3, 15-18
Psalm 149 (*or* Psalm 150)
Ephesians 1:11-23
Luke 6:20-31

November 1–7
Haggai 1:15b–2:9
Psalm 145:1-5, 17-21
2 Thessalonians 2:1-5, 13-17
Luke 20:27-38

November 8–14
Isaiah 65:17-25
Isaiah 12 (*or* Psalm 118)
2 Thessalonians 3:6-13
Luke 21:5-19

November 15–21
REIGN OF CHRIST
Jeremiah 23:1-6
Luke 1:68-79
Colossians 1:11-20
Luke 23:33-43

November 22–28
FIRST SUNDAY OF ADVENT
Isaiah 2:1-5
Psalm 122
Romans 13:11-14
Matthew 24:36-44

November 25
THANKSGIVING DAY (USA)
Deuteronomy 26:1-11
Psalm 100
Philippians 4:4-9
John 6:25-35

November 29–December 5
SECOND SUNDAY OF ADVENT
Isaiah 11:1-10
Psalm 72:1-7, 18-19
Romans 15:4-13
Matthew 3:1-12

December 6–12
THIRD SUNDAY OF ADVENT
Isaiah 35:1-10
Psalm 146:5-10
  (*or* Luke 1:47-55)
James 5:7-10
Matthew 11:2-11

December 13–19
FOURTH SUNDAY OF ADVENT
Isaiah 7:10-16
Psalm 80:1-7, 17-19
Romans 1:1-7
Matthew 1:18-25

December 20–26
FIRST SUNDAY AFTER
CHRISTMAS DAY
Isaiah 63:7-9
Psalm 148
Hebrews 2:10-18
Matthew 2:13-23

December 24
CHRISTMAS EVE
Isaiah 9:2-7
Psalm 96
Titus 2:11-14
Luke 2:1-20

December 25
CHRISTMAS DAY
Isaiah 52:7-10
Psalm 98
Hebrews 1:1-12
John 1:1-14

December 27–January 2
Jeremiah 31:7-14
Psalm 147:12-20
Ephesians 1:3-14
John 1:1-18